SOPHISMS

OF THE

PROTECTIONISTS.

BY THE LATE

M. FREDERIC BASTIAT,

Member of the Institute of France.

Part I. Sophisms of Protection—First Series.
Part II. Sophisms of Protection—Second Series.
Part III. Spoliation and Law.
Part IV. Capital and Interest.

TRANSLATED FROM THE PARIS EDITION OF 1863.

NEW-YORK:
AMERICAN FREE TRADE LEAUGE.

1870.

PREFACE.

A previous edition of this work has been published under the title of "Essays on Political Economy, by the late M. Frederic Bastiat." When it became necessary to issue a second edition, the Free-Trade League offered to buy the stereotype plates and the copyright, with a view to the publication of the book on a large scale and at a very low price. The primary object of the League is to educate public opinion; to convince the people of the United States of the folly and wrongfulness of the Protective system. The methods adopted by the League for the purpose have been the holding of public meetings and the publication of books, pamphlets, and tracts, some of which are for sale at the cost of publication, and others given away gratuitously.

In publishing this book the League feels that it is offering the most effective and most popular work on political economy that has as yet been written. M. Bastiat not only enlivens a dull subject with his wit, but also reduces the propositions of the Protectionists to absurdities.

Free-Traders can do no better service in the cause of truth, justice, and humanity, than by circulating this little book among their friends. It is offered you at what it costs to print it Will not every Free-Trader put a copy of the book into the hands of his Protectionist friends?

It would not be proper to close this short preface without an expression on the part of the League of its obligation to the able translator of the work from the French, Mr. Horace White, of Chicago.

OFFICE OF THE AMERICAN FREE-TRADE LEAGUE,
9 Nassau Street, New-York, June, 1870.

PREFACE TO FIRST EDITION.

THIS compilation, from the works of the late M. Bastiat, is given to the public in the belief that the time has now come when the people, relieved from the absorbing anxieties of the war, and the subsequent strife on reconstruction, are prepared to give a more earnest and thoughtful attention to economical questions than was possible during the previous ten years. That we have retrograded in economical science during this period, while making great strides in moral and political advancement by the abolition of slavery and the enfranchisement of the freedmen, seems to me incontestable. Professor Perry has described very concisely the steps taken by the manufacturers in 1861, after the Southern members had left their seats in Congress, to reverse the policy of the government in reference to foreign trade.* He has noticed but has not laid so much stress as he might on the fact that while there was

* Elements of Political Economy, p. 461.

no considerable public opinion to favor them, there was none at all to oppose them. Not only was the attention of the people diverted from the tariff by the dangers then impending, but the Republican party, which then came into power, had, in its National Convention, offered a bribe to the State of Pennsylvania for its vote in the Presidential election, which bribe was set forth in the following words:

> "*Resolved*, That while providing revenue for the support of the General Government by duties upon imports, sound policy requires such an adjustment of these imposts as to encourage the development of the industrial interests o the whole country; and we commend that policy of national exchanges which secures to the workingmen liberal wages, to agriculture remunerative prices, to mechanics and manufacturers an adequate reward for their skill, labor and enterprise, and to the nation commercial prosperity and independence."—*Chicago Convention Platform*, 1860.

It is true that this resolution did not commit anybody to the doctrine that the industrial interests of the whole country are promoted by taxes levied upon imported property, however "adjusted," but it was understood, by the Pennsylvanians at least, to be a promise that if the Republican party were successful in the coming election, the doctrine of protection, which had been overthrown in 1846, and had been in an extremely languishing state ever since, should be put upon its legs again. I am far from asserting that this overture was needed to secure the vote of Pennsylvania for Mr. Lincoln in 1860, or that that State was governed by less worthy motives in her political action than other States. I only remark that her delegates in the convention thought such a resolution would be extremely useful, and such was the anxiety to secure her vote in the election that a much stronger resolution might have been conceded if it had been required. I affirm, however, that there was no agitation on the tariff question in any other quarter. New England had united in passing the tariff of 1857, which lowered the duties imposed by the act of 1846 about fifty per cent., *i. e.*, one-half of the previously existing scale. The Western States had not petitioned Congress or the convention to disturb the tariff; nor had New York done so, although Mr. Greeley, then as now, was invoking, more or less frequently, the shade of Henry Clay to help re-establish what is deftly styled the "American System."

The protective policy was restored, after its fifteen years' sleep, under the auspices of Mr. Morrill, a Representative (now a Senator) from Vermont. Latterly I have noticed in the speeches and votes of this gentleman (who is, I think, one of the most conscientious, as he is one of the most amiable, men in public life), a reluctance to follow to their logical conclusion the principles embodied in the "Morrill tariff" of 1861. His remarks upon the copper bill, during the recent session of Congress, indicate that, in his opinion, those branches of American industry which are engaged in producing articles sent abroad in exchange for the products of foreign nations, are entitled to some consideration. This is an important admission, but not so important as another, which he made in his speech on the national finances, January 24, 1867, in which, referring to the bank note circulation existing in the year 1860, he said: "*And that was a year of as large production and as much general prosperity as any, perhaps, in our history.*" * If the year immediately preceding the enactment of the Morrill tariff was a year of as large production and as much general prosperity as any in our history, of what use has the Morrill tariff been? We have seen that it was not demanded by any public agitation. We now see that it has been of no public utility.

In combating, by arguments and illustrations adapted to the comprehension of the mass of mankind, the errors and sophisms with which protectionists deceive themselves and others, M. Bastiat is the most lucid and pointed of all writers on economical science with whose works I have any acquaintance. It is not necessary to accord to him a place among the architects of the science of political economy, although some of his admirers rank him among

* Congressional Globe, Second Session Thirty-Ninth Congress, Part I, p. 724.

the highest.* It is enough to count him among the greatest of its expounders and demonstrators. His death, which occurred at Pisa, Italy, on the 24th December, 1850, at the age of 49, was a serious loss to France and to the world. His works, though for the most part fragmentary, and given to the public from time to time through the columns of the *Journal des Economistes*, the *Journal des Debats*, and the *Libre Echange*, remain a monument of a noble intellect guided by a noble soul. They have been collected and published (including the *Harmonies Economiques*, which the author left in manuscript) by Guillaumin & Co., the proprietors of the *Journal des Economistes*, in two editions of six volumes each, 8vo. and 12mo. When we reflect that these six volumes were produced between April, 1844, and December, 1850, by a young man of feeble constitution, who commenced life as a clerk in a mercantile establishment, and who spent much of his time during these six years in delivering public lectures, and laboring in the National Assembly, to which he was chosen in 1848, our admiration for such industry is only modified by the thought that if he had

* Mr. Macleod (*Dictionary of Political Economy*, vol. I, p. 246) speaks of Bastiat's definition of Value as "the greatest revolution that has been effected in any science since the days of Galileo."

See also Professor Perry's pamphlet, *Recent Phases of Thought in Political Economy*, read before the American Social Science Association, October, 1868, in which, it appears to me, that Bastiat's theory of Rent, in announcing which he was anticipated by Mr. Carey, is too highly praised.

been more saving of his strength, he might have rendered even greater services to his country and to mankind.

The *Sophismes Economiques*, which fill the larger portion of this volume, were not expected by their author to outlast the fallacies which they sought to overthrow. But these fallacies have lived longer and have spread over more of the earth's surface than any one *a priori* could have believed possible. It is sometimes useful, in opposing doctrines which people have been taught to believe are peculiar to their own country and time, to show that the same doctrines have been maintained in other countries and times, and have been exploded in other languages. By what misuse of words the doctrine of Protection came to be denominated the "American System," I could never understand. It prevailed in England nearly two hundred years before our separation from the mother country. Adam Smith directed the first formidable attack against it in the very year that our independence was declared. It held its ground in England until it had starved and ruined almost every branch of industry—agriculture, manufactures, and commerce alike.* It was not

* It is so often affirmed by protectionists that the superiority of Great Britain in manufactures was attained by means of protection, that it is worth while to dispel that illusion. The facts are precisely the reverse. Protection had brought Great Britain in the year 1842 to the last stages of penury and decay, and it wanted but a year or two more of the same regimen to have precipitated the country into a bloody revolution. I quote a paragraph from Miss Martineau's "History of England from 1816 to 1854," Book VI, Chapter 5:

wholly overthrown until 1846, the same year that witnessed its discomfiture in the United States, as already shown. It still exists in a subdued and declining way in

"Serious as was the task of the Minister (Sir R. Peel) in every view, the most immediate sympathy was felt for him on account of the fearful state of the people. The distress had now so deepened in the manufacturing districts as to render it clearly inevitable that many must die, and a multitude be lowered to a state of sickness and irritability from want of food; while there seemed no chance of any member of the manufacturing classes coming out of the struggle at last with a vestige of property wherewith to begin the world again. The pressure had long extended beyond the interests first affected, and when the new Ministry came into power, there seemed to be no class that was not threatened with ruin. In Carlisle, the Committee of Inquiry reported that a fourth of the population was in a state bordering on starvation—actually certain to die of famine, unless relieved by extraordinary exertions. In the woollen districts of Wiltshire, the allowance to the independent laborer was not two-thirds of the minimum in the workhouse, and the large existing population consumed only a fourth of the bread and meat required by the much smaller population of 1820. In Stockport, more than half the master spinners had failed before the close of 1842; dwelling houses to the number of 3,000, were shut up; and the occupiers of many hundreds more were unable to pay rates at all. Five thousand persons were walking the streets in compulsory idleness, and the Burnley guardians wrote to the Secretary of State that the distress was far beyond their management; so that a government commissioner and government funds were sent down without delay. At a meeting in Manchester, where humble shopkeepers were the speakers, anecdotes were related which told more than declamation. Rent collectors were afraid to meet their principals, as no money could be collected. Provision dealers were subject to incursions from a wolfish man prowling for food for his children, or from a half frantic woman, with her dying baby at her breast; or from parties of ten or a dozen desperate wretches who were levying contributions along the street. The linen draper told how new clothes had become out of the question with his customers, and they bought only remnants and patches, to mend the old ones. The baker was more and more surprised at the number of people who bought half-pennyworths of bread. A provision dealer used to throw away outside scraps; but now respectable customers of twenty years' standing bought them in pennyworths to moisten their potatoes. These shopkeepers contemplated nothing but ruin from the impoverished condition of their customers. While poor-rates were increasing beyond all precedent, their trade was only one-half, or one-third, or even one-tenth what it had been three years before. In that neighborhood, a gentleman, who had retired from business in 1833, leaving a property worth £60,000 to his sons, and who had, early in the distress, become security for them, was showing the works for the benefit of the creditors, at a salary of £1 a week. In families where the father had hitherto earned £2 per week, and laid by a portion weekly, and where all was now gone but the sacks of shavings they slept on, exertions were made to get 'blue milk' for children to moisten their oatmeal with; but soon they could have it only on alternate days; and soon water must do. At Leeds the pauper stone-heap amounted to 150,000 tons; and the guardians offered the paupers 6s. per week for doing nothing, rather than 7s. 6d. per week for stone-breaking. The millwrights and other trades were offering a premium on emigration, to induce their hands to go away. At Hinckley,

France, despite the powerful and brilliant attacks of Say, Bastiat, and Chevalier, but its end cannot be far distant in that country. The Cobden-Chevalier treaty with England has been attended by consequences so totally at variance with the theories and prophecies of the protectionists that it must soon succumb.

As these pages are going through the press, a telegram announces that the French Government has abolished the discriminating duties levied upon goods imported in foreign bottoms, and has asked our government to abolish the like discrimination which our laws have created. Commercial freedom is making rapid progress in Prussia, Austria,

one-third of the inhabitants were paupers; more than a fifth of the houses stood empty; and there was not work enough in the place to employ properly one-third of the weavers. In Dorsetshire a man and his wife had for wages 2s. 6d. per week, and three loaves; and the ablest laborer had 6s. or 7s. In Wiltshire, the poor peasants held open-air meetings after work—which was necessarily after dark. There, by the light of one or two flaring tallow candles, the man or the woman who had a story to tell stood on a chair, and related how their children were fed and clothed in old times—poorly enough, but so as to keep body and soul together; and now, how they could nohow manage to do it. The bare details of the ages of their children, and what the little things could do, and the prices of bacon and bread, and calico and coals, had more pathos in them than any oratory heard elsewhere."

"But all this came from the Corn Laws," is the ready reply of the American protectionist. The Corn Laws were the doctrine of protection applied to breadstuffs, farm products, "raw materials." But it was not only protection for corn that vexed England in 1842, but protection for every thing and every body, from the landlord and the mill-owner to the kelp gatherer. Every species of manufacturing industry had asked and obtained protection. The nation had put in force, logically and thoroughly, the principle of denying themselves any share in the advantages which nature or art had conferred upon other climates and peoples, (which is the principle of protection), and with the results so pathetically described by Miss Martineau. The prosperity of British manufactures dates from the year 1846. That they maintained any kind of existence prior to that time is a most striking proof of the vitality of human industry under the persecution of bad laws.

Italy, and even in Spain. The United States alone, among civilized nations, hold to the opposite principle. Our anomalous position in this respect is due, as I think, to our anomalous condition during the past eight or nine years, already adverted to—a condition in which the protected classes have been restrained by no public opinion—public opinion being too intensely preoccupied with the means of preserving the national existence to notice what was doing with the tariff. But evidences of a reawakening are not wanting.

There is scarcely an argument current among the protectionists of the United States that was not current in France at the time Bastiat wrote the *Sophismes Economiques*. Nor was there one current in his time that is not performing its bad office among us. Hence his demonstrations of their absurdity and falsity are equally applicable to our time and country as to his. They may have even greater force among us if they thoroughly dispel the notion that Protection is an "American system." Surely they cannot do less than this.

There are one or two arguments current among the protectionists of the United States that were not rife in France when Bastiat wrote his *Sophismes*. It is said, for instance, that protection has failed to achieve all the good results expected from it, because the policy of the government has been variable. If we could have a steady course of protection for a sufficient period of time (nobody being bold enough to say what time would be sufficient), and could be *assured* of having it, we should see wonderful progress. But, inasmuch as the policy of the government is uncertain, protection has never yet had a fair trial. This is like saying, "if the stone which I threw in the air had staid there, my head would not have been broken by its fall." It would not stay there. The law of gravitation is committed against its staying there. Its only resting-place is on the earth. They begin by violating natural laws and natural rights—the right to exchange services for services—and then complain because these natural laws war against them and finally overcome them. But it is not true that protection has not had a fair trial in the United States. The protection has been greater at some times than at others, that is all. Prior to the late war, all our revenue was raised from customs; and while the tariffs of 1846 and 1857 were designated "free trade tariffs," to distinguish them from those existing before and since, they were necessarily protective to a certain extent.

Again, it is said that there is need of diversifying our industry—as though industry would not diversify itself sufficiently through the diverse tastes and predilections of individuals—as though it were necessary to supplement the work of the Creator in this behalf, by human enactments founded upon reciprocal rapine. The only rational object of diversifying industry is to make people better and happier. Do men and women become better and happier by being huddled together in mills and factories, in a stifling atmosphere, on scanty wages, ten hours each day and 313 days each year, than when cultivating our free and fertile lands? Do they have equal opportunities for mental and moral improvement? The trades-unions tell us, No. Whatever may be the experience of other countries, where the land is either owned by absentee lords, who take all the product except what is necessary to give the tenant a bare subsistence, or where it is cut up in parcels not larger than an American garden patch, it is an undeniable fact that no other class of American workingmen are so independent, so intelligent, so well provided with comforts and leisure, or so rapidly advancing in prosperity, as our agriculturists; and this notwithstanding they are enormously overtaxed to maintain other branches of industry, which, according to the protective theory, cannot support themselves. The natural tendency of our people to flock to the cities, where their eyes and ears are gratified at the expense of their other senses, physical and moral, is sufficiently marked not to need the influence of legislation to stimulate it.

It is not the purpose of this preface to anticipate the admirable arguments of M. Bastiat; but there is another theory in vogue which deserves a moment's consideration.

Mr. H. C. Carey tells us, that a country which exports its food, in reality exports its soil, the foreign consumers not giving back to the land the fertilizing elements abstracted from it. Mr. Mill has answered this argument, upon philosophical principles, at some length, showing that whenever it ceases to be advantageous to America to export breadstuffs, she will cease to do so; also, that when it becomes necessary to manure her lands, she will either import manure or make it at home.* A shorter answer is, that the lands are no better manured by having the bread consumed in Lowell, or Pittsburgh, or even in Chicago, than in Birmingham or Lyons. But it seems to me that Mr. Carey does not take into account the fact that the total amount of breadstuffs exported from any country must be an exceedingly small fraction of the whole amount taken from the soil, and scarcely appreciable as a source of manure, even if it were practically utilized in that way. Thus, our exportation of flour and meal, wheat and Indian corn, for the year 1860, as compared with the total crop produced, was as follows:

TOTAL CROP.†

Flour and Meal, bbls.	Wheat, bu.	Corn, bu.
55,217,800	173,104,924	838,792,740

* Principles of Political Economy (People's Ed.), London, 1865, page 557.

† These figures are taken from the census report for the year 1860. In this report the total production of flour and meal is given, not in barrels, but in value. The quantity is ascertained by dividing the total value by the average price per barrel in New York during the year, the fluctuations

Exportation.

Flour and Meal, bbls.	Wheat, bu.	Corn, bu.
2,845,305	4,155,153	1,314,155
Percentage of Exportation to Total Crop.		
5.15	2.40	.39

This was the result for the year preceding the enactment of the Morrill tariff. It is true that our exports of wheat and Indian corn rose in the three years following the enactment of the Morrill tariff, from an average of eight million bushels to an average of forty-six million bushels, but this is contrary to the theory that high tariffs tend to keep breadstuffs at home, and low ones to send them abroad. There is need of great caution in making generalizations as to the influence of tariffs on the movement of breadstuffs. Good or bad harvests in various countries exercise an uncontrollable influence upon their movement, far beyond the reach of any legislation short of prohibition. The market for breadstuffs in the world is as the number of consumers; that is, of population. It is sometimes said in the way of reproach, (and it is a curious travesty of Mr. Carey's manure argument,) that foreign nations *will not* take our breadstuffs. It is not true; but if it were, that would not be a good reason for our passing laws to prevent them from doing so; that is,

then being very slight. Flour being a manufactured article, is it not a little curious that we exported under the "free trade tariff" twice as large a per centage of breadstuffs in that form as we did of the "raw material," wheat?

to deprive them of the means to pay for them. Every country must pay for its imports with its exports. It must pay for the services which it receives with the services which it renders. If foreign nations are not allowed to render services to us, how shall we render them the service of bread?

The first series of Bastiat's *Sophismes* were published in 1845, and the second series in 1848. The first series were translated in 1848, by Mrs. D. J. McCord, and published the same year by G. P. Putnam, New York. Mrs. McCord's excellent translation has been followed (by permission of her publisher, who holds the copyright,) in this volume, having been first compared with the original, in the Paris edition of 1863. A very few verbal alterations have been made, which, however, have no bearing on the accuracy and faithfulness of her work. The translation of the essay on "Capital and Interest" is from a duodecimo volume published in London a year or two ago, the name of the translator being unknown to me. The second series of the *Sophismes*, and the essay entitled "Spoliation and Law," are, I believe, presented in English for the first time in these pages.

H. W.

CHICAGO, August 1, 1869.

PART I.

SOPHISMS OF PROTECTION.

FIRST SERIES.

INTRODUCTION.

My object in this little volume has been to refute some of the arguments usually advanced against Free Trade.

I am not seeking a combat with the protectionists. I merely advance a principle which I am anxious to present clearly to the minds of sincere men, who hesitate because they doubt.

I am not of the number of those who maintain that protection is supported by interests. I believe that it is founded upon errors, or, if you will, upon *incomplete truths.* Too many fear free trade, for this apprehension to be other than sincere.

My aspirations are perhaps high; but I confess that it would give me pleasure to hope that this little work might become, as it were, a *manual* for such men as may be called upon to decide between the two principles. When one has not made oneself perfectly familiar with the doctrines of free trade, the sophisms of protection perpetually return to the mind under one form or another; and, on each occasion, in order to counteract their effect, it is necessary to enter into a long and laborious analysis. Few, and least of all legislators, have leisure for this labor, which I would, on this account, wish to present clearly drawn up to their hand.

But it may be said, are then the benefits of free trade so hidden as to be perceptible only to economists by profession?

Yes; we confess it; our adversaries in the discussion have a signal advantage over us. They can, in a few words, present an incomplete truth; which, for us to show that it is incomplete, renders necessary long and uninteresting dissertations.

This results from the fact that protection accumulates upon a single point the good which it effects, while the evil inflicted is infused throughout the mass. The one strikes the eye at a first glance, while the other becomes perceptible only to close investigation. With regard to free trade, precisely the reverse is the case.

It is thus with almost all questions of political economy.

If you say, for instance: There is a machine which has turned out of employment thirty workmen;

Or again: There is a spendthrift who encourages every kind of industry;

Or: The conquest of Algiers has doubled the commerce of Marseilles;

Or, once more: The public taxes support one hundred thousand families;

You are understood at once; your propositions are clear, simple, and true in themselves. If you deduce from them the principle that

Machines are an evil;

That sumptuous extravagance, conquest, and heavy imposts are blessings;

Your theory will have the more success, because you will be able to base it upon indisputable facts.

But we, for our part, cannot stop at a cause and its immediate effect; for we know that this effect may in its turn become itself a cause. To judge of a measure, it is necessary that we should follow it from step to step, from result to result, until through the successive links of the chain of events we arrive at the final effect. We must, in short, *reason*.

But here we are assailed by clamorous exclamations: You are theorists, metaphysicians, ideologists, utopians, men of maxims! and immediately all the prejudices of the public are against us.

What then shall we do? We must invoke the patience and candor of the reader, giving to our deductions, if we are capable of it, sufficient clearness to throw forward at once, without disguise or palliation, the true and the false, in order, once for all, to determine whether the victory should be for Restriction or Free Trade.

I wish here to make a remark of some importance.

Some extracts from this volume have appeared in the "*Journal des Economistes.*"

In an article otherwise quite complimentary published by the Viscount de Romanet (see *Moniteur Industriel* of the 15th and 18th of May, 1845), he intimates that I ask for the *suppression of custom houses.* Mr. de Romanet is mistaken. I ask for the suppression of the *protective policy.* We do not dispute the right of *government* to impose taxes, but would, if possible, dissuade *producers* from taxing one another. It was said by Napoleon that duties should never be a fiscal instrument, but a means of protecting industry. We plead the contrary, and say, that duties should never be made an instrument of reciprocal rapine; but that they may be employed as a useful fiscal machine. I am so far from asking for the suppression of duties, that I look upon them as the anchor on which the future salvation of our finances will depend. I believe that they may bring immense receipts into the treasury, and, to give my entire and undisguised opinion, I am inclined, from the slow progress of healthy, economical doctrines, and from the magnitude of our budget, to hope more for the cause of commercial reform from the necessities of the Treasury than from the force of an enlightened public opinion.

I.

ABUNDANCE — SCARCITY.

WHICH is the best for man or for society, abundance or scarcity?

How, it may be exclaimed, can such a question be asked? Has it ever been pretended, is it possible to maintain, that scarcity can be the basis of a man's happiness?

Yes; this has been maintained, this is daily maintained; and I do not hesitate to say that the *scarcity theory* is by far the most popular of the day. It furnishes the subject of discussions, in conversations, journals, books, courts of justice; and extraordinary as it may appear, it is certain that political economy will have fulfilled its task and its practical mission, when it shall have rendered common and irrefutable the simple proposition that "in abundance consist man's riches."

Do we not hear it said every day, "Foreign nations are inundating us with their productions"? Then we fear abundance.

Has not Mr. de Saint Cricq said, "Production is superabundant"? Then he fears abundance.

Do we not see workmen destroying and breaking machinery? They are frightened by the excess of production; in other words, they fear abundance.

Has not Mr. Bugeaud said, "Let bread be dear and the agriculturist will be rich"? Now bread can only be dear because it is scarce. Then Mr. Bugeaud lauded scarcity.

Has not Mr. d'Argout produced the fruitfulness of the sugar culture as an argument against it? Has he not said, "The beet cannot have a permanent and extended cultivation, because a few acres given up to it in each department, would furnish sufficient for the consumption of all France"? Then, in his opinion, good consists in sterility and scarcity, evil in fertility and abundance.

"*La Presse*," "*Le Commerce*," and the majority of our journals, are, every day, publishing articles whose aim is to prove to the chambers and to government that a wise policy should seek to raise prices by tariffs; and do we not daily see these powers obeying these injunctions of the press? Now, tariffs can only raise prices by diminishing the quantity of goods offered for sale. Then, here we see newspapers, the legislature, the ministry, all guided by the scarcity theory, and I was correct in my statement that this theory is by far the most popular.

How then has it happened, that in the eyes at once of laborers, editors and statesmen, abundance should appear alarming, and scarcity advantageous? It is my intention to endeavor to show the origin of this delusion.

A man becomes rich, in proportion to the profitableness of his labor; that is to say, *in proportion as he sells his productions at a high price.* The price of his productions is high in proportion to their scarcity. It is plain then, that, as far as regards him at least, scarcity enriches him. Applying successively this mode of reasoning to each class of laborers individually, the *scarcity theory* is deduced from it. To put this theory into practice, and in order to favor each class of labor, an artificial scarcity is forced in every kind of production, by prohibition, restriction, suppression of machinery, and other analogous measures.

In the same manner it is observed that when an article is abundant it brings a small price. The gains of the producer are, of course, less. If this is the case with all produce, all producers are then poor. Abundance then ruins society. And as any strong conviction will always seek to force itself into practice, we see, in many countries, the laws aiming to prevent abundance.

This sophism, stated in a general form, would produce but a slight impression. But when applied to any particular order of facts, to any particular article of industry, to any one class of labor, it is extremely specious, because it is a syllogism which is not *false*, but *incomplete.* And what is true in a syllogism always necessarily presents itself to the mind, while the *incomplete*, which is a negative quality, an unknown value, is easily forgotten in the calculation.

Man produces in order to consume. He is at once producer and consumer. The argument given above, considers him only under the first point of view. Let us look at him in the second character and the conclusion will be different. We may say,

The consumer is rich in proportion as he *buys* at a low price. He buys at a low price in proportion to the abundance of the article in demand; abundance then enriches him. This reasoning extended to all consumers must lead to the *theory of abundance!*

It is the imperfectly understood notion of exchange of produce which leads to these fallacies. If we consult our individual interest, we perceive immediately that it is double. As *sellers* we are interested in high prices, consequently in scarcity. As *buyers* our advantage is in cheapness, or what is the same thing, abundance. It is impossible then to found a proper system of reasoning upon either the one or the other of these separate interests before determining which of the two coincides and identifies itself with the general and permanent interests of mankind.

If man were a solitary animal, working exclusively for himself, consuming the fruit of his own personal labor; if, in a word, he did not exchange his produce, the theory of scarcity could never have introduced itself into the world. It would be too strikingly evident, that abundance, whencesoever derived, is advantageous to him, whether this abundance might be the result of his own labor, of ingenious tools, or of powerful machinery; whether due to the fertility of the soil, to the liberality of nature, or to an *inundation* of foreign goods, such as the sea bringing from distant regions might cast upon his shores. Never would the solitary man have dreamed, in order to encourage his own labor, of destroying his instruments for facilitating his work, of neutralizing the fertility of the soil, or of casting back into the sea the produce of its bounty. He would understand that his labor was a *means* not an *end*, and that it would be absurd to reject the object, in order to encourage the means. He would understand that if he has required two hours per day to supply his necessities, any thing which spares him an hour of this labor, leaving the result the same, gives him this hour to dispose of as he pleases in adding to his comforts. In a word, he would understand that every step in the *saving of labor*, is a step in the improvement of his condition. But traffic clouds our vision in the contemplation of this simple truth. In a state of society with the division of labor to which it leads, the production and consumption of an article no longer belong to the same individual. Each now looks upon his labor not as a means, but as an end. The exchange of produce creates with regard to each object two separate interests, that of the producer and that of the consumer; and these two interests are always directly opposed to each other.

It is essential to analyze and study the nature of each. Let us then suppose a producer of whatever kind; what is his immediate interest? It consists in two things: 1st, that the smallest possible number of individuals should devote themselves to the business which he follows; and 2dly, that the greatest possible number should seek the articles of his produce. In the more succinct terms of Political Economy, the supply should be small, the demand large; or yet in other words: limited competition, unlimited consumption.

What on the other side is the immediate interest of the consumer? That the supply should be large, the demand small.

As these two interests are immediately opposed to each other, it follows that if one coincides with the general interest of society the other must be adverse to it.

Which then, if either, should legislation favor as contributing most to the good of the community?

To determine this question, it suffices to inquire in which the secret desires of the majority of men would be accomplished.

Inasmuch as we are producers, it must be confessed that we have each of us anti-social desires. Are we vine-growers? It would not distress *us* were the frost to nip all the vines in the world except our own: *this is the scarcity theory.* Are we iron-workers? We would desire (whatever might be the public need) that the market should offer no iron but our own; and precisely for the reason that this need, painfully felt and imperfectly supplied, causes us to receive a high price for *our* iron: *again here is the theory of scarcity.* Are we agriculturists? We say with Mr. Bugeaud, let bread be dear, that is to say scarce, and our business goes well: *again the theory of scarcity.*

Are we physicians? We cannot but see that certain physical ameliorations, such as the improved climate of the country, the development of certain moral virtues, the progress of knowledge pushed to the extent of enabling each individual to take care of his own health, the discovery of certain simple remedies easily applied, would be so many fatal blows to our profession. As physicians, then, our secret desires are anti-social. I must not be understood to imply that physicians allow themselves to form such desires. I am happy to believe that they would hail with joy a universal panacea. But in such a sentiment it is the man, the Christian, who manifests himself, and who by a praiseworthy abnegation of self, takes that point of view of the question, which belongs to the consumer. As a physician exercising his profession, and gaining from this profession his standing in society, his comforts, even the means of existence of his family, it is impossible but that his desires, or if you please so to word it, his interests, should be anti-social.

Are we manufacturers of cotton goods? We desire to sell them at the price most advantageous to *ourselves.* We would willingly consent to the suppression of all rival manufactories. And if we dare not publicly express this desire, or pursue the complete realization of it with some success, we do so, at least to a certain extent, by indirect means; as for example, the exclusion of foreign goods, in order to diminish the *quantity offered,* and to produce thus by forcible means, and for our own profits, a *scarcity* of clothing.

We might thus pass in review every business and every profession, and should always find that the producers, *in their character of producers,* have invariably anti-social interests. "The shop-keeper (says Montaigne) succeeds in his business through the extravagance of youth; the laborer by the high price of grain; the architect by the decay of houses; officers of justice by lawsuits and quarrels. The standing and occupation even of ministers of religion are drawn from our death and our vices. No physician takes pleasure in the health even of his friends; no soldier in the peace of his country; and so on with all."

If then the secret desires of each producer were realized, the world would rapidly retrograde towards barbarism. The sail would proscribe steam; the oar would proscribe the sail, only in its turn to give way to wagons, the wagon to the mule, and the mule to the foot-peddler. Wool would exclude cotton; cotton would exclude wool; and thus on, until the scarcity and want of every thing would cause man himself to disappear from the face of the globe.

If we now go on to consider the immediate interest of the *consumer*, we shall find it in perfect harmony with the public interest, and with the well-being of humanity. When the buyer presents himself in the market, he desires to find it abundantly furnished. He sees with pleasure propitious seasons for harvesting; wonderful inventions putting within his reach the largest possible quantity of produce; time and labor saved; distances effaced; the spirit of peace and justice diminishing the weight of taxes; every barrier to improvement cast down; and in all this his interest runs parallel with an enlightened public interest. He may push his secret desires to an absurd and chimerical height, but never can they cease to be humanizing in their tendency. He may desire that food and clothing, house and hearth, instruction and morality, security and peace, strength and health, should come to us without limit and without labor or effort on our part, as the water of the stream, the air which we breathe, and the sunbeams in which we bask, but never could the realization of his most extravagant wishes run counter to the good of society.

It may be said, perhaps, that were these desires granted, the labor of the producer constantly checked would end by being entirely arrested for want of support. But why? Because in this extreme supposition every imaginable need and desire would be completely satisfied. Man, like the All-powerful, would create by the single act of his will. How in such an hypothesis could laborious production be regretted?

Imagine a legislative assembly composed of producers, of whom each member should cause to pass into a law his secret desire as a *producer;* the code which would emanate from such an assembly could be nothing but systematized monopoly; the scarcity theory put into practice.

In the same manner, an assembly in which each member should consult only his immediate interest of *consumer* would aim at the systematizing of free trade; the suppression of every restrictive measure; the destruction of artificial barriers; in a word, would realize the theory of abundance.

It follows then,

That to consult exclusively the immediate interest of the producer, is to consult an anti-social interest.

To take exclusively for basis the interest of the consumer, is to take for basis the general interest.

Let me be permitted to insist once more upon this point of view, though at the risk of repetition.

A radical antagonism exists between the seller and the buyer.

The former wishes the article offered to be *scarce*, supply small, and at a high price.

The latter wishes it *abundant*, supply large, and at a low price.

The laws, which should at least remain neutral, take part for the seller against the buyer; for the producer against the consumer; for high against low prices; for scarcity against abundance. They act, if not intentionally at least logically, upon the principle that *a nation is rich in proportion as it is in want of every thing.*

For, say they, it is necessary to favor the producer by securing him a profitable disposal of his goods. To effect this, their price must be raised; to raise the price the supply must be diminished; and to diminish the supply is to create scarcity.

Let us suppose that at this moment, with these laws in full action, a complete inventory should be made, not by value, but by weight, measure and quantity, of all articles now in France calculated to supply the necessities and pleasures of its inhabitants; as grain, meat, woollen and cotton goods, fuel, etc.

Let us suppose again that to-morrow every barrier to the introduction of foreign goods should be removed.

Then, to judge of the effect of such a reform, let a new inventory be made three months hence.

Is it not certain that at the time of the second

inventory, the quantity of grain, cattle, goods, iron, coal, sugar, etc., will be greater than at the first?

So true is this, that the sole object of our protective tariffs is to prevent such articles from reaching us, to diminish the supply, to prevent low prices, or which is the same thing, the abundance of goods.

Now I ask, are the people under the action of these laws better fed because there is *less* bread, *less* meat, and *less* sugar in the country? Are they better dressed because there are *fewer* goods? Better warmed because there is *less* coal? Or do they prosper better in their labor because iron, copper, tools and machinery are scarce?

But, it is answered, if we are inundated with foreign goods and produce, our coin will leave the country.

Well, and what matters that? Man is not fed with coin. He does not dress in gold, nor warm himself with silver. What difference does it make whether there be more or less coin in the country, provided there be more bread in the cupboard, more meat in the larder, more clothing in the press, and more wood in the cellar?

To Restrictive Laws, I offer this dilemma:

Either you allow that you produce scarcity, or you do not allow it.

If you allow it, you confess at once that your end is to injure the people as much as possible. If you do not allow it, then you deny your power to diminish the supply, to raise the price, and consequently you deny having favored the producer.

You are either injurious or inefficient. You can never be useful

---

II.

OBSTACLE — CAUSE.

THE obstacle mistaken for the cause—scarcity mistaken for abundance. The sophism is the same. It is well to study it under every aspect.

Man naturally is in a state of entire destitution.

Between this state and the satisfying of his wants, there exists a multitude of *obstacles* which it is the object of labor to surmount. It is interesting to seek how and why he could have been led to look even upon these obstacles to his happiness as the cause of it.

I wish to take a journey of some hundred miles. But, between the point of my departure and my destination, there are interposed, mountains, rivers, swamps, forests, robbers—in a word, *obstacles;* and to conquer these obstacles, it is necessary that I should bestow much labor and great efforts in opposing them;—or, what is the same thing, if others do it for me, I must pay them the value of their exertions. It is evident that I should have been better off had these obstacles never existed.

Through the journey of life, in the long series of days from the cradle to the tomb, man has many difficulties to oppose him in his progress. Hunger, thirst, sickness, heat, cold, are so many obstacles scattered along his road. In a state of isolation, he would be obliged to combat them all by hunting, fishing, agriculture, spinning, weaving, architecture, etc., and it is very evident that it would be better for him that these difficulties should exist to a less degree, or even not at all. In a state of society he is not obliged, personally, to struggle with each of these obstacles, but others do it for him; and he, in return, must remove some one of them for the benefit of his fellow-men.

Again it is evident, that, considering mankind as a whole, it would be better for society that these obstacles should be as weak and as few as possible.

But if we examine closely and in detail the phenomena of society, and the private interests of men as modified by exchange of produce, we perceive, without difficulty, how it has happened that wants have been confounded with riches, and the obstacle with the cause.

The separation of occupations, which results from the habits of exchange, causes each man, instead of struggling against all surrounding obstacles to combat only *one;* the effort being made not for himself alone, but for the benefit of his fellows, who, in their turn, render a similar service to him.

Now, it hence results, that this man looks upon the obstacle which he has made it his profession to combat for the benefit of others, as the immediate cause of his riches. The greater, the more serious, the more stringent may be this obstacle, the more he is remunerated for the conquering of it, by those who are relieved by his labors.

A physician, for instance, does not busy himself in baking his bread, or in manufacturing his clothing and his instruments; others do it for him, and he, in return, combats the maladies with which his patients are afflicted. The more dangerous and frequent these maladies are, the more others are willing, the more, even, are they forced, to work in his service. Disease, then, which is an obstacle to the happiness of mankind, becomes to him the source of his comforts. The reasoning of all producers is, in what concerns themselves, the same. As the doctor draws his profits from disease, so does the ship owner from the obstacle called *distance;* the agriculturist from that named *hunger;* the cloth manufacturer from *cold;* the schoolmaster lives upon *ignorance,* the jeweler upon *vanity,* the lawyer upon *quarrels,* the notary upon *breach of faith.* Each profession has then an immediate interest in the continuation, even in the extension, of the particular obstacle to which its attention has been directed.

Theorists hence go on to found a system upon these individual interests, and say: Wants are riches: Labor is riches: The obstacle to well-being is well-being: To multiply obstacles is to give food to industry.

Then comes the statesman;—and as the developing and propagating of obstacles is the developing and propagating of riches, what more natural than that he should bend his efforts to that point? He says, for instance: If we prevent a large importation of iron, we create a difficulty in procuring it. This obstacle severely felt, obliges individuals to pay, in order to relieve themselves from it. A certain number of our citizens, giving themselves up to the combating of this obstacle, will thereby make their fortunes. In proportion, too, as the obstacle is great, and the mineral scarce, inaccessible, and of difficult and distant transportation, in the same proportion will be the number of laborers maintained by the various branches of this industry.

The same reasoning will lead to the suppression of machinery.

Here are men who are at a loss how to dispose of their wine-harvest. This is an obstacle which other men set about removing for them by the manufacture of casks. It is fortunate, say our statesmen, that this obstacle exists, since it occupies a portion of the labor of the nation, and enriches a certain number of our citizens. But here is presented to us an ingenious machine, which cuts down the oak, squares it, makes it into staves, and, gathering these together, forms them into casks. The obstacle is thus diminished, and with it the profits of the coopers. We must prevent this. Let us proscribe the machine!

To sift thoroughly this sophism, it is sufficient to remember that human labor is not an *end*, but a *means*. *It is never without employment.* If one obstacle is removed, it seizes another, and mankind is delivered from two obstacles by the same effort which was at first necessary for one. If the labor of coopers becomes useless, it must take another direction. But with what, it may be asked, will they be remunerated? Precisely with what they are at present remunerated. For if a certain quantity of labor becomes free from its original occupation, to be otherwise disposed of, a corresponding quantity of wages must thus also become free. To maintain that human labor can end by wanting employment, it would be necessary to prove that mankind will cease to encounter obstacles. In such a case, labor would be not only impossible, it would be superfluous. We should have nothing to do, because we should be all-powerful, and our *fiat* alone would satisfy at once our wants and our desires.

III.

EFFORT—RESULT.

We have seen that between our wants and their gratification many obstacles are interposed. We conquer or weaken these by the employment of our faculties. It may be said, in general terms, that industry is an effort followed by a result.

But by what do we measure our well-being? By the *result* of our effort, or by the *effort itself?* There exists always a proportion between the effort employed and the result obtained. Does progress consist in the relative increase of the second or of the first term of this proportion?

Both propositions have been sustained, and in political economy opinions are divided between them.

According to the first system, riches are the result of labor. They increase in the same ratio as *the result does to the effort.* Absolute perfection, of which *God* is the type, consists in the infinite distance between these two terms in this relation, viz., effort none, result infinite.

The second system maintains that it is the effort itself which forms the measure of, and constitutes, our riches. Progression is the increase of the *proportion of the effort to the result.* Its ideal extreme may be represented by the eternal and fruitless efforts of Sisyphus.*

The first system tends naturally to the encouragement of every thing which diminishes difficulties, and augments production,—as powerful machinery, which adds to the strength of man; the exchange of produce, which allows us to profit by the various natural agents distributed in different degrees over the surface of our globe; the intellect which discovers, experience which proves, and emulation which excites.

The second as logically inclines to every thing which can augment the difficulty and diminish the product; as privileges, monopolies, restrictions, prohibitions, suppression of machinery, sterility, etc.

It is well to remark here that the universal practice of men is always guided by the principle of the first system. Every *workman*, whether agriculturist, manufacturer, merchant, soldier, writer or philosopher, devotes the strength of his intellect to do better, to do more quickly, more economically,—in a word, *to do more with less.*

The opposite doctrine is in use with legislators, editors, statesmen, men whose business is to make experiments upon society. And even of these we may observe, that in what personally concerns *themselves*, they act, like every body else, upon the

* We will therefore beg the reader to allow us in future, for the sake of conciseness, to designate this system under the term of *Sisyphism*.

principle of obtaining from their labor the greatest possible quantity of useful results.

It may be supposed that I exaggerate, and that there are no true *Sisyphists.*

I grant that in practice the principle is not pushed to its extremest consequences. And this must always be the case when one starts upon a wrong principle, because the absurd and injurious results to which it leads, cannot but check it in its progress. For this reason, practical industry never can admit of *Sisyphism.* The error is too quickly followed by its punishment to remain concealed. But in the speculative industry of theorists and statesmen, a false principle may be for a long time followed up, before the complication of its consequences, only half understood, can prove its falsity; and even when all is revealed, the opposite principle is acted upon, self is contradicted, and justification sought, in the incomparably absurd modern axiom, that in political economy there is no principle universally true.

Let us see then, if the two opposite principles I have laid down do not predominate, each in its turn; —the one in practical industry, the other in industrial legislation.

I have already quoted some words of Mr. Bugeaud; but we must look on Mr. Bugeaud in two separate characters, the agriculturist and the legislator.

As agriculturist, Mr. Bugeaud makes every effort to attain the double object of sparing labor, and obtaining bread cheap. When he prefers a good plough to a bad one, when he improves the quality of his manures; when, to loosen his soil, he substitutes as much as possible the action of the atmosphere for that of the hoe or the harrow; when he calls to his aid every improvement that science and experience have revealed, he has, and can have, but one object, viz., *to diminish the proportion of the effort to the result.* We have indeed no other means of judging of the success of an agriculturist, or of the merits of his system, but by observing how far he has succeeded in lessening the one, while he increases the other; and as all the farmers in the world act upon this principle, we may say that all mankind are seeking, no doubt for their own advantage, to obtain at the lowest price, bread, or whatever other article of produce they may need, always diminishing the effort necessary for obtaining any given quantity thereof.

This incontestable tendency of human nature, once proved, would, one might suppose, be sufficient to point out the true principle to the legislator, and to show him how he ought to assist industry (if indeed it is any part of his business to assist it at all), for it would be absurd to say that the laws of men should operate in an inverse ratio from those of Providence.

Yet we have heard Mr. Bugeaud in his character of legislator, exclaim, "I do not understand this theory of cheapness; I would rather see bread dear, and work more abundant." And consequently the deputy from Dordogne votes in favor of legislative measures whose effect is to shackle and impede commerce, precisely because by so doing we are prevented from procuring by exchange, and at low price, what direct production can only furnish more expensively.

Now it is very evident that the system of Mr. Bugeaud the deputy, is directly opposed to that of Mr. Bugeaud the agriculturist. Were he consistent with himself, he would as legislator vote against all restriction; or else as farmer, he would practice in his fields the same principle which he proclaims in the public councils. We should then see him sowing his grain in his most sterile fields, because he would thus succeed in *laboring much*, to *obtain little*. We should see him forbidding the use of the plough, because he could, by scratching up the soil with his nails, fully gratify his double wish of "*dear bread* and *abundant labor*."

Restriction has for its avowed object, and acknowledged effect, the augmentation of labor. And again, equally avowed and acknowledged, its object and effect are, the increase of prices;—a synonymous term for scarcity of produce. Pushed then to its greatest extreme, it is pure *Sisyphism* as we have defined it: *labor infinite; result nothing.*

Baron Charles Dupin, who is looked upon as the oracle of the peerage in the science of political economy, accuses railroads of *injuring shipping*, and it is certainly true that the most perfect means of attaining an object must always limit the use of a less perfect means. But railways can only injure shipping by drawing from it articles of transportation; this they can only do by transporting more cheaply; and they can only transport more cheaply, by *diminishing the proportion of the effort employed to the result obtained;* for it is in this that cheapness consists. When, therefore, Baron Dupin laments the suppression of labor in attaining a given result, he maintains the doctrine of *Sisyphism.* Logically, if he prefers the vessel to the railway, he should also prefer the wagon to the vessel, the pack-saddle to the wagon, and the wallet to the pack-saddle; for this is, of all known means of transportation, the one which requires the greatest amount of labor, in proportion to the result obtained.

"Labor constitutes the riches of the people," said Mr. de Saint Cricq, a minister who has laid not a few shackles upon our commerce. This was no elliptical expression, meaning that the "results of labor constitute the riches of the people." No,—this statesman intended to say, that it is the *intensity* of labor, which measures riches; and the proof of this is, that from step to step, from restriction to restriction, he forced on France (and in so doing believed that he was doing well) to give to the procuring, of, for instance, a certain quantity of iron, double the necessary labor. In England, iron was then at eight francs; in France it cost sixteen. Supposing the day's work to be worth one franc, it is evident that France could, by barter, procure a quintal of iron by eight days' labor taken from the labor of the nation. Thanks to the restrictive measures of Mr. de Saint Cricq, sixteen days' work were necessary to procure it, by direct production. Here then we have double labor for an identical result; therefore double riches; and riches, measured not by the result, but by the intensity of labor. Is not this pure and unadulterated *Sisyphism?*

That there may be nothing equivocal, the minister carries his idea still farther, and on the same principle that we have heard him call the intensity of labor *riches*, we will find him calling the abundant results of labor, and the plenty of every thing proper to the satisfying of our wants, *poverty.* "Every where," he remarks, "machinery has pushed aside manual labor; every where production is superabundant; every where the equilibrium is destroyed between the power of production and that of consumption." Here then we see that, according to Mr. de Saint Cricq, if France was in a critical situation, it was because her productions were too abundant;

there was too much intelligence, too much efficiency in her national labor. We were too well fed, too well clothed, too well supplied with every thing; the rapid production was more than sufficient for our wants. It was necessary to put an end to this calamity, and therefore it became needful to force us, by restrictions, to work more, in order to produce less.

I also touched upon an opinion expressed by another minister of commerce, Mr. d'Argout, which is worthy of being a little more closely looked into. Wishing to give a death blow to the beet, he said: "The culture of the beet is undoubtedly useful, *but this usefulness is limited.* It is not capable of the prodigious developments which have been predicted of it. To be convinced of this it is enough to remark that the cultivation of it must necessarily be confined within the limits of consumption. Double, treble if you will, the present consumption of France, and *you will still find that a very small portion of her soil will suffice for this consumption.* (Truly a most singular cause of complaint!) Do you wish the proof of this? How many hectares were planted in beets in the year 1828? 3,130, which is 1-10540th of our cultivable soil. How many are there at this time, when our domestic sugar supplies one-third of the consumption of the country? 16,700 hectares, or 1-1978th of the cultivable soil, or 45 centiares for each commune. Suppose that our domestic sugar should monopolize the supply of the whole consumption, we still would have but 48,000 hectares or 1-689th of our cultivable soil in beets."*

There are two things to consider in this quotation. The facts and the doctrine. The facts go to prove that very little soil, capital, and labor would be necessary for the production of a large quantity of sugar; and that each commune of France would be abundantly provided with it by giving up one hectare to its cultivation. The peculiarity of the doctrine consists in the looking upon this facility of production as an unfortunate circumstance, and the regarding the very fruitfulness of this new branch of industry as a *limitation to its usefulness.*

It is not my purpose here to constitute myself the defender of the beet, or the judge of the singular facts stated by Mr. d'Argout, but it is worth the trouble of examining into the doctrines of a statesman, to whose judgment France, for a long time, confided the fate of her agriculture and her commerce.

I began by saying that a variable proportion exists in all industrial pursuits, between the effort and the result. Absolute imperfection consists in an infinite effort, without any result; absolute per-

* In justice to Mr. d'Argout we should say that this singular language is given by him as the argument of the enemies of the beet. But he made it his own, and sanctioned it by the law in justification of which he adduced it.

fection in an unlimited result, without any effort; and perfectibility, in the progressive diminution of the effort, compared with the result.

But Mr. d'Argout tells us, that where we looked for life, we shall find only death. The importance of any object of industry is, according to him, in direct proportion to its feebleness. What, for instance, can we expect from the beet? Do you not see that 48,000 hectares of land, with capital and labor in proportion, will suffice to furnish sugar to all France? It is then an object of *limited usefulness;* limited, be it understood, in the *work* which it calls for; and this is the sole measure, according to our minister, of the usefulness of any pursuit. This usefulness would be much more limited still, if, thanks to the fertility of the soil, or the richness of the beet, 24,000 hectares would serve instead of 48,000. If there were only needed twenty times, a hundred times more soil, more capital, more labor, to *attain the same result*—Oh! then some hopes might be founded upon this article of industry; it would be worthy of the protection of the state, for it would open a vast field to national labor. But to produce much with little is a bad example, and the laws ought to set things to rights.

What is true with regard to sugar, cannot be false with regard to bread. If therefore the usefulness of an object of industry is to be calculated, not by the comforts which it can furnish with a certain quantum of labor, but, on the contrary, by the increase of labor which it requires in order to furnish a certain quantity of comforts, it is evident that we ought to desire, that each acre of land should produce little corn, and that each grain of corn should furnish little nutriment; in other words, that our territory should be sterile enough to require a considerably larger proportion of soil, capital, and labor to nourish its population. The demand for human labor could not fail to be in direct proportion to this sterility, and then truly would the wishes of Messrs. Bugeaud, Saint Cricq, Dupin, and d'Argout be satisfied; bread would be dear, work abundant, and France would be rich—rich according to the understanding of these gentlemen.

All that we could have further to hope for, would be, that human intellect might sink and become extinct; for, while intellect exists, it can but seek continually to increase the *proportion of the end to the means; of the product to the labor.* Indeed it is in this continuous effort, and in this alone, that intellect consists.

Sisyphism has then been the doctrine of all those who have been intrusted with the regulation of the industry of our country. It would not be just to reproach them with this; for this principle becomes that of our ministry, only because it prevails in the chambers; it prevails in the chambers, only because it is sent there by the electoral body; and the electoral body is imbued with it, only because public opinion is filled with it to repletion.

Let me repeat here, that I do not accuse such men as Messrs. Bugeaud, Dupin, Saint Cricq, and d'Argout, of being absolutely and always *Sisyphists.* Very certainly they are not such in their personal transactions; very certainly each one of them will procure for himself *by barter*, what by *direct production* would be attainable only at a higher price. But I maintain that they are *Sisyphists* when they prevent the country from acting upon the same principle.

IV.

EQUALIZING OF THE FACILITIES OF PRODUCTION.

It is said . . . . . . but, for fear of being accused of manufacturing Sophisms for the mouths of the protectionists, I will allow one of their most able reasoners to speak for himself.

"It is our belief that protection should correspond to, should be the representation of, the difference which exists between the price of an article of home production and a similar article of foreign production. . . . . . A protecting duty calculated upon such a basis does nothing more than secure free competition; ..... free competition can only exist where there is an equality in the facilities of production. In a horse-race the load which each horse carries is weighed and all advantages equalized; otherwise there could be no competition. In commerce, if one producer can undersell all others, he ceases to be a competitor and becomes a monopolist. ..... Suppress the protection which represents the difference of price according to each, and foreign productions must immediately inundate and obtain the monopoly of our market."*

"Every one ought to wish, for his own sake and for that of the community, that the productions of the country should be protected against foreign competition, *whenever the latter may be able to undersell the former.*"†

This argument is constantly recurring in all writings of the protectionist school. It is my intention to make a careful investigation of its merits, and I must begin by soliciting the attention and the patience of the reader. I will first examine into the inequalities which depend upon natural causes, and afterwards into those which are caused by diversity of taxes.

Here, as elsewhere, we find the theorists who favor protection, taking part with the producer. Let us consider the case of the unfortunate consumer, who

* M. le Vicomte de Romanet.

† Mathieu de Dombasle.

seems to have entirely escaped their attention. They compare the field of production to the *turf.* But on the turf, the race is at once a *means and an end.* The public has no interest in the struggle, independent of the struggle itself. When your horses are started in the course with the single object of determining which is the best runner, nothing is more natural than that their burdens should be equalized. But if your object were to send an important and critical piece of intelligence, could you without incongruity place obstacles to the speed of that one whose fleetness would secure the best means of attaining your end? And yet this is your course in relation to industry. You forget the end aimed at, which is the *well-being* of the community.

But we cannot lead our opponents to look at things from our point of view, let us now take theirs; let us examine the question as producers.

I will seek to prove

1. That equalizing the facilities of production is to attack the foundations of all trade.

2. That it is not true that the labor of one country can be crushed by the competition of more favored climates.

3. That, even were this the case, protective duties cannot equalize the facilities of production.

4. That freedom of trade equalizes these conditions as much as possible; and

5. That the countries which are the least favored

by nature are those which profit most by freedom of trade.

I. The equalizing of the facilities of production, is not only the shackling of certain articles of commerce, but it is the attacking of the system of mutual exchange in its very foundation principle. For this system is based precisely upon the very diversities, or, if the expression be preferred, upon the inequalities of fertility, climate, temperature, capabilities, which the protectionists seek to render null. If Guyenne sends its wines to Brittany, and Brittany sends corn to Guyenne, it is because these two provinces are, from different circumstances, induced to turn their attention to the production of different articles. Is there any other rule for international exchanges? Again, to bring against such exchanges the very inequalities of condition which excite and explain them, is to attack them in their very cause of being. The protective system, closely followed up, would bring men to live like snails, in a state of complete isolation. In short, there is not one of its Sophisms, which if carried through by vigorous deductions, would not end in destruction and annihilation.

II. It is not true that the unequal facility of production, in two similar branches of industry, should necessarily cause the destruction of the one which is the least fortunate. On the turf, if one horse gains the prize, the other loses it; but when two horses work to produce any useful article, each produces in proportion to his strength; and because the stronger is the more useful, it does not follow that the weaker is good for nothing. Wheat is cultivated in every department of France, although there are great differences in the degree of fertility existing among them. If it happens that there be one which does not cultivate it, it is because, even to itself, such cultivation is not useful. Analogy will show us, that under the influence of an unshackled trade, notwithstanding similar differences, wheat would be produced in every kingdom of Europe; and if any one were induced to abandon entirely the cultivation of it, this would only be, because it would *be her interest* to employ otherwise her lands, her capital, and her labor. And why does not the fertility of one department paralyze the agriculture of a neighboring and less favored one? Because the phenomena of political economy have a suppleness, an elasticity, and, so to speak, *a self-leveling power*, which seems to escape the attention of the school of protectionists. They accuse us of being theorists, but it is themselves who are theorists to a supreme degree, if being theoretic consists in building up systems upon the experience of a single fact, instead of profiting by the experience of a series of facts. In the above example, it is the difference in the value of lands, which compensates for the difference in their fertility. Your field produces three times as much as mine. Yes. But it has cost you three times as much, and therefore I can still compete with you: this is the sole mystery. And observe how the advantage on one point leads to disadvantage on the other. Precisely because your soil is more fruitful, it is more dear. It is not *accidentally* but *necessarily* that the equilibrium is established, or at least inclines to establish itself; and can it be denied that perfect freedom in exchanges is, of all the systems, the one which favors this tendency?

I have cited an agricultural example; I might as easily have taken one from any trade. There are tailors at Quimper, but that does not prevent tailors from being in Paris also, although the latter have to pay a much higher rent, as well as higher price for furniture, workmen, and food. But their customers are sufficiently numerous not only to re-establish the balance, but also to make it lean on their side.

When therefore the question is about equalizing the advantages of labor, it would be well to consider whether the natural freedom of exchange is not the best umpire.

This self-leveling faculty of political phenomena is so important, and at the same time so well calculated to cause us to admire the providential wisdom which presides over the equalizing government of society, that I must ask permission a little longer, to turn to it the attention of the reader.

The protectionists say, Such a nation has the advantage over us, in being able to procure cheaply, coal, iron, machinery, capital; it is impossible for us to compete with it.

We must examine the proposition under other aspects. For the present, I stop at the question, whether, when an advantage and a disadvantage are placed in juxtaposition, they do not bear in themselves, the former a descending, the latter an ascending power, which must end by placing them in a just equilibrium.

Let us suppose the countries A and B. A has every advantage over B; you thence conclude that labor will be concentrated upon A, while B must be abandoned. A, you say, sells much more than it buys; B buys more than it sells. I might dispute this, but I will meet you upon your own ground.

In the hypothesis, labor, being in great demand in A, soon rises in value; while labor, iron, coal, lands, food, capital, all being little sought after in B, soon fall in price.

Again: A being always selling and B always buying, cash passes from B to A. It is abundant in A—very scarce in B.

But where there is abundance of cash, it follows that in all purchases a large proportion of it will be needed. Then in A, *real dearness*, which proceeds from a very active demand, is added to *nominal dearness*, the consequence of a superabundance of the precious metals.

Scarcity of money implies that little is necessary for each purchase. Then in B, a *nominal cheapness* is combined with *real cheapness.*

Under these circumstances, industry will have the strongest possible motives for deserting A, to establish itself in B.

Now, to return to what would be the true course of things. As the progress of such events is always gradual, industry from its nature being opposed to sudden transits, let us suppose that, without waiting the extreme point, it will have gradually divided itself between A and B, according to the laws of supply and demand; that is to say, according to the laws of justice and usefulness.

I do not advance an empty hypothesis when I say, that were it possible that industry should concentrate itself upon a single point, there must, from its nature, arise spontaneously, and in its midst, an irresistible power of decentralization.

We will quote the words of a manufacturer to the Chamber of Commerce at Manchester (the figures brought into his demonstration are suppressed):

"Formerly we exported goods; this exportation gave way to that of thread for the manufacture of goods; later, instead of thread, we exported machinery for the making of thread; then capital for the construction of machinery ; and lastly, workmen and talent, which are the source of capital. All these elements of labor have, one after the other, transferred themselves to other points, where their profits were increased, and where the means of subsistence being less difficult to obtain, life is maintained at a less cost. There are at present to be seen in Prussia, Austria, Saxony, Switzerland, and Italy, immense manufacturing establishments, founded entirely by English capital, worked by English labor, and directed by English talent."

We may here perceive, that Nature, or rather Providence, with more wisdom and foresight than the narrow rigid system of the protectionists can suppose, does not permit the concentration of labor, the monopoly of advantages, from which they draw their arguments as from an absolute and irremediable fact. It has, by means as simple as they are infallible, provided for dispersion, diffusion, mutual dependence, and simultaneous progress; all of which, your restrictive laws paralyze as much as is in their power, by their tendency towards the isolation of nations. By this means they render much more decided the differences existing in the conditions of production; they check the self-leveling power of industry, prevent fusion of interests, and fence in each nation within its own peculiar advantages and disadvantages.

III. To say that by a protective law the conditions of production are equalized, is to disguise an error under false terms. It is not true that an import duty equalizes the conditions of production. These remain after the imposition of the duty just as they were before. The most that the law can do is to equalize the *conditions of sale.* If it should be said that I am playing upon words, I retort the accusation upon my adversaries. It is for them to prove that *production* and *sale* are synonymous terms, which if they cannot do, I have a right to accuse them, if not of playing upon words, at least of confounding them.

Let me be permitted to exemplify my idea.

Suppose that several Parisian speculators should determine to devote themselves to the production of oranges. They know that the oranges of Portugal can be sold in Paris at ten centimes, whilst on account of the boxes, hot-houses, etc., which are necessary to ward against the severity of our climate, it is impossible to raise them at less than a franc apiece. They accordingly demand a duty of ninety centimes upon Portugal oranges. With the help of this duty, say they, the *conditions of production* will be equalized. The legislative body, yielding as usual to this argument, imposes a duty of ninety centimes on each foreign orange.

Now I say that the *relative conditions of production* are in no wise changed. The law can take nothing from the heat of the sun in Lisbon, nor from the severity of the frosts in Paris. Oranges continuing to mature themselves *naturally* on the banks of the Tagus, and artificially upon those of the Seine, must continue to require for their production much more labor on the latter than the former. The law can only equalize the *conditions of sale.* It is evident that while the Portuguese sell their oranges at a franc apiece, the ninety centimes which go to pay the tax are taken from the French consumer. Now look at the whimsicality of the result. Upon each Portuguese orange, the country loses nothing; for the ninety centimes which the consumer pays to satisfy the tax, enter into the treasury. There is improper distribution, but no loss. Upon each French orange consumed, there will be about ninety centimes lost; for while the buyer very certainly loses them, the seller just as certainly does not gain them, for even according to the hypothesis, he will receive only the price of production. I will leave it to the protectionists to draw their conclusion.

IV. I have laid some stress upon this distinction between the conditions of production and those of sale, which perhaps the prohibitionists may consider as paradoxical, because it leads me on to what they will consider as a still stranger paradox. This is: If you really wish to equalize the facilities of production, leave trade free.

This may surprise the protectionists; but let me

entreat them to listen, if it be only through curiosity, to the end of my argument. It shall not be long. I will now take it up where we left off.

If we suppose for the moment, that the common and daily profits of each Frenchman amount to one franc, it will indisputably follow that to produce an orange by *direct* labor in France, one day's work, or its equivalent, will be requisite; whilst to produce the cost of a Portuguese orange, only one-tenth of this day's labor is required; which means simply this, that the sun does at Lisbon what labor does at Paris. Now is it not evident, that if I can produce an orange, or, what is the same thing, the means of buying it, with one-tenth of a day's labor, I am placed exactly in the same condition as the Portuguese producer himself, excepting the expense of the transportation? It is then certain that freedom of commerce equalizes the conditions of production direct or indirect, as much as it is possible to equalize them; for it leaves but the one inevitable difference, that of transportation.

I will add that free trade equalizes also the facilities for attaining enjoyments, comforts, and general consumption; the last an object which is, it would seem, quite forgotten, and which is nevertheless all important; since consumption is the main object of all our industrial efforts. Thanks to freedom of trade, we would enjoy here the results of the Portuguese sun, as well as Portugal itself; and the inhabitants of Havre, would have in their reach, as well as those of London, and with the same facilities, the advantages which nature has in a mineralogical point of view conferred upon Newcastle.

The protectionists may suppose me in a paradoxical humor, for I go farther still. I say, and I sincerely believe, that if any two countries are placed in unequal circumstances as to advantages of production, *that one of the two which is the least favored by nature, will gain most by freedom of commerce.* To prove this, I shall be obliged to turn somewhat aside from the form of reasoning which belongs to this work. I will do so, however; first, because the question in discussion turns upon this point; and again, because it will give me the opportunity of exhibiting a law of political economy of the highest importance, and which, well understood, seems to me to be destined to lead back to this science all those sects which, in our days, are seeking in the land of chimeras that social harmony which they have been unable to discover in nature. I speak of the law of consumption, which the majority of political economists may well be reproached with having too much neglected.

Consumption is the *end*, the final cause, of all the phenomena of political economy, and, consequently, in it is found their final solution.

No effect, whether favorable or unfavorable, can be arrested permanently upon the producer. The advantages and the disadvantages, which, from his relations to nature and to society, are his, both equally pass gradually from him, with an almost insensible tendency to be absorbed and fused into the community at large; the community considered as consumers. This is an admirable law, alike in its cause and its effects, and he who shall succeed in making it well understood, will have a right to say, "I have not, in my passage through the world, forgotten to pay my tribute to society."

Every circumstance which favors the work of production is of course hailed with joy by the producer, for its *immediate effect* is to enable him to render greater services to the community, and to exact from it a greater remuneration. Every circumstance which injures production, must equally be the source of uneasiness to him; for its *immediate effect* is to diminish his services, and consequently his remuneration. This is a fortunate and necessary law of nature. The immediate good or evil of favorable or unfavorable circumstances must fall upon the producer, in order to influence him invincibly to seek the one and to avoid the other.

Again, when a workman succeeds in his labor, the *immediate* benefit of this success is received by him. This again is necessary, to determine him to devote his attention to it. It is also just; because it is just that an effort crowned with success should bring its own reward.

But these effects, good and bad, although permanent in themselves, are not so as regards the producer. If they had been so, a principle of progressive and consequently infinite *inequality* would have been introduced among men. This good, and this evil, both therefore pass on, to become absorbed in the general destinies of humanity.

How does this come about? I will try to make it understood by some examples.

Let us go back to the thirteenth century. Men who gave themselves up to the business of copying, received for this service *a remuneration regulated by the general rate of profits.* Among them is found one, who seeks and finds the means of multiplying rapidly copies of the same work. He invents printing. The first effect of this is, that the individual is enriched, while many more are impoverished. At the first view, wonderful as the discovery is, one hesitates in deciding whether it is not more injurious than useful. It seems to have introduced into the world, as I said above, an element of infinite inequality. Guttenberg makes large profits by this invention, and perfects the invention by the profits, until all other copyists are ruined. As for the public,—the consumer,—it gains but little, for Guttenberg takes care to lower the price of books only just so much as is necessary to undersell all rivals.

But the great Mind which put harmony into the movements of celestial bodies, could also give it to the internal mechanism of society. We will see the advantages of this invention escaping from the individual, to become forever the common patrimony of mankind.

The process finally becomes known. Guttenberg is no longer alone in his art; others imitate him. Their profits are at first considerable. They are recompensed for being the first who make the effort to imitate the processes of the newly invented art. This again was necessary, in order that they might be induced to the effort, and thus forward the great and final result to which we approach. They gain much; but they gain less than the inventor, for *competition* has commenced its work. The price of books now continually decreases. The gains of the imitators diminish in proportion as the invention becomes older; and in the same proportion imitation becomes less meritorious. Soon the new object of industry attains its normal condition; in other words, the remuneration of printers is no longer an exception to the general rules of remuneration, and, like that of copyists formerly, it is only regulated *by the general rate of profits.* Here then the producer, as such, holds only the old position. The discovery, however, has been made; the saving of time, labor, effort, for a fixed result, for a certain number of volumes, is realized. But in what is this manifested? In the cheap price of books. For the good of whom? For the good of the consumer,—of society,—of humanity. Printers, having no longer any peculiar merit, receive no longer a peculiar remuneration. As men,—as consumers,—they no doubt participate in the advantages which the invention confers upon the community; but that is all. As printers, as producers, they are placed upon the ordinary footing of all other producers. Society pays them for their labor, and not for the usefulness of the invention. *That* has become a gratuitous benefit, a common heritage to mankind.

What has been said of printing can be extended to every agent for the advancement of labor; from the nail and the mallet, up to the locomotive and the electric telegraph. Society enjoys all, by the abundance of its use, its consumption; and it *enjoys all gratuitously.* For as their effect is to diminish prices, it is evident that just so much of the price as is taken off by their intervention, renders the production in so far *gratuitous.* There only remains the actual labor of man to be paid for; and the remainder, which is the result of the invention, is subtracted; at least after the invention has run through the cycle which I have just described as its destined course. I send for a workman; he brings a saw with him; I pay him two francs for his day's labor, and he saws me twenty-five boards. If the saw had not been invented, he would perhaps not have been able to make one board, and I would have paid him the same for his day's labor. The *usefulness* then of the saw, is for me a gratuitous gift of nature, or rather it is a portion of the inheritance which, *in common* with my brother men, I have received from the genius of my ancestors. I have two workmen in my field; the one directs the handle of a plough, the other that of a spade. The result of their day's labor is very different, but the price is the same, because the remuneration is proportioned, not to the usefulness of the result, but to the effort, the labor given to attain it.

I invoke the patience of the reader, and beg him to believe, that I have not lost sight of free trade: I entreat him only to remember the conclusion at which I have arrived: *Remuneration is not proportioned to the usefulness of the articles brought by the producer into the market, but to the labor.**

I have so far taken my examples from human inventions, but will now go on to speak of natural advantages.

In every article of production, nature and man must concur. But the portion of nature is always gratuitous. Only so much of the usefulness of an article as is the result of human labor becomes the object of mutual exchange, and consequently of remuneration. The remuneration varies much, no doubt, in proportion to the intensity of the labor, of the skill which it requires, of its being *à propos*

* It is true that labor does not receive a uniform remuneration; because labor is more or less intense, dangerous, skillful, etc. Competition establishes for each category a price current; and it is of this variable price that I speak.

to the demand of the day, of the need which exists for it, of the momentary absence of competition, etc. But it is not the less true in principle, that the assistance received from natural laws, which belongs to all, counts for nothing in the price.

We do not pay for the air we breathe, although so useful to us, that we could not live two minutes without it. We do not pay for it, because Nature furnishes it without the intervention of man's labor. But if we wish to separate one of the gases which compose it, for instance, to fill a balloon, we must take some trouble and labor; or if another takes it for us, we must give him an equivalent in something which will have cost us the trouble of production. From which we see that the exchange is between troubles, efforts, labors. It is certainly not for hydrogen gas that I pay, for this is every where at my disposal, but for the work that it has been necessary to accomplish in order to disengage it; work which I have been spared, and which I must refund. If I am told that there are other things to pay for; as expense, materials, apparatus; I answer, that still in these things it is the work that I pay for. The price of the coal employed is only the representation of the labor necessary to dig and transport it.

We do not pay for the light of the sun, because Nature alone gives it to us. But we pay for the light of gas, tallow, oil, wax, because here is labor to be remunerated;—and remark, that it is so entirely labor and not utility to which remuneration is proportioned, that it may well happen that one of these means of lighting, while it may be much more effective than another, may still cost less. To cause this, it is only necessary that less human labor should be required to furnish it.

When the water-carrier comes to supply my house, were I to pay him in proportion to the *absolute utility* of the water, my whole fortune would not be sufficient. But I pay him only for the trouble he has taken. If he requires more, I can get others to furnish it, or finally go and get it myself. The water itself is not the subject of our bargain; but the labor taken to get the water. This point of view is so important, and the consequences that I am going to draw from it so clear, as regards the freedom of international exchanges, that I will still elucidate my idea by a few more examples.

The alimentary substance contained in potatoes does not cost us very dear, because a great deal of it is attainable with little work. We pay more for wheat, because, to produce it Nature requires more labor from man. It is evident that if Nature did for the latter what she does for the former, their prices would tend to the same level. It is impossible that the producer of wheat should permanently gain more than the producer of potatoes. The law of competition cannot allow it.

If by a happy miracle the fertility of all arable

lands were to be increased, it would not be the agriculturist, but the consumer, who would profit by this phenomenon; for the result of it would be, abundance and cheapness. There would be less labor incorporated into an acre of grain, and the agriculturist would be therefore obliged to exchange it for a less labor incorporated into some other article. If, on the contrary, the fertility of the soil were suddenly to deteriorate, the share of Nature in production would be less, that of labor greater, and the result would be higher prices. I am right then in saying that it is in consumption, in mankind, that at length all political phenomena find their solution. As long as we fail to follow their effects to this point, and look only at *immediate* effects, which act but upon individual men or classes of men *as producers,* we know nothing more of political economy than the quack does of medicine, when, instead of following the effects of a prescription in its action upon the whole system, he satisfies himself with knowing how it affects the palate and the throat.

The tropical regions are very favorable to the production of sugar and coffee; that is to say, Nature does most of the business and leaves but little for labor to accomplish. But who reaps the advantage of this liberality of Nature? Not these regions, for they are forced by competition to receive simply remuneration for their labor. It is mankind who is the gainer; for the result of this liberality is *cheapness*, and cheapness belongs to the world.

Here in the temperate zone, we find coal and iron ore, on the surface of the soil; we have but to stoop and take them. At first, I grant, the immediate inhabitants profit by this fortunate circumstance. But soon comes competition, and the price of coal and iron falls, until this gift of Nature becomes gratuitous to all, and human labor is only paid according to the general rate of profits.

Thus natural advantages, like improvements in the process of production, are, or have a constant tendency to become, under the law of competition, the common and *gratuitous* patrimony of consumers, of society, of mankind. Countries therefore which do not enjoy these advantages, must gain by commerce with those which do; because the exchanges of commerce are between *labor and labor;* subtraction being made of all the natural advantages which are combined with these labors; and it is evidently the most favored countries which can incorporate into a given labor the largest proportion of these *natural advantages.* Their produce representing less labor, receives less recompense; in other words, is *cheaper.* If then all the liberality of Nature results in cheapness, it is evidently not the producing, but the consuming country, which profits by her benefits.

Hence we may see the enormous absurdity of the consuming country, which rejects produce precisely because it is cheap. It is as though we should say: "We will have nothing of that which Nature gives you. You ask of us an effort equal to two, in order to furnish ourselves with articles only attainable at home by an effort equal to four. You can do it because with you Nature does half the work. But we will have nothing to do with it; we will wait till your climate, becoming more inclement, forces you to ask of us a labor equal to four, and then we can treat with you *upon an equal footing.*"

A is a favored country; B is maltreated by Nature. Mutual traffic then is advantageous to both, but principally to B, because the exchange is not between *utility* and *utility*, but between *value* and *value.* Now A furnishes a greater *utility in a similar value*, because the *utility* of any article includes at once what Nature and what labor have done; whereas the *value* of it only corresponds to the portion accomplished by labor. B then makes an entirely advantageous bargain; for by simply paying the producer from A for his labor, it receives in return not only the results of that labor, but in addition there is thrown in whatever may have accrued from the superior bounty of Nature.

We will lay down the general rule.

Traffic is an exchange of *values;* and as value is reduced by competition to the simple representation of labor, traffic is the exchange of equal labors. Whatever Nature has done towards the production of the articles exchanged, is given on both sides *gratuitously;* from whence it necessarily follows, that the most advantageous commerce is transacted with those countries which are the most favored by Nature.

The theory of which I have attempted, in this chapter, to trace the outlines, would require great developments. But perhaps the attentive reader will have perceived in it the fruitful seed which is destined in its future growth to smother Protection, at once with Fourierism, Saint Simonism, Commonism, and the various other schools whose object is to exclude the law of COMPETITION from the government of the world. Competition, no doubt, considering man as producer, must often interfere with his individual and *immediate* interests. But if we consider the great object of all labor, the universal good, in a word, *Consumption*, we cannot fail to find that Competition is to the moral world what the law of equilibrium is to the material one. It is the foundation of true Commomism, of true Socialism, of the equality of comforts and condition, so much sought after in our day; and if so many sincere reformers, so many earnest friends to the public rights, seek to reach their end by commercial *legislation*, it is only because they do not yet understand *commercial freedom.*

V.

OUR PRODUCTIONS ARE OVERLOADED WITH TAXES.

This is but a new wording of the last Sophism. The demand made is, that the foreign article should be taxed, in order to neutralize the effects of the tax, which weighs down national produce. It is still then but the question of equalizing the facilities of production. We have but to say that the tax is an artificial obstacle, which has exactly the same effect as a natural obstacle, i. e. the increasing of the price. If this increase is so great that there is more loss in producing the article in question than in attracting it from foreign parts by the production of an equivalent value, let it alone. Individual interest will soon learn to choose the lesser of two evils. I might refer the reader to the preceding demonstration for an answer to this Sophism; but it is one which recurs so often in the complaints and the petitions, I had almost said the demands, of the protectionist school, that it deserves a special discussion.

If the tax in question should be one of a special kind, directed against fixed articles of production, I agree that it is perfectly reasonable that foreign produce should be subjected to it. For instance, it would be absurd to free foreign salt from impost duty; not that in an economical point of view France would lose any thing by it; on the contrary, whatever may be said, principles are invariable, and France would gain by it, as she must always gain by avoiding an obstacle whether natural or artificial. But here the obstacle has been raised with a fiscal object. It is necessary that this end should be attained; and if foreign salt were to be sold in our market free from duty, the treasury would not receive its revenue, and would be obliged to seek it from some thing else. There would be evident inconsistency in creating an obstacle with a given object, and then avoiding the attainment of that object. It would have been better at once to seek what was needed in the other impost without taxing French salt. Such are the circumstances under which I would allow upon any foreign article a duty, *not protecting* but fiscal.

But the supposition that a nation, because it is subjected to heavier imposts than those of another neighboring nation, should protect itself by tariffs against the competition of its rival, is a Sophism, which it is now my purpose to attack.

I have said more than once, that I am opposing only the theory of the protectionists, with the hope of discovering the source of their errors. Were I disposed to enter into controversy with them, I would say: Why direct your tariffs principally against England and Belgium, both countries more overloaded with taxes than any in the world? Have I not a right to look upon your argument as a mere pretext? But I am not of the number of those who believe that prohibitionists are guided by interest, and not by conviction. The doctrine of Protection is too popular not to be sincere. If the majority could believe in freedom, we would be free. Without doubt it is individual interest which weighs us down with tariffs; but it acts upon conviction.

The State may make either a good or a bad use of taxes; it makes a good use of them when it renders to the public services equivalent to the value received from them; it makes a bad use of them when it expends this value, giving nothing in return.

To say in the first case that they place the country which pays them in more disadvantageous conditions for production, than the country which is free from them, is a Sophism. We pay, it is true, twenty millions for the administration of justice, and the maintenance of the police, but we have justice and the police; we have the security which they give, the time which they save for us; and it is most probable that production is neither more easy nor more active among nations, where (if there be such) each individual takes the administration of justice into his own hands. We pay, I grant, many hundred millions for roads, bridges, ports, railways; but we have these railways, these ports, bridges and roads, and unless we maintain that it is a losing business to establish them, we cannot say that they place us in a position inferior to that of nations who have, it is true, no taxes for public works, but who likewise have no public works. And here we see why (even while we accuse internal taxes of being a cause of industrial inferiority) we direct our tariffs precisely against those nations which are the most taxed. It is because these taxes, well used, far from injuring, have ameliorated the *conditions of production* to these nations. Thus we again arrive at the conclusion that the protectionist Sophisms not only wander from, but are the contrary—the very antithesis of truth.

As to unproductive imposts, suppress them if you can; but surely it is a most singular idea to suppose, that their evil effect is to be neutralized by the addition of individual taxes to public taxes. Many thanks for the compensation! The State, you say, has taxed us too much; surely this is no reason why we should tax each other!

A protective duty is a tax directed against foreign produce, but which returns, let us keep in mind, upon the national consumer. Is it not then a singular argument to say to him, "Because the taxes are heavy, we will raise prices higher for you; and because the State takes a part of your revenue, we will give another portion of it to benefit a monopoly?

But let us examine more closely this Sophism so accredited among our legislators; although, strange to say, it is precisely those who keep up the unproductive imposts (according to our present hypothesis) who attribute to them afterwards our supposed inferiority, and seek to re-establish the equilibrium by further imposts and new clogs.

It appears to me to be evident that protection, without any change in its nature and effects, might have taken the form of a direct tax, raised by the State, and distributed as a premium to privileged industry.

Let us admit that foreign iron could be sold in our market at eight francs, but not lower; and French iron at not lower than twelve francs.

In this hypothesis there are two ways in which the State can secure the national market to the home producer.

The first, is to put upon foreign iron a duty of five francs. This, it is evident, would exclude it, because it could no longer be sold at less than thirteen francs; eight francs for the cost price, five for the tax; and at this price it must be driven from the market by French iron, which we have supposed to cost twelve francs. In this case the buyer, the consumer, will have paid all the expenses of the protection given.

The second means would be to lay upon the public a tax of five francs, and to give it as a premium to the iron manufacturer. The effect would in either case be equally a protective measure. Foreign iron would, according to both systems, be alike excluded; for our iron manufacturer could sell at seven francs, what, with the five francs premium, would thus bring him in twelve. While the price of sale being seven francs, foreign iron could not obtain a market at eight.

In these two systems the principle is the same; the effect is the same. There is but this single difference; in the first case the expense of protection is paid by a part, in the second by the whole of the community.

I frankly confess my preference for the second system, which I regard as more just, more economical and more legal. More just, because, if society wishes to give bounties to some of its members, the whole community ought to contribute; more economical, because it would banish many difficulties, and save the expenses of collection; more legal, lastly, because the public would see clearly into the operation, and know what was required of it.

But if the protective system had taken this form, would it not have been laughable enough to hear it said, "We pay heavy taxes for the army, the navy, the judiciary, the public works, the schools, the public debt, etc. These amount to more than a thousand million. It would therefore be desirable that the State should take another thousand million, to relieve the poor iron manufacturers; or the suffering stockholders of coal mines; or those unfortunate lumber dealers, or the useful codfishery."

This, it must be perceived, by an attentive investigation, is the result of the Sophism in question. In vain, gentlemen, are all your efforts; you cannot *give money* to one without taking it from another. If you are absolutely determined to exhaust the funds of the taxable community, well; but, at least, do not mock them; do not tell them, "We take from you again, in order to compensate you for what we have already taken."

It would be a too tedious undertaking to endeavor to point out all the fallacies of this Sophism. I will therefore limit myself to the consideration of it in three points.

You argue that France is overburthened with taxes, and deduce thence the conclusion that it is necessary to protect such and such an article of produce. But protection does not relieve us from the payment of these taxes. If, then, individuals devoting themselves to any one object of industry, should advance this demand: "We, from our participation in the payment of taxes, have our expenses of production increased, and therefore ask for a protective duty which shall raise our price of sale;" what is this but a demand on their part to be allowed to free themselves from the burthen of the tax, by laying it on the rest of the community?

Their object is to balance, by the increased price of their produce, the amount which *they* pay in taxes. Now, as the whole amount of these taxes must enter into the treasury, and the increase of price must be paid by society, it follows that (where this protective duty is imposed) society has to bear, not only the general tax, but also that for the protection of the article in question. But it is answered, let *every thing* be protected. Firstly, this is impossible; and, again, were it possible, how could such a system give relief? *I* will pay for you, *you* will pay for me; but not the less, still there remains the tax to be paid.

Thus you are the dupes of an illusion. You determine to raise taxes for the support of an army, a navy, the church, university, judges, roads, etc. Afterwards you seek to disburthen from its portion of the tax, first one article of industry, then another, then a third; always adding to the burthen of the mass of society. You thus only create interminable complications. If you can prove that the increase of price resulting from protection, falls upon the foreign producer, I grant something specious in your argument. But if it be true that the French people paid the tax before the passing of the protective duty, and afterwards that it has paid not only the tax, but the protective duty also, truly I do not perceive wherein it has profited.

But I go much further, and maintain that the

more oppressive our taxes are, the more anxiously ought we to open our ports and frontiers to foreign nations, less burthened than ourselves. And why? In order that we may share with them, as much as possible, the burthen which we bear. Is it not an incontestable maxim in political economy, that taxes must, in the end, fall upon the consumer? The greater then our commerce, the greater the portion which will be reimbursed to us, of taxes incorporated in the produce, which we will have sold to foreign consumers; whilst we, on our part, will have made to them only a lesser reimbursement, because (according to our hypothesis) their produce is less taxed than ours.

Again, finally, has it ever occurred to you to ask yourself, whether these heavy taxes which you adduce as a reason for keeping up the prohibitive system, may not be the result of this very system itself? To what purpose would be our great standing armies, and our powerful navies, if commerce were free?

VI.

BALANCE OF TRADE.

OUR adversaries have adopted a system of tactics, which embarrasses us not a little. Do we prove our doctrine? They admit the truth of it in the most respectful manner. Do we attack their principles? They abandon them with the best possible grace. They only ask that our doctrine, which they acknowledge to be true, should be confined to books; and that their principles, which they allow to be false, should be established in practice. If we will give up to them the regulation of our tariffs, they will leave us triumphant in the domain of theory.

"Assuredly," said Mr. Gauthier de Roumilly, lately, "assuredly no one wishes to call up from their graves the defunct theories of the balance of trade." And yet Mr. Gauthier, after giving this passing blow to error, goes on immediately afterwards, and for two hours consecutively, to reason as though this error were a truth.

Give me Mr. Lestiboudois. Here we have a consistent reasoner! a logical arguer! There is nothing in his conclusions which cannot be found in his premises. He asks nothing in practice which he does not justify in theory. His principles may perchance be false, and this is the point in question. But he has a principle. He believes, he proclaims aloud, that if France gives ten to receive fifteen, she loses five; and surely, with such a belief, nothing is more natural than that he should make laws consistent with it.

He says: "What it is important to remark, is, that constantly the amount of importation is augmenting, and surpassing that of exportation. Every year France buys more foreign produce, and sells less of its own produce. This can be proved by figures. In 1842, we see the importation exceed the exportation by two hundred millions. This appears to me to prove, in the clearest manner, that national labor *is not sufficiently protected*, that we are provided by foreign labor, and that the competition of our rivals *oppresses* our industry. The law in question, appears to me to be a consecration of the fact, that our political economists have assumed a false position in declaring, that in proportion to produce bought, there is always a corresponding quantity sold. It is evident that purchases may be made, not with the habitual productions of a country, not with its revenue, not with the results of actual labor, but with its capital, with the accumulated savings which should serve for reproduction. A country may spend, dissipate its profits and savings, may impoverish itself, and by the consumption of its national capital, progress gradually to its ruin. *This is precisely what we are doing. We give, every year, two hundred millions to foreign nations.*"

Well! here, at least, is a man whom we can understand. There is no hypocrisy in this language. The balance of trade is here clearly maintained and defended. France imports two hundred millions more than she exports. Then France loses two hundred millions yearly. And the remedy? It is to check importation. The conclusion is perfectly consistent.

It is, then, with Mr. Lestiboudois that we will argue, for how is it possible to do so with Mr. Gauthier? If you say to the latter, the balance of trade is a mistake, he will answer, So I have declared it in my exordium. If you exclaim, But it is a truth, he will say, Thus I have classed it in my conclusions.

Political economists may blame me for arguing with Mr. Lestiboudois. To combat the balance of trade, is, they say, neither more nor less than to fight against a windmill.

But let us be on our guard. The balance of trade is neither so old, nor so sick, nor so dead, as Mr. Gauthier is pleased to imagine; for all the legislature, Mr. Gauthier himself included, are associated by their votes with the theory of Mr. Lestiboudois.

However, not to fatigue the reader, I will not seek to investigate too closely this theory, but will content myself with subjecting it to the experience of facts.

It is constantly alleged in opposition to our principles, that they are good only in theory. But, gentlemen, do you believe that merchants' books are good in practice? It does appear to me that if there is any thing which can have a practical authority, when the object is to prove profit and loss, that this must be commercial accounts. We cannot suppose that all the merchants of the world, for centuries back, should have so little understood their own affairs, as to have kept their books in such a manner as to represent gains as losses, and losses as gains. Truly it would be easier to believe that Mr. Lestiboudois is a bad political economist.

A merchant, one of my friends, having had two business transactions, with very different results, I have been curious to compare on this subject the accounts of the counter with those of the custom-house, interpreted by Mr. Lestiboudois with the sanction of our six hundred legislators.

Mr. T.. despatched from Havre a vessel, freighted, for the United States, with French merchandise, principally Parisian articles, valued at 200,000 francs. Such was the amount entered at the custom-house. The cargo, on its arrival at New Orleans, had paid ten per cent. expenses, and was liable to thirty per cent. duties; which raised its value to 280,000 francs. It was sold at twenty per cent. profit on its original value, which being 40,000 francs, the price of sale was 320,000 francs, which the assignee converted into cotton. This cotton, again, had to pay for expenses of transportation, insurance, commissions, etc., ten per cent.: so that when the return cargo arrived at Havre, its value had risen to 352,000 francs, and it was thus entered at the custom-house. Finally, Mr. T... realized again on this return cargo twenty per cent. profits; amounting to 70,400 francs. The cotton thus sold for the sum of 422,400 francs.

If Mr. Lestiboudois requires it, I will send him an extract from the books of Mr. T... He will there see, *credited* to the account of *profit and loss*, that is to say, set down as gained, two sums; the one of 40,000, the other of 70,000 francs, and Mr. T... feels perfectly certain that as regards these, there is no mistake in his accounts.

Now what conclusion does Mr. Lestiboudois draw from the sums entered into the custom-house, in this operation? He thence learns that France has exported 200,000 francs, and imported 352,000; from whence the honorable deputy concludes "*that she has spent, dissipated the profits of her previous savings; that she is impoverishing herself and progressing to her ruin; and that she has squandered on a foreign nation* 152,000 *francs of her capital.*"

Some time after this transaction, Mr. T... despatched another vessel, again freighted with domestic produce, to the amount of 200,000 francs. But the vessel foundered after leaving the port, and Mr. T... had only farther to inscribe on his books two little items, thus worded:

"*Sundries due to X*, 200,000 francs, for purchase of divers articles despatched by vessel N.

"*Profit and loss due to sundries*, 200,000 *francs, for final and total loss of cargo.*"

In the meantime the custom-house inscribed 200,000 francs upon its list of *exportations*, and as there can of course be nothing to balance this entry on the list of *importations*, it hence follows that Mr. Lestiboudois and the Chamber must see in this wreck *a clear profit* to France of 200,000 francs.

We may draw hence yet another conclusion, viz.: that according to the Balance of Trade theory, France has an exceedingly simple manner of constantly doubling her capital. It is only necessary, to accomplish this, that she should, after entering into the custom-house her articles for exportation, cause them to be thrown into the sea. By this course, her exportations can speedily be made to equal her capital; importations will be nothing, and our gain will be, all which the ocean will have swallowed up.

You are joking, the protectionists will reply. You know that it is impossible that we should utter such absurdities. Nevertheles, I answer, you do utter them, and what is more, you give them life, you exercise them practically upon your fellow citizens, as much, at least, as is in your power to do.

The truth is, that the theory of the Balance of Trade should be precisely *reversed*. The profits accruing to the nation from any foreign commerce should be calculated by the overplus of the importation above the exportation. This overplus, after the deduction of expenses, is the real gain. Here we have the true theory, and it is one which leads directly to freedom in trade. I now, gentlemen, abandon you this theory, as I have done all those of the preceding chapters. Do with it as you please, exaggerate it as you will; it has nothing to fear. Push it to the farthest extreme; imagine, if it so please you, that foreign nations should inundate us with useful produce of every description, and ask nothing in return; that our importations should be *infinite*, and our exportations *nothing*. Imagine all this, and still I defy you to prove that we will be the poorer in consequence.

VII.

PETITION FROM THE MANUFACTURERS OF CANDLES, WAX-LIGHTS, LAMPS, CHANDELIERS, REFLECTORS, SNUFFERS, EXTINGUISHERS; AND FROM THE PRODUCERS OF TALLOW, OIL, RESIN, ALCOHOL, AND GENERALLY OF EVERY THING USED FOR LIGHTS.

To the Honorable the Members of the Chamber of Deputies:

"GENTLEMEN,—You are in the right way: you reject abstract theories; abundance, cheapness, concerns you little. You are entirely occupied with the interest of the producer, whom you are anxious to free from foreign competition. In a word, you wish to secure the *national market* to *national labor*.

"We come now to offer you an admirable opportunity for the application of your —— what shall we say? your theory? no, nothing is more deceiving than theory;—your doctrine? your system? your principle? But you do not like doctrines; you hold systems in horror; and, as for principles, you declare that there are no such things in political economy. We will say then, your practice; your practice without theory, and without principle.

"We are subjected to the intolerable competition of a foreign rival, who enjoys, it would seem, such superior facilities for the production of light, that he is enabled to *inundate* our *national market* at so exceedingly reduced a price, that, the moment he makes his appearance, he draws off all custom from us; and thus an important branch of French industry, with all its innumerable ramifications, is suddenly reduced to a state of complete stagnation. This rival, who is no other than the sun, carries on so bitter a war against us, that we have every reason to believe that he has been excited to this course by our perfidious neighbor England. (Good diplomacy this, for the present time!) In this belief we are confirmed by the fact that in all his transactions with this proud island, he is much more moderate and careful than with us.

"Our petition is, that it would please your honorable body to pass a law whereby shall be directed the shutting up of all windows, dormers, sky-lights, shutters, curtains, vasistas, œil-de-bœufs, in a word, all openings, holes, chinks and fissures through which the light of the sun is used to penetrate into our dwellings, to the predjudice of the profitable manufactures which we flatter ourselves we have been enabled to bestow upon the country; which country cannot, therefore, without ingratitude, leave us now to struggle unprotected through so unequal a contest.

"We pray your honorable body, not to mistake our petition for a satire, nor to repulse us without at least hearing the reasons which we have to advance in its favor.

"And first, if, by shutting out as much as possible all access to natural light, you thus create the necessity for artificial light, is there in France an industrial pursuit which will not, through some connection with this important object, be benefited by it?

"If more tallow be consumed, there will arise a necessity for an increase of cattle and sheep. Thus artificial meadows must be in greater demand; and meat, wool, leather, and above all, manure, this basis of agricultural riches, must become more abundant.

"If more oil be consumed, it will cause an increase in the cultivation of the olive-tree. This plant, luxuriant and exhausting to the soil, will come in good time to profit by the increased fertility which the raising of cattle will have communicated to our fields.

"Our heaths will become covered with resinous trees. Numerous swarms of bees will gather upon our mountains the perfumed treasures, which are now cast upon the winds, useless as the blossoms from which they emanate. There is, in short, no branch of agriculture which would not be greatly developed by the granting of our petition.

"Navigation would equally profit. Thousands of vessels would soon be employed in the whale fisheries, and thence would arise a navy capable of sustaining the honor of France, and of responding to the patriotic sentiments of the undersigned petitioners, candle merchants, etc.

"But what words can express the magnificence which *Paris* will then exhibit! Cast an eye upon the future and behold the gildings, the bronzes, the magnificent crystal chandeliers, lamps, reflectors and candelabras, which will glitter in the spacious stores, compared with which the splendor of the present day will appear trifling and insignificant.

"There is none, not even the poor manufacturer of resin in the midst of his pine forests, nor the miserable miner in his dark dwelling, but who would enjoy an increase of salary and of comforts.

"Gentlemen, if you will be pleased to reflect, you cannot fail to be convinced that there is perhaps not one Frenchman, from the opulent stockholder of Anzin down to the poorest vender of matches, who is not interested in the success of our petition.

"We foresee your objections, gentlemen; but there is not one that you can oppose to us which you will not be obliged to gather from the works of the partisans of free trade. We dare challenge you to pronounce one word against our petition, which is not equally opposed to your own practice and the principle which guides your policy.

"Do you tell us, that if we gain by this protection, France will not gain, because the consumer must pay the price of it?

"We answer you:

"You have no longer any right to cite the interest of the consumer. For whenever this has been found to compete with that of the producer, you have invariably sacrificed the first. You have done this to *encourage labor*, to *increase the demand for labor.* The same reason should now induce you to act in the same manner.

"You have yourselves already answered the objection. When you were told: The consumer is interested in the free introduction of iron, coal, corn, wheat, cloths, etc., your answer was: Yes, but the producer is interested in their exclusion. Thus, also, if the consumer is interested in the admission of light, we, the producers, pray for its interdiction.

"You have also said, the producer and the consumer are one. If the manufacturer gains by protection, he will cause the agriculturist to gain also; if agriculture prospers, it opens a market for manufactured goods. Thus we, if you confer upon us the monopoly of furnishing light during the day, will as a first consequence buy large quantities of tallow, coals, oil, resin, wax, alcohol, silver, iron, bronze, crystal, for the supply of our business; and then we and our numerous contractors having become rich, our consumption will be great, and will become a means of contributing to the comfort and competency of the workers in every branch of national labor.

"Will you say that the light of the sun is a gratuitous gift, and that to repulse gratuitous gifts, is to repulse riches under pretence of encouraging the means of obtaining them?

"Take care,—you carry the death-blow to your own policy. Remember that hitherto you have always repulsed foreign produce, *because* it was an approach to a gratuitous gift, and *the more in proportion* as this approach was more close. You have, in obeying the wishes of other monopolists, acted only from a *half-motive;* to grant our petition there is a much *fuller inducement.* To repulse us, precisely for the reason that our case is a more complete one than any which have preceded it, would be to lay down the following equation: $+ \times + = -$;

in other words, it would be to accumulate absurdity upon absurdity.

"Labor and Nature concur in different proportions, according to country and climate, in every article of production. The portion of Nature is always gratuitous; that of labor alone regulates the price.

"If a Lisbon orange can be sold at half the price of a Parisian one, it is because a natural and gratuitous heat does for the one, what the other only obtains from an artificial and consequently expensive one.

"When, therefore, we purchase a Portuguese orange, we may say that we obtain it half gratuitously and half by the right of labor; in other words, at *half price* compared to those of Paris.

"Now it is precisely on account of this *demi-gratuity* (excuse the word) that you argue in favor of exclusion. How, you say, could national labor sustain the competition of foreign labor, when the first has every thing to do, and the last is rid of half the trouble, the sun taking the rest of the business upon himself? If then the *demi-gratuity* can determine you to check competition, on what principle can the *entire gratuity* be alleged as a reason for admitting it? You are no logicians if, refusing the demi-gratuity as hurtful to human labor, you do not *à fortiori*, and with double zeal, reject the full gratuity.

"Again, when any article, as coal, iron, cheese, or cloth, comes to us from foreign countries with less labor than if we produced it ourselves, the difference in price is a *gratuitous gift* conferred upon us; and the gift is more or less considerable, according as the difference is greater or less. It is the quarter, the half, or the three-quarters of the value of the produce, in proportion as the foreign merchant requires the three-quarters, the half, or the quarter of the price. It is as complete as possible when the producer offers, as the sun does with light, the whole in free gift. The question is, and we put it formally, whether you wish for France the benefit of gratuitous consumption, or the supposed advantages of laborious production. Choose, but be consistent. And does it not argue the greatest inconsistency to check as you do the importation of coal, iron, cheese, and goods of foreign manufacture, merely because and even in proportion as their price approaches *zero*, while at the same time you freely admit, and without limitation, the light of the sun, whose price is during the whole day at *zero?*"

VIII.

DISCRIMINATING DUTIES.

A poor laborer of Gironde had raised, with the greatest possible care and attention, a nursery of vines, from which, after much labor, he at last succeeded in producing a pipe of wine, and forgot, in the joy of his success, that each drop of this precious nectar had cost a drop of sweat to his brow. I will sell it, said he to his wife, and with the proceeds I will buy thread, which will serve you to make a *trousseau* for our daughter. The honest countryman, arriving in the city, there met an Englishman and a Belgian. The Belgian said to him, Give me your wine, and I in exchange, will give you fifteen bundles of thread. The Englishman said, Give it to me, and I will give you twenty bundles, for we English can spin cheaper than the Belgians. But a custom-house officer standing by, said to the laborer, My good fellow, make your exchange, if you choose, with the Belgian, but it is my duty to prevent your doing so with the Englishman. What! exclaimed the countryman, you wish me to take fifteen bundles of Brussels thread, when I can have twenty from Manchester? Certainly; do you not see that France would be a loser, if you were to receive twenty bundles instead of fifteen?

I can scarcely understand this, said the laborer. Nor can I explain it, said the custom-house officer, but there is no doubt of the fact; for deputies, ministers, and editors, all agree that a people is impoverished in proportion as it receives a large compensation for any given quantity of its produce. The countryman was obliged to conclude his bargain with the Belgian. His daughter received but three-fourths of her *trousseau*; and these good folks are still puzzling themselves to discover how it can happen that people are ruined by receiving four instead of three; and why they are richer with three dozen towels instead of four.

IX.

WONDERFUL DISCOVERY!

At this moment, when all minds are occupied in endeavoring to discover the most economical means of transportation; when, to put these means into practice, we are leveling roads, improving rivers, perfecting steamboats, establishing railroads, and attempting various systems of traction, atmospheric, hydraulic, pneumatic, electric, etc.,—at this moment when, I believe, every one is seeking in sincerity and with ardor the solution of this problem—

"*To bring the price of things in their place of consumption, as near as possible to their price in that of production*"—

I would believe myself acting a culpable part towards my country, towards the age in which I live, and towards myself, if I were longer to keep secret the wonderful discovery which I have just made.

I am well aware that the self-illusions of inventors have become proverbial, but I have, nevertheless, the most complete certainty of having discovered an infallible means of bringing the produce of the entire world into France, and reciprocally to transport ours, with a very important reduction of price.

Infallible! and yet this is but a single one of the advantages of my astonishing invention, which requires neither plans nor devices, neither preparatory studies, nor engineers, nor machinists, nor capital, nor stockholders, nor governmental assistance! There is no danger of shipwrecks, of explosions, of shocks, of fire, nor of displacement of rails! It can be put into practice without preparation from one day to another!

Finally, and this will, no doubt, recommend it to the public, it will not increase taxes one cent; but the contrary. It will not augment the number of government functionaries, nor the exigencies of government officers; but the contrary. It will put in hazard the liberty of no one; but the contrary.

I have been led to this discovery not from accident, but observation, and I will tell you how.

I had this question to determine:

"Why does any article made, for instance, at Brussels, bear an increased price on its arrival at Paris?"

It was immediately evident to me that this was the result of *obstacles* of various kinds existing between Brussels and Paris. First, there is *distance*, which cannot be overcome without trouble and loss of time; and either we must submit to these in our own person, or pay another for bearing them for us. Then come rivers, swamps, accidents, heavy and muddy roads; these are so many *difficulties* to be overcome; in order to do which, causeways are constructed, bridges built, roads cut and paved, railroads established, etc. But all this is costly, and the article transported must bear its portion of the expense. There are robbers, too, on the roads, and this necessitates guards, a police, etc.

Now, among these *obstacles*, there is one which we ourselves have placed, and that at no little expense, between Brussels and Paris. This consists of men planted along the frontier, armed to the teeth, whose business it is to place *difficulties* in the way of the transportation of goods from one country to another.

These men are called custom-house officers, and their effect is precisely similar to that of steep and boggy roads. They retard and put obstacles in the way of transportation, thus contributing to the difference which we have remarked between the price of production and that of consumption; to diminish which difference as much as possible, is the problem which we are seeking to resolve.

Here, then, we have found its solution. *Let our tariff be diminished.* We will thus have constructed a Northern Railroad which will cost us nothing. Nay, more, we will be saved great expenses, and will begin from the first day to save capital.

Really, I cannot but ask myself, in surprise, how our brains could have admitted so whimsical a piece of folly, as to induce us to pay many millions to destroy the *natural obstacles* interposed between France and other nations, only at the same time to pay so many millions more in order to replace them by *artificial obstacles*, which have exactly the same effect; so that the obstacle removed, and the obstacle created, neutralize each other; things go on as before, and the only result of our trouble, is, a double expense.

An article of Belgian production is worth at Brussels twenty francs, and, from the expenses of transportation, thirty francs at Paris. A similar article of Parisian manufacture costs forty francs. What is our course under these circumstances?

First, we impose a duty of at least ten francs on the Belgian article, so as to raise its price to a level with that of the Parisian; the government withal, paying numerous officials to attend to the levying of this duty. The article thus pays ten francs for transportation, ten for the tax.

This done, we say to ourselves: Transportation between Brussels and Paris is very dear; let us spend two or three millions in railways, and we will reduce it one-half. Evidently the result of such a course will be to get the Belgian article at Paris for thirty-five francs, viz:

20 francs—price at Brussels.
10 " duty.
5 " transportation by railroad.
—
35 francs—total, or market price at Paris.

Could we not have attained the same end by lowering the tariff to five francs? We would then have—

20 francs—price at Brussels.
5 " duty.
10 " transportation on the common road.
—
35 francs—total, or market price at Paris.

And this arrangement would have saved us the 200,000,000 spent upon the railroad, besides the expense saved in custom-house surveillance, which would of course diminish in proportion as the temptation to smuggling would become less.

But it is answered, the duty is necessary to protect Parisian industry. So be it; but do not then destroy the effect of it by your railroad.

For if you persist in your determination to keep the Belgian article on a par with the Parisian at forty francs, you must raise the duty to fifteen francs, in order to have:—

20 francs—price at Brussels.
15 " protective duty.
5 " transportation by railroad.
—
40 francs—total, at equalized prices.

And I now ask, of what benefit, under these circumstances, is the railroad?

Frankly, is it not humiliating to the nineteenth century, that it should be destined to transmit to future ages the example of such puerilities seriously and gravely practiced? To be the dupe of another, is bad enough; but to employ all the forms and ceremonies of legislation in order to cheat one's self,—to doubly cheat one's self, and that too in a mere mathematical account,—truly this is calculated to lower a little the pride of this *enlightened age.*

X.

RECIPROCITY.

WE have just seen that all which renders transportation difficult, acts in the same manner as protection; or, if the expression be preferred, that protection tends towards the same result as obstacles to transportation.

A tariff may then be truly spoken of, as a swamp, a rut, a steep hill; in a word, an *obstacle,* whose effect is to augment the difference between the price of consumption and that of production. It is equally incontestable that a swamp, a bog, etc., are veritable protective tariffs.

There are people (few in number, it is true, but such there are) who begin to understand that obstacles are not the less obstacles, because they are artificially created, and that our well-being is more advanced by freedom of trade than by protection; precisely as a canal is more desirable than a sandy, hilly, and difficult road.

But they still say, this liberty ought to be reciprocal. If we take off our taxes in favor of Spain, while Spain does not do the same towards us, it is evident that we are duped. Let us then make *treaties of commerce* upon the basis of a just reciprocity; let us yield where we are yielded to; let us make the *sacrifice* of buying that we may obtain the advantage of selling.

Persons who reason thus, are (I am sorry to say), whether they know it or not, governed by the protectionist principle. They are only a little more inconsistent than the pure protectionists, as these are more inconsistent than the absolute prohibitionists.

I will illustrate this by a fable.

STULTA AND PUERA (FOOL-TOWN AND BOY-TOWN).

There were, it matters not where, two towns, *Stulta* and *Puera*, which at great expense had a road built which connected them with each other. Some time after this was done, the inhabitants of *Stulta* became uneasy, and said: *Puera* is overwhelming us with its productions; this must be attended to. They established therefore a corps of *Obstructors*, so called because their business was to place obstacles in the way of the wagon trains which arrived from *Puera*. Soon after, *Puera* also established a corps of Obstructors.

After some centuries, people having become more enlightened, the inhabitants of *Puera* began to discover that these reciprocal obstacles might possibly be reciprocal injuries. They sent therefore an ambassador to *Stulta*, who (passing over the official phraseology) spoke much to this effect: "We have built a road, and now we put obstacles in the way of this road. This is absurd. It would have been far better to have left things in their original position, for then we would not have been put to the expense of building our road, and afterwards of creating difficulties. In the name of *Puera*, I come to propose to you, not to renounce at once our system of mutual obstacles, for this would be acting according to a theory, and we despise theories as much as you do; but to lighten somewhat these obstacles, weighing at the same time carefully our respective *sacrifices*." The ambassador having thus spoken, the town of *Stulta* asked time to reflect; manufacturers, agriculturists were consulted; and at last, after some years' deliberation, it was declared that the negotiations were broken off.

At this news, the inhabitants of *Puera* held a council. An old man (who it has always been supposed had been secretly bribed by *Stulta*) rose and said: "The obstacles raised by *Stulta* are injurious to our sales; this is a misfortune. Those which we ourselves create, injure our purchases; this is a second misfortune. We have no power over the first, but the second is entirely dependent upon ourselves. Let us then at least get rid of one, since we cannot be delivered from both. Let us suppress our corps of *Obstructors*, without waiting for *Stulta* to do the same. Some day or other she will learn to understand better her own interests."

A second counselor, a man of practice and of

facts, uncontrolled by theories and wise in ancestral experience, replied: "We must not listen to this dreamer, this theorist, this innovator, this utopian, this political economist, this friend to *Stulta*. We would be entirely ruined if the embarrassments of the road were not carefully weighed and exactly equalized, between *Stulta* and *Peura*. There would be more difficulty in going than in coming; in exportation than in importation. We would be, with regard to *Stulta*, in the inferior condition in which Havre, Nantes, Bordeaux, Lisbon, London, Hamburg, and New Orleans, are, in relation to cities placed higher up the rivers Seine, Loire, Garonne, Tagus, Thames, the Elbe, and the Mississippi; for the difficulties of ascending must always be greater than those of descending rivers. (A voice exclaims: 'But the cities near the mouths of rivers have always prospered more than those higher up the stream.') This is not possible. (The same voice: 'But it is a fact.') Well, they have then prospered *contrary to rule*." Such conclusive reasoning staggered the assembly. The orator went on to convince them thoroughly and conclusively by speaking of national independence, national honor, national dignity, national labor, overwhelming importation, tributes, ruinous competition. In short, he succeeded in determining the assembly to continue their system of obstacles, and I can now point out a certain country where you may see roadbuilders and *Obstructors* working with the best possible understanding, by the decree of the same legislative assembly, paid by the same citizens; the first to improve the road, the last to embarrass it.

XI.

ABSOLUTE PRICES.

If we wish to judge between freedom of trade and protection, to calculate the probable effect of any political phenomenon, we should notice how far its influence tends to the production of *abundance or scarcity*, and not simply of *cheapness or dearness* of price. We must beware of trusting to *absolute prices*, it would lead to inextricable confusion.

Mr. Mathieu de Dombasle, after having established the fact that protection raises prices, adds:

"The augmentation of price increases the expenses of life, and consequently the price of labor, and every one finds in the increase of the price of his produce the same proportion as in the increase of his expenses. Thus, if every body pays as consumer, every body receives also as producer."

It is evident that it would be easy to reverse the argument and say: If every body receives as producer, every body must pay as consumer.

Now, what does this prove? Nothing whatever, unless it be that protection *transfers* riches, uselessly and unjustly. Robbery does the same.

Again, to prove that the complicated arrangements of this system give even simple compensation, it is necessary to adhere to the "*consequently*" of Mr. de Dombasle, and to convince one's self that the price of labor rises with that of the articles protected. This is a question of fact, which I refer to Mr. Moreau de Jonnès, begging him to examine whether the rate of wages was found to increase with the stock of the mines of Anzin. For my own part I do not believe in it, because I think that the price of labor, like every thing else, is governed by the proportion existing between the supply and the demand. Now I can perfectly well understand that *restriction* will diminish the supply of coal, and consequently raise its price; but I do not as clearly see that it increases the demand for labor, thereby raising the rate of wages. This is the less conceivable to me, because the sum of labor required depends upon the quantity of disposable capital; and protection, while it may change the direction of capital, and transfer it from one business to another, cannot increase it one penny.

This question, which is of the highest interest, we will examine elsewhere. I return to the discussion of *absolute prices*, and declare that there is no absurdity which cannot be rendered specious by such reasoning as that of Mr. de Dombasle.

Imagine an isolated nation possessing a given quantity of cash, and every year wantonly burning the half of its produce. I will undertake to prove by the theory of Mr. de Dombasle that this nation will not be the less rich in consequence of such a procedure.

For, the result of the conflagration must be, that every thing would double in price. An inventory made before this event would offer exactly the same nominal value, as one made after it. Who then would be the loser? If John buys his cloth dearer, he also sells his corn at a higher price; and if Peter makes a loss on the purchase of his corn, he gains it back by the sale of his cloth. Thus "every one finds in the increase of the price of his produce, the same proportion as in the increase of his expenses; and thus if every body pays as consumer, every body also receives as producer."

All this is nonsense. The simple truth is: that whether men destroy their corn and cloth by fire or by use, the effect is the same *as regards price*, but not *as regards riches*, for it is precisely in the enjoyment of the use, that riches—in other words, comfort, well-being—exist.

Protection may, in the same way, while it lessens the abundance of things, raise their prices, so as to leave each individual as rich, *numerically speaking*, as when unembarrassed by it. But because we put down in an inventory three hectolitres of corn at

20 francs, or four hectolitres at 15 francs, and sum up the nominal value of each at 60 francs, does it thence follow that they are equally capable of contributing to the necessities of the community?

To this view of consumption, it will be my continual endeavor to lead the protectionists; for in this is the end of all my efforts, the solution of every problem. I must continually repeat to them that restriction, by impeding commerce, by limiting the division of labor, by forcing it to combat difficulties of situation and temperature, must in its results diminish the quantity produced by any fixed quantum of labor. And what can it benefit us that the smaller quantity produced under the protective system bears the same *nominal value* as the greater quantity produced under the free trade system? Man does not live on *nominal values*, but on real articles of produce; and the more abundant these articles are, no matter what price they may bear, the richer is he.

XII.

DOES PROTECTION RAISE THE RATE OF WAGES?

WORKMEN, your situation is singular! you are robbed, as I will presently prove to you....But no; I retract the word; we must avoid an expression which is violent; perhaps indeed incorrect; inasmuch as this spoliation, wrapped in the sophisms which disguise it, is practiced, we must believe, without the intention of the spoiler, and with the consent of the spoiled. But it is nevertheless true that you are deprived of the just compensation of your labor, while no one thinks of causing *justice* to be rendered to you. If you could be consoled by noisy appeals to philanthropy, to powerless charity, to degrading alms-giving, or if high-sounding words would relieve you, these indeed you can have in abundance. But *justice*, simple *justice*—nobody thinks of rendering you this. For would it not be *just* that after a long day's labor, when you have received your little wages, you should be permitted to exchange them for the largest possible sum of comforts that you can obtain voluntarily from any man whatsoever upon the face of the earth?

Let us examine if *injustice* is not done to you, by the legislative limitation of the persons from whom you are allowed to buy those things which you need; as bread, meat, cotton and woolen cloths, etc.; thus fixing (so to express myself) the artificial price which these articles must bear.

Is it true that protection, which avowedly raises prices, and thus injures you, raises proportionably the rate of wages?

On what does the rate of wages depend?

One of your own class has energetically said: "When two workmen run after a master, wages fall; when two masters run after a workman, wages rise."

Allow me, in more laconic phrase, to employ a more scientific, though perhaps a less striking expression: "The rate of wages depends upon the proportion which the supply of labor bears to the demand."

On what depends the *demand* for labor?

On the quantity of disposable national capital. And the law which says, "such or such an article shall be limited to home production and no longer imported from foreign countries," can it in any degree increase this capital? Not in the least. This law may withdraw it from one course, and transfer it to another; but cannot increase it one penny. Then it cannot increase the demand for labor.

While we point with pride to some prosperous manufacture, can we answer, from whence comes the capital with which it is founded and maintained? Has it fallen from the moon? or rather is it not drawn either from agriculture, or navigation, or other industry? We here see why, since the reign of protective tariffs, if we see more workmen in our mines and our manufacturing towns, we find also fewer sailors in our ports, and fewer laborers and vine-growers in our fields and upon our hill-sides.

I could speak at great length upon this subject, but prefer illustrating my thought by an example.

A countryman had twenty acres of land, with a capital of 10,000 francs. He divided his land into four parts, and adopted for it the following changes of crops: 1st, maize; 2d, wheat; 3d, clover; and 4th, rye. As he needed for himself and family but a small portion of the grain, meat, and dairy-produce of the farm, he sold the surplus and bought oil, flax, wine, etc. The whole of his capital was yearly distributed in wages and payments of accounts to the workmen of the neighborhood. This capital was, from his sales, again returned to him, and even increased from year to year. Our countryman, being fully convinced that idle capital produces nothing, caused to circulate among the working classes this annual increase, which he devoted to the inclosing and clearing of lands, or to improvements in his farming utensils and his buildings. He deposited some sums in reserve in the hands of a neighboring banker, who on his part did not leave these idle in his strong box, but lent them to various tradesmen, so that the whole came to be usefully employed in the payment of wages.

The countryman died, and his son, become master of the inheritance, said to himself: "It must be confessed that my father has, all his life, allowed himself to be duped. He bought oil, and thus paid *tribute* to Province, while our own land could, by an effort, be made to produce olives. He bought wine, flax, and oranges, thus paying *tribute* to Brittany, Medoc, and the Hiera islands very unnecessarily, for wine, flax and oranges may be forced to grow upon our own lands. He paid tribute to the miller and the weaver; our own servants could very well weave our linen, and crush our wheat between two stones. He did all he could to ruin himself, and gave to strangers what ought to have been kept for the benefit of his own household."

Full of this reasoning, our headstrong fellow determined to change the routine of his crops. He divided his farm into twenty parts. On one he cultivated the olive; on another the mulberry; on a third flax; he devoted the fourth to vines, the fifth to wheat, etc., etc. Thus he succeeded in rendering himself *independent*, and furnished all his family supplies from his own farm. He no longer received any thing from the general circulation; neither, it is true, did he cast any thing into it. Was he the richer for this course? No, for his land did not suit the cultivation of the vine; nor was the climate favorable to the olive. In short, the family supply of all these articles was very inferior to what it had been during the time when the father had obtained them all by exchange of produce.

With regard to the demand for labor, it certainly was no greater than formerly. There were, to be sure, five times as many fields to cultivate, but they were five times smaller. If oil was raised, there was less wheat; and because there was no more flax bought, neither was there any more rye sold. Besides, the farmer could not spend in wages more than his capital, and his capital, instead of increasing, was now constantly diminishing. A great part of it was necessarily devoted to numerous buildings and utensils, indispensable to a person who determines to undertake every thing. In short, the supply of labor continued the same, but the means of paying becoming less, there was, necessarily, a reduction of wages.

The result is precisely similar, when a nation isolates itself by the prohibitive system. Its number of industrial pursuits is certainly multiplied, but their importance is diminished. In proportion to their number, they become less productive, for the same capital and the same skill are obliged to meet a greater number of difficulties. The fixed capital absorbs a greater part of the circulating capital; that is to say, a greater part of the funds destined to the payment of wages. What remains, ramifies itself in vain, the quantity cannot be augmented. It is like the water of a pond, which, distributed in a multitude of reservoirs, appears to be more abundant, because it covers a greater quantity of soil, and presents a larger surface to the sun, while we hardly perceive that, precisely on this account, it absorbs, evaporates, and loses itself the quicker.

Capital and labor being given, the result is, a sum of production, always the less great, in proportion as obstacles are numerous. There can be no doubt that protective tariffs, by forcing capital and labor to struggle against greater difficulties of soil and climate, must cause the general production to be less, or, in other words, diminish the portion of comforts which would thence result to mankind. If, then, there be a general diminution of comforts, how, workmen, can it be possible that *your* portion should be increased? Under such a supposition, it would be necessary to believe that the rich, those who made the law, have so arranged matters, that not only they subject themselves to their own proportion of the general loss, but taking the whole of it upon themselves, that they submit also to a further loss, in order to increase your gains. Is this credible? Is this possible? It is, indeed, a most suspicious act of generosity, and if you act wisely, you will reject it.

XIII.

THEORY — PRACTICE.

PARTISANS of free-trade, we are accused of being theorists, and not relying sufficiently upon practice.

What a powerful argument against Mr. Say (says Mr. Ferrier,) is the long succession of distinguished ministers, the imposing league of writers who have all differed from him; and Mr. Say is himself conscious of this, for he says: "It has been said, in support of old errors, that there must necessarily be some foundation for ideas so generally adopted by all nations. Ought we not, it is asked, to distrust observations and reasoning which run counter to every thing which has been looked upon as certain up to this day, and which has been regarded as undoubted by so many who were to be confided in, alike on account of their learning and of their philanthropic intentions? This argument is, I confess, calculated to make a profound impression, and might cast a doubt upon the most incontestable facts, if the world had not seen so many opinions, now universally recognized as false, as universally maintain, during a long series of ages, their dominion over the human mind. The day is not long passed since all nations, from the most ignorant to the most enlightened, and all men, the wisest as well as the most uninformed, admitted only four elements. Nobody dreamed of disputing this doctrine, which is, nevertheless, false, and to-day universally decried."

Upon this passage Mr. Ferrier makes the following remarks:

"Mr. Say is strangely mistaken, if he believes that he has thus answered the very strong objections which he has himself advanced. It is natural enough that, for ages, men otherwise well informed, might mistake upon a question of natural history; this proves nothing. Water, air, earth, and fire, elements or not, were not the less useful to man. . . . . Such errors as this are of no importance. They do not lead to revolutions, nor do they cause mental uneasiness; above all, they clash with no interests, and might, therefore, without inconvenience, last for millions of years. The physical world progresses as though they did not exist. But can it be thus with errors which affect the moral world? Can it be conceived that a system of government absolutely false, consequently injurious, could be followed for many centuries, and among many nations, with the general consent of well-informed men? Can it be explained how such a system could be connected with the constantly increasing prosperity of these nations? Mr. Say confesses that the argument which he combats is calculated to make a profound impression. Most certainly it is; and this impression remains; for Mr. Say has rather increased than diminished it."

Let us hear Mr. de Saint Chamans.

"It has been only towards the middle of the last, the eighteenth century, when every subject and every principle have without exception been given up to the discussion of book-makers, that these furnishers of *speculative* ideas, applied to every thing and applicable to nothing, have begun to write upon the subject of political economy. There existed previously a system of political economy, not written, but *practiced* by governments. Colbert was, it is said, the inventor of it; and Colbert gave the law to every state of Europe. Strange to say, he does so still, in spite of contempt and anathemas, in spite too of the discoveries of the modern school. This system, which has been called by our writers the *mercantile system*, consisted in . . . . . checking by prohibition or import duties such foreign productions as were calculated to ruin our manufactures by competition. . . . . This system has been declared, by all writers on political economy, of every school,* to be weak, absurd, and calculated to impoverish the countries where it prevails. Banished from books, it has taken refuge in

* Might we not say: It is a powerful argument against Messrs. Ferrier and de Saint Chamans, that all writers on political economy, of *every school*, that is to say, all men who have studied the question, come to this conclusion: After all, freedom is better than restriction, and the laws of God wiser than those of Mr. Colbert.

the practice of all nations, greatly to the surprise of those who cannot conceive that in what concerns the wealth of nations, governments should, rather than be guided by the wisdom of authors, prefer the *long experience* of a system, etc. . . . . It is above all inconceivable to them that the French government . . . . . should obstinately resist the new lights of political economy, and maintain in its *practice* the old errors, pointed out by all our writers. . . . . But I am devoting too much time to this mercantile system, which, unsustained by writers, *has only facts* in its favor!"

Would it not be supposed from this language that political economists, in claiming for each individual the *free disposition of his own property*, have, like the Fourierists, stumbled upon some new, strange, and chimerical system of social government, some wild theory, without precedent in the annals of human nature? It does appear to me, that, if in all this there is any thing doubtful, and of fanciful or theoretic origin, it is not free trade, but protection; not the operating of exchanges, but the custom-house, the duties, imposed to overturn artificially the natural order of things.

The question, however, is not here to compare and judge of the merits of the two systems, but simply to know which of the two is sanctioned by experience.

You, Messrs. monopolists, maintain that *facts* are for you, and that we on our side have only *theory*.

You even flatter yourselves that this long series of public acts, this old experience of Europe which you invoke, appeared imposing to Mr. Say; and I confess that he has not refuted you, with his habitual sagacity.

I, for my part, cannot consent to give up to you the domain of *facts;* for while on your side you can advance only limited and special facts, *we* can oppose to them universal facts, the free and voluntary acts of all men.

What do *we* maintain? and what do *you* maintain?

We maintain that "it is best to buy from others what we ourselves can produce only at a higher price."

You maintain that "it is best to make for ourselves, even though it should cost us more than to buy from others."

Now gentlemen, putting aside theory, demonstration, reasoning, (things which seem to nauseate you,) which of these assertions is sanctioned by *universal practice?*

Visit our fields, workshops, forges, stores; look above, below, and around you; examine what is passing in your own household; observe your own actions at every moment, and say which principle it is, that directs these laborers, workmen, contractors, and merchants; say what is your own personal *practice.*

Does the agriculturist make his own clothes? Does the tailor produce the grain which he consumes? Does not your housekeeper cease to make her bread at home, as soon as she finds it more economical to buy it from the baker? Do you lay down your pen to take up the blacking-brush in order to avoid paying tribute to the shoe-black? Does not the whole economy of society depend upon a separation of occupations, a division of labor, in a word, upon mutual exchange of production, by which we, one and all, make a calculation which causes us to discontinue direct production, when indirect acquisition offers us a saving of time and labor.

You are not then sustained by *practice*, since it would be impossible, were you to search the world, to show us a single man who acts according to your principle.

You may answer that you never intended to make your principle the rule of individual relations. You confess that it would thus destroy all social ties, and force men to the isolated life of snails. You only contend that it governs *in fact*, the relations which are established between the agglomerations of the human family.

We say that this assertion too is erroneous. A family, a town, county, department, province, all are so many agglomerations, which, without any exception, all *practically* reject your principle; never, indeed, even think of it. Each of these procures by barter, what would be more expensively procured by production. Nations would do the same, did you not *by force* prevent them.

We, then, are the men who are guided by practice and experience. For to combat the interdict which you have specially put upon some international exchanges, we bring forward the practice and experience of all individuals, and of all agglomerations of individuals, whose acts being voluntary, render them proper to be given as proof in the question. But you, on your part, begin by *forcing*, by *hindering*, and then, adducing forced or forbidden acts, you exclaim: "Look; we can prove ourselves justified by example!"

You exclaim against our *theory*, and even against *all theory*. But are you certain, in laying down your principles, so antagonistic to ours, that you too are not building up theories? Truly, you too have your theory; but between yours and ours there is this difference:

Our theory is formed upon the observation of universal *facts*, universal sentiments, universal calculations and acts. We do nothing more than classify and arrange these, in order to better understand them. It is so little opposed to practice, that it is in fact only *practice explained.* We look upon the actions of men as prompted by the instinct of self-preservation and of progress. What they do freely, willingly,—this is what we call *Political Economy*, or economy of society. We must repeat constantly that each man is *practically* an excellent political economist, producing or exchanging, as his advantage dictates. Each by experience raises himself to the science; or rather the science is nothing more than experience, scrupulously observed and methodically expounded.

But *your* theory is *theory* in the worst sense of the word. You imagine procedures which are sanctioned by the experience of no living man, and then call to your aid constraint and prohibition. You cannot avoid having recourse to force; because, wishing to make men produce what they can *more advantageously* buy, you require them to give up an advantage, and to be led by a doctrine which implies contradiction even in its terms.

I defy you too, to take this doctrine, which by your own avowal would be absurd in individual relations, and apply it, even in speculation, to transactions between families, towns, departments, or provinces. You yourselves confess that it is only applicable to internal relations.

Thus it is that you are daily forced to repeat:

"Principles can never be universal. What is *well* in an individual, a family, commune, or province, is *ill* in a nation. What is good in detail—for instance: purchase rather than production, where purchase is more advantageous—is *bad* in a society.

The political economy of individuals is not that of nations;" and other such idle stuff, *ejusdem farinæ.*

And all this for what? To prove to us, that we consumers, we are your property! that we belong to you, soul and body! that you have an exclusive right on our stomachs and our limbs! that it is your right to feed and dress us at your own price, however great your ignorance, your rapacity, or the inferiority of your work.

Truly, then, your system is one not founded upon practice; it is one of abstraction—of extortion.

XIV.

CONFLICTING PRINCIPLES.

THERE is one thing which embarrasses me not a little; and it is this:

Sincere men, taking upon the subject of political economy the point of view of producers, have arrived at this double formula:

"A government should dispose of consumers subject to its laws in favor of home industry."

"It should subject to its laws foreign consumers, in order to dispose of them in favor of home industry."

The first of the formulas is that of *Protection;* the second that of *Outlets.*

Both rest upon this proposition, called the *Balance of Trade*, that

"A people is impoverished by importations and enriched by exportations."

For if every foreign purchase is a *tribute paid*, a loss, nothing can be more natural than to restrain, even to prohibit importations.

And if every foreign sale is a *tribute received*, a gain, nothing more natural than to create *outlets*, even by force.

Protective System; Colonial System.—These are only two aspects of the same theory. To *prevent* our citizens from buying from foreigners, and to *force* foreigners to buy from our citizens. Two consequences of one identical principle.

It is impossible not to perceive that according to this doctrine, if it be true, the welfare of a country depends upon *monopoly* or domestic spoliation, and upon *conquest* or foreign spoliation.

Let us take a glance into one of these huts, perched upon the side of our Pyrenean range.

The father of a family has received the little wages of his labor; but his half-naked children are shivering before a biting northern blast, beside a fireless hearth, and an empty table. There is wool, and wood, and corn, on the other side of the mountain, but these are forbidden to them; for the other side of the mountain is not France. Foreign wood must not warm the hearth of the poor shepherd; his children must not taste the bread of Biscay, nor cover their numbed limbs with the wool of Navarre. It is thus that the general good requires!

The disposing by law of consumers, forcing them to the support of home industry, is an encroachment upon their liberty, the forbidding of an action (mutual exchange) which is in no way opposed to morality! In a word, it is an act of *injustice.*

But this, it is said, is necessary, or else home labor will be arrested, and a severe blow will be given to public prosperity.

Thus then we must come to the melancholy conclusion, that there is a radical incompatibility between the Just and the Useful.

Again, if each people is interested in *selling,* and not in *buying,* a violent action and reaction must form the natural state of their mutual relations; for each will seek to force its productions upon all, and all will seek to repulse the productions of each.

A sale in fact implies a purchase, and since, according to this doctrine, to sell is beneficial, and to buy injurious, every international transaction must imply the benefiting of one people by the injuring of another.

But men are invincibly inclined to what they feel to be advantageous to themselves, while they also, instinctively resist that which is injurious. From hence then we must infer that each nation bears within itself a natural force of expansion, and a not less natural force of resistance, which are equally injurious to all others. In other words, antagonism and war are the *natural* state of human society.

Thus then the theory in discussion resolves itself into the two following axioms. In the affairs of a nation,

Utility is incompatible with the internal administration of justice.

Utility is incompatible with the maintenance of external peace.

Well, what embarrasses and confounds me is, to explain how any writer upon public rights, any statesman who has sincerely adopted a doctrine of which the leading principle is so antagonistic to other incontestable principles, can enjoy one moment's repose or peace of mind.

For myself, if such were my entrance upon the threshold of science, if I did not clearly perceive that Liberty, Utility, Justice, and Peace, are not only compatible, but closely connected, even identical, I would endeavor to forget all I have learned; I would say:

"Can it be possible that God can allow men to attain prosperity only through injustice and war? Can he so direct the affairs of mortals, that they can only renounce war and injustice by, at the same time, renouncing their own welfare?

"Am I not deceived by the false lights of a science which can lead me to the horrible blasphemy implied in this alternative, and shall I dare to take it upon myself to propose this as a basis for the legislation of a great people? When I find a long succession of illustrious and learned men, whose researches in the same science have led to more consoling results; who, after having devoted their lives to its study, affirm that through it they see Liberty and Utility indissolubly linked with Justice and Peace, and find these great principles destined to continue on through eternity in infinite parallels, have they not in their favor the presumption which results from all that we know of the goodness and wisdom of God as manifested in the sublime harmony of material creation? Can I lightly believe, in opposition to such a presumption and such imposing authorities, that this same God has been pleased to put disagreement and antagonism in the laws of the moral world? No; before I can believe that all social principles oppose, shock and neutralize each other; before I can think them in constant, anarchical and eternal conflict; above all, before I can seek to impose upon my fellow-citizens the impious system to which my reasonings have led me, I must retrace my steps, hoping, perchance, to find some point where I have wandered from my road."

And if, after a sincere investigation twenty times repeated, I should still arrive at the frightful conclusion that I am driven to choose between the Desirable and the Good, I would reject the science, plunge into a voluntary ignorance, above all, avoid participation in the affairs of my country, and leave to others the weight and responsibility of so fearful a choice.

XV.

RECIPROCITY AGAIN.

Mr. de Saint Cricq has asked: "Are we sure that our foreign customers will buy from us as much as they sell us?"

Mr. de Dombasle says: "What reason have we for believing that English producers will come to seek their supplies from us, rather than from any other nation, or that they will take from us a value equivalent to their exportations into France?"

I cannot but wonder to see men who boast, above all things, of being *practical*, thus reasoning wide of all practice!

In practice, there is perhaps no traffic which is a direct exchange of produce for produce. Since the use of money, no man says, I will seek shoes, hats, advice, lessons, only from the shoemaker, the hatter, the lawyer, or teacher, who will buy from me the exact equivalent of these in corn. Why should nations impose upon themselves so troublesome a restraint?

Suppose a nation without any exterior relations. One of its citizens makes a crop of corn. He casts it into the *national* circulation, and receives in exchange—what? Money, bank bills, securities, divisible to any extent, by means of which it will be lawful for him to withdraw when he pleases, and, unless prevented by just competition from the national circulation, such articles as he may wish. At the end of the operation, he will have withdrawn from the mass the exact equivalent of what he first cast into it, and in value, *his consumption will exactly equal his production.*

If the exchanges of this nation with foreign nations are free, it is no longer into the *national* circulation but into the *general* circulation that each individual casts his produce, and from thence his consumption is drawn. He is not obliged to calculate whether what he casts into this general circulation is purchased by a countryman or by a foreigner; whether the notes he receives are given to him by a Frenchman or an Englishman, or whether the articles which he procures through means of this money are manufactured on this or the other side of the Rhine or the Pyrenees. One thing is certain; that each individual finds an exact balance between what he casts in and what he withdraws from the great common reservoir; and if this be true of each individual, it is not less true of the entire nation.

The only difference between these two cases is, that in the last, each individual has open to him a larger market both for his sales and his purchases, and has, consequently, a more favorable opportunity of making both to advantage.

The objection advanced against us here, is, that if all were to combine in not withdrawing from circulation the produce from any one individual, he, in his turn, could withdraw nothing from the mass. The same, too, would be the case with regard to a nation.

Our answer is: If a nation can no longer withdraw any thing from the mass of circulation, neither will it any longer cast any thing into it. It will work for itself. It will be obliged to submit to what, in advance, you wish to force upon it, viz., *Isolation.* And here you have the ideal of the prohibitive system.

Truly, then, is it not ridiculous enough that you should inflict upon it now, and unnecessarily, this system, merely through fear that some day or other it might chance to be subjected to it without your assistance?

XVI.

OBSTRUCTED RIVERS PLEADING FOR THE PROHIBITIONISTS.

SOME years since, being at Madrid, I went to the meeting of the Cortes. The subject in discussion was a proposed treaty with Portugal, for improving the channel of the Douro. A member rose and said: If the Douro is made navigable, transportation must become cheaper, and Portuguese grain will come into formidable competition with our *national labor.* I vote against the project, unless ministers will agree to increase our tariff so as to re-establish the equilibrium.

Three months after, I was in Lisbon, and the same question came before the Senate. A noble Hidalgo said: Mr. President, the project is absurd. You guard at great expense the banks of the Douro, to prevent the influx into Portugal of Spanish grain, and at the same time you now propose, at great expense, *to facilitate such an event.* There is in this a want of consistency in which I can have no part. Let the Douro descend to our Sons as we have received it from our Fathers.

XVII.

A NEGATIVE RAILROAD.

I HAVE already remarked that when the observer has unfortunately taken his point of view from the position of producer, he cannot fail in his conclusions to clash with the general interest, because the producer, as such, must desire the existence of efforts, wants, and obstacles.

I find a singular exemplification of this remark in a journal of Bordeaux.

Mr. Simiot puts this question:

Ought the railroad from Paris into Spain to present a break or terminus at Bordeaux?

This question he answers affirmatively. I will only consider one among the numerous reasons which he adduces in support of his opinion.

The railroad from Paris to Bayonne ought (he says) to present a break or terminus at Bordeaux, in order that goods and travelers stopping in this city should thus be forced to contribute to the profits of the boatmen, porters, commission merchants, hotel-keepers, etc.

It is very evident that we have here again the interest of the agents of labor put before that of the consumer.

But if Bordeaux would profit by a break in the

road, and if such profit be conformable to the public interest, then Angoulême, Poictiers, Tours, Orleans, and still more all the intermediate points, as Ruffec, Châtellerault, etc., etc., would also petition for breaks; and this too would be for the general good and for the interest of national labor. For it is certain, that in proportion to the number of these breaks or termini, will be the increase in consignments, commissions, lading, unlading, etc. This system furnishes us the idea of a railroad made up of successive breaks; *a negative railroad.*

Whether or not the Protectionists will allow it, most certain it is, that the *restrictive principle* is identical with that which would maintain *this system of breaks:* it is the sacrifice of the consumer to the producer, of the end to the means.

XVIII.

"THERE ARE NO ABSOLUTE PRINCIPLES."

THE facility with which men resign themselves to ignorance in cases where knowledge is all-important to them, is often astonishing; and we may be sure that a man has determined to rest in his ignorance, when he once brings himself to proclaim as a maxim that there are no absolute principles.

We enter into the legislative halls, and find that the question is, to determine whether the law will or will not allow of international exchanges.

A deputy rises and says, If we tolerate these exchanges, foreign nations will overwhelm us with their produce. We will have cotton goods from England, coal from Belgium, woolens from Spain, silks from Italy, cattle from Switzerland, iron from Sweden, corn from Prussia, so that no industrial pursuit will any longer be possible to us.

Another answers: Prohibit these exchanges, and the divers advantages with which nature has endowed these different countries, will be for us as though they did not exist. We will have no share in the benefits resulting from English skill, or Belgian mines, from the fertility of the Polish soil, or the Swiss pastures; neither will we profit by the cheapness of Spanish labor, or the heat of the Italian climate. We will be obliged to seek by a forced and laborious production, what, by means of exchanges, would be much more easily obtained.

Assuredly one or other of these deputies is mistaken. But which? It is worth the trouble of examining. There lie before us two roads, one of which leads inevitably to *wretchedness*. We must choose.

To throw off the feeling of responsibility, the answer is easy: There are no absolute principles.

This maxim, at present so fashionable, not only pleases idleness, but also suits ambition.

If either the theory of prohibition, or that of free trade, should finally triumph, one little law would form our whole economical code. In the first case this would be: *foreign trade is forbidden;* in the second: *foreign trade is free;* and thus, many great personages would lose their importance.

But if trade has no distinctive character, if it is capriciously useful or injurious, and is governed by no natural law, if it finds no spur in its usefulness, no check in its inutility, if its effects cannot be appreciated by those who exercise it; in a word, if it has no absolute principles,—oh! then it is necessary to deliberate, weigh, and regulate transactions, the conditions of labor must be equalized, the level of profits sought. This is an important charge, well calculated to give to those who execute it, large salaries, and extensive influence.

Contemplating this great city of Paris, I have thought to myself: Here are a million of human beings who would die in a few days, if provisions of every kind did not flow in towards this vast metropolis. The imagination is unable to calculate the multiplicity of objects which to-morrow must enter its gates, to prevent the life of its inhabitants from terminating in famine, riot, or pillage. And yet at this moment all are asleep, without feeling one moment's uneasiness, from the contemplation of this frightful possibility. On the other side, we see eighty departments who have this day labored, without concert, without mutual understanding, for the victualing of Paris. How can each day bring just what is necessary, nothing less, nothing more, to this gigantic market? What is the ingenious and secret power which presides over the astonishing regularity of such complicated movements, a regularity in which we all have so implicit, though thoughtless, a faith; on which our comfort, our very existence depends? This power is an *absolute principle*, the principle of freedom in exchanges. We have faith in that inner light which Providence has placed in the heart of all men; confiding to it the preservation and amelioration of our species; *interest*, since we must give its name, so vigilant, so active, having so much forecast when allowed its free action. What would be your condition, inhabitants of Paris, if a minister, however superior his abilities, should undertake to substitute, in the place of this power, the combinations of his own genius? If he should think of subjecting to his own supreme direction this prodigious mechanism, taking all its springs into his own hand, and deciding by whom, how, and on what conditions each article should be produced, transported, exchanged and consumed? Ah! although there is much suffering within your walls; although misery, despair, and perhaps starvation, may call forth more tears than your warmest charity can wipe away, it is probable, it is certain, that the arbitrary intervention of government would infinitely multiply these sufferings, and would extend among you the evils which now reach but a small number of your citizens.

If then we have such faith in this principle as applied to our private concerns, why should we not extend it to international transactions, which are assuredly less numerous, less delicate, and less complicated? And if it be not necessary for the prefect of Paris to regulate our industrial pursuits, to weigh our profits and our losses, to occupy himself with the quantity of our cash, and to equalize the conditions of our labor in internal commerce, on what principle can it be necessary that the custom-house, going beyond its fiscal mission, should pretend to exercise a protective power over our external commerce?

XIX.

NATIONAL INDEPENDENCE.

Among the arguments advanced in favor of a restrictive system, we must not forget that which is drawn from the plea of *national independence.*

"What will we do," it is asked, "in case of war, if we are at the mercy of England for our iron and coal?"

The English monopolists, on their side, do not fail to exclaim: "What will become of Great Britain in case of war if she depends upon France for provisions?"

One thing appears to be quite lost sight of, and this is, that the dependence which results from commercial transactions, is a *reciprocal* dependence. We can only be dependent upon foreign supplies, in so far as foreign nations are dependent upon us. This is the essence of *society*. The breaking off of natural relations places a nation, not in an independent position, but in a state of isolation.

And remark that the reason given for this isolation, is that it is a necessary provision for war, while the act is itself a commencement of war. It renders war easier, less burdensome, and consequently less unpopular. If nations were to one another permanent outlets for mutual produce; if their respective relations were such that they could not be broken without inflicting the double suffering of privation and of over-supply, there could then no longer be any need of these powerful fleets which ruin, and these great armies which crush them; the peace of the world could no more be compromised by the whim of a Thiers or a Palmerston, and wars would cease, from want of resources, motives, pretexts, and popular sympathy.

I know that I shall be reproached (for it is the fashion of the day) for placing interest, vile and prosaic interest, at the foundation of the fraternity of nations. It would be preferred that this should be based upon charity, upon love; that there should be in it some self-denial, and that clashing a little with the material welfare of men, it should bear the merit of a generous sacrifice.

When will we have done with such puerile declamations? We contemn, we revile *interest*, that is to say, the good and the useful, (for if all men are interested in an object, how can this object be other than good in itself?) as though this interest were not the necessary, eternal, and indestructible mover, to the guidance of which Providence has confided human perfectibility! One would suppose that the utterers of such sentiments must be models of disinterestedness; but does the public not begin to perceive with disgust, that this affected language is the stain of those pages for which it oftenest pays the highest price?

What! because comfort and peace are correlative, because it has pleased God to establish so beautiful a harmony in the moral world, you would blame me when I admire and adore his decrees, and for accepting with gratitude his laws, which make justice a requisite for happiness! You will consent to have peace only when it clashes with your welfare, and liberty is irksome if it imposes no sacrifices! What then prevents you, if self-denial has so many charms, from exercising it as much as you desire in your private actions? Society will be benefited by your so doing, for some one must profit by your sacrifices. But it is the height of absurdity to wish to impose such a principle upon mankind generally; for the self-denial of all, is the sacrifice of all. This is evil systematized into theory.

But, thanks be to Heaven! these declamations may be written and read, and the world continues nevertheless to obey its great mover, its great cause of action, which, spite of all denials, is *interest.*

It is singular enough, too, to hear sentiments of such sublime self-abnegation quoted in support even of Spoliation; and yet to this tends all this pompous show of disinterestedness! These men so sensitively delicate, that they are determined not to enjoy even peace, if it must be propped by the vile *interest* of men, do not hesitate to pick the pockets of other men, and above all of poor men. For what tariff protects the poor? Gentlemen, we pray you, dispose as you please of what belongs to yourselves, but let us entreat you to allow us to use, or to exchange, according to our own fancy, the fruit of our own labor, the sweat of our own brows. Declaim as you will about self-sacrifice; that is all pretty enough; but we beg of you, do not at the same time forget to be honest.

XX.

HUMAN LABOR—NATIONAL LABOR.

DESTRUCTION of machinery—prohibition of foreign goods. These are two acts proceeding from the same doctrine.

We do meet with men who, while they rejoice over the revelation of any great invention, favor nevertheless the protective policy; but such men are very inconsistent.

What is the objection they adduce against free trade? That it causes us to seek from foreign and more easy production, what would otherwise be the result of home production. In a word, that it injures domestic industry.

On the same principle, can it not be objected to machinery, that it accomplishes through natural agents what would otherwise be the result of manual labor, and that it is thus injurious to human labor?

The foreign laborer, enjoying greater facilities of production than the French laborer, is, with regard to the latter, a veritable *economical machine*, which crushes him by competition. Thus, a piece of machinery capable of executing any work at a less price than could be done by any given number of hands, is, as regards these hands, in the position of a *foreign competitor*, who paralyzes them by his rivalry.

If then it be judicious to protect *home labor* against the competition of *foreign labor*, it cannot be less so to protect *human labor* against *mechanical labor.*

Whoever adheres to the protective system, ought not, if his brain be possessed of any logical powers, to stop at the prohibition of foreign produce, but should extend this prohibition to the produce of the loom and of the plough.

I approve therefore of the logic of those who, whilst they cry out against the *inundation* of foreign merchandise, have the courage to declaim equally against the *excessive production* resulting from the inventive power of mind.

Of this number is Mr. de Saint Chamans. "One of the strongest arguments, (says he) which can be adduced against free trade, and the too extensive employment of machines, is, that many workmen are deprived of work, either by foreign competition, which depresses manufactures, or by machinery, which takes the place of men in workshops."

Mr. de St. Chamans saw clearly the analogy, or rather the identity which exists between *importation* and *machinery*, and was, therefore, in favor of proscribing both. There is some pleasure in having to do with intrepid arguers, who, even in error, thus carry through a chain of reasoning.

But let us look at the difficulty into which they are here led.

If it be true, *à priori*, that the domain of *invention*, and that of *labor*, can be extended only to the injury of one another, it would follow that the fewest *workmen* would be employed in countries (Lancashire, for instance) where there is the most *machinery*. And if it be, on the contrary, proved, that machinery and manual labor coexist to a greater extent among rich nations than among savages, it must necessarily follow, that these two powers do not interfere with one another.

I cannot understand how a thinking being can rest satisfied with the following dilemma:

Either the inventions of man do not injure labor; and this, from general facts, would appear to be the case, for there exists more of both among the English and the French, than among the Sioux and the Cherokees. If such be the fact, I have gone upon a wrong track, although unconscious at what point. I have wandered from my road, and I would commit high treason against humanity, were I to introduce such an error into the legislation of my country.

Or else the results of the inventions of mind limit manual labor, as would appear to be proved from limited facts; for every day we see some machine rendering unnecessary the labor of twenty, or perhaps a hundred workmen. If this be the case, I am forced to acknowledge, as a fact, the existence of a flagrant, eternal, and incurable antagonism between the intellectual and the physical power of man; between his improvement and his welfare. I cannot avoid feeling that the Creator should have bestowed upon man either reason or bodily strength; moral force, or brutal force; and that it has been a bitter mockery to confer upon him faculties which must inevitably counteract and destroy one another.

This is an important difficulty, and how is it put aside? By this singular apothegm:

"*In political economy there are no absolute principles.*"

There are no principles! Why, what does this mean, but that there are no facts? Principles are only formulas, which recapitulate a whole class of well-proved facts.

Machinery and Importation must certainly have effects. These effects must be either good or bad. Here there may be a difference of opinion as to which is the correct conclusion, but whichever is adopted, it must be capable of being submitted to the formula of one or other of these principles, viz.: Machinery is a good, or, Machinery is an evil. Importations are beneficial, or, Importations are injurious. But to say *there are no principles*, is certainly the last degree of debasement to which the human mind can lower itself, and I confess that I blush for my country, when I hear so monstrous an absurdity uttered before, and approved by, the French Chambers, the *élite* of the nation, who thus justify themselves for imposing upon the country laws, of the merits or demerits of which they are perfectly ignorant.

But, it may be said to me, finish, then, by destroying the *Sophism.* Prove to us that machines are not injurious to *human labor*, nor importations to *national labor.*

In a work of this nature, such demonstrations cannot be very complete. My aim is rather to point out than to explain difficulties, and to excite reflection rather than to satisfy it. The mind never attains to a firm conviction which is not wrought out by its own labor. I will, however, make an effort to put it upon the right track.

The adversaries of importations and of machinery are misled by allowing themselves to form too hasty a judgment from immediate and transitory effects, instead of following these up to their general and final consequences.

The immediate effect of an ingenious piece of machinery, is, that it renders superfluous, in the production of any given result, a certain quantity of manual labor. But its action does not stop here. This result being obtained at less labor, is given to the public at a less price. The amount thus saved to the buyers, enables them to procure other comforts, and thus to encourage general labor, precisely in proportion to the saving they have made upon the one article which the machine has given to them at an easier price. Thus the standard of labor is not lowered, though that of comfort is raised.

Let me endeavor to render this double fact more striking by an example.

I suppose that ten million of hats, at fifteen francs each, are yearly consumed in France. This would give to those employed in this manufacture one hundred and fifty millions. A machine is invented which enables the manufacturer to furnish hats at ten francs. The sum given to the maintenance of this branch of industry, is thus reduced (if we suppose the consumption not to be increased) to one hundred millions. But the other fifty millions are not, therefore, withdrawn from the maintenance of *human labor*. The buyers of hats are, from the surplus saved upon the price of that article, enabled to satisfy other wants, and thus, in the same proportion, to encourage general industry. John buys a pair of shoes; James, a book; Jerome, an article of furniture, etc. Human labor, as a whole, still receives the encouragement of the whole one hundred and fifty millions, while the consumers, with the same supply of hats as before, receive also the increased number of comforts accruing from the fifty millions, which the use of the machine has been the means of saving to them. These comforts are the net gain which France has received from the invention. It is a gratuitous gift; a tribute exacted from nature by the genius of man. We grant that, during this process, a certain sum of labor will have been *displaced*, forced to change its direction; but we cannot allow that it has been destroyed or even diminished.

The case is the same with regard to importations. I will resume my hypothesis.

France, according to our supposition, manufactured ten millions of hats at fifteen francs each. Let us now suppose that a foreign producer brings them into our market at ten francs. I maintain that *national labor* is thus in no wise diminished. It will be obliged to produce the equivalent of the hundred millions which go to pay for the ten millions of hats at ten francs, and then there remains to each buyer five francs, saved on the purchase of his hat, or, in total, fifty millions, which serve for the acquisition of other comforts, and the encouragement of other labor.

The mass of labor remains, then, what it was, and the additional comforts accruing from the fifty millions saved in the purchase of hats, are the net profit of importation or free trade.

It is no argument to try and alarm us by a picture of the sufferings which, in this hypothesis, would result from the displacement or change of labor.

For, if prohibition had never existed, labor

would have classed itself in accordance with the laws of trade, and no displacement would have taken place.

If prohibition has led to an artificial and unproductive classification of labor, then it is prohibition, and not free trade, which is responsible for the inevitable displacement which must result in the transition from evil to good.

It is a rather singular argument to maintain that, because an abuse which has been permitted a temporary existence, cannot be corrected without wounding the interests of those who have profited by it, it ought, therefore, to claim perpetual duration.

XXI.

RAW MATERIAL.

It is said that no commerce is so advantageous as that in which manufactured articles are exchanged for raw material; because the latter furnishes aliment for *national labor.*

And it is hence concluded:

That the best regulation of duties, would be to give the greatest possible facilities to the importation of raw material, and at the same time to check that of the finished article.

There is, in political economy, no more generally accredited Sophism than this. It serves for argument not only to the protectionists, but also to the pretended free trade school; and it is in the latter capacity that its most mischievous tendencies are called into action. For a good cause suffers much less in being attacked, than in being badly defended.

Commercial liberty must probably pass through the same ordeal as liberty in every other form. It can only dictate laws, after having first taken thorough possession of men's minds. If, then, it be true that a reform, to be firmly established, must be generally understood, it follows that nothing can so much retard it, as the misleading of public opinion. And what more calculated to mislead opinion than writings, which, while they proclaim free trade, support the doctrines of monopoly?

It is some years since three great cities of France, viz., Lyons, Bordeaux, and Havre, combined in opposition to the restrictive system. France, all Europe, looked anxiously and suspiciously at this apparent declaration in favor of free trade. Alas! it was still the banner of monopoly which they followed! a monopoly, only a little more sordid, a little more absurd than that of which they seemed to desire the destruction! Thanks to the Sophism which I would now endeavor to deprive of its disguise, the petitioners only reproduced, with an additional incongruity, the old doctrine of *protection to national labor.* What is, in fact, the prohibitive system? We will let Mr. de Saint Cricq answer for us.

"Labor constitutes the riches of a nation, because it creates supplies for the gratification of our necessities; and universal comfort consists in the abundance of these supplies." Here we have the principle.

"But this abundance ought to be the result of *national labor.* If it were the result of foreign labor, national labor must receive an inevitable check." Here lies the error. (See the preceding Sophism).

"What, then, ought to be the course of an agricultural and manufacturing country? It ought to reserve its market for the produce of its own soil and its own industry." Here is the object.

"In order to effect this, it ought, by restrictive, and, if necessary, by prohibitive duties, to prevent the influx of produce from foreign soils and foreign industry." Here is the means.

Let us now compare this system with that of the petition from Bordeaux.

This divided articles of merchandise into three classes. "The first class includes articles of food and *raw material untouched by human labor. A judicious system of political economy would require that this class should be exempt from taxation.*" Here we have the principle of no labor, no protection.

"The second class is composed of articles which have received *some preparation* for manufacture. This preparation would render reasonable the imposition of *some duties.*" Here we find the commencement of protection, because, at the same time, likewise commences the demand for *national labor.*

"The third class comprehends finished articles, which can, under no circumstances, furnish material for national labor. We consider this as the most fit for taxation." Here we have at once the maximum of labor, and, consequently, of production.

The petitioners then, as we here see, proclaimed foreign labor as injurious to national labor. This is the *error* of the prohibitive system.

They desired the French market to be reserved for *French labor.* This is the *object* of the prohibitive system.

They demanded that foreign labor should be subjected to restrictions and taxes. These are the *means* of the prohibitive system.

What difference, then, can we possibly discover to exist between the Bordalese petitioners and the Corypheus of restriction? One, alone; and that is simply the greater or less extension which is given to the signification of the word *labor.*

Mr. de Saint Cricq, taking it in its widest sense, is, therefore, in favor of *protecting* every thing.

"Labor," he says, "constitutes *the whole* wealth of a nation. Protection should be for the agricultural interest, and *the whole* agricultural interest; for the manufacturing interest, and *the whole* manufacturing interest; and this principle I will continually endeavor to impress upon this Chamber."

The petitioners consider no labor but that of the manufacturers, and accordingly, it is that, and that alone, which they would wish to admit to the favors of protection.

"Raw material being entirely *untouched by human labor*, our system should exempt it from taxes. Manufactured articles furnishing no material for national labor, we consider as the most fit for taxation."

There is no question here as to the propriety of protecting national labor. Mr. de Saint Cricq and the Bordalese agree entirely upon this point. We have, in our preceding chapters, already shown how entirely we differ from both of them.

The question to be determined, is, whether it is Mr. de Saint Cricq, or the Bordalese, who give to the word *labor* its proper acceptation. And we must confess that Mr. de Saint Cricq is here decidedly in the right. The following dialogue might be supposed between them:

Mr. de Saint Cricq.—You agree that national labor ought to be protected. You agree that no foreign labor can be introduced into our market, without destroying an equal quantity of our national labor. But you contend that there are numerous articles of merchandise possessing *value*, for they are sold, and which are nevertheless *untouched by human labor.* Among these you name corn, flour, meat, cattle, bacon, salt, iron, copper, lead, coal, wool, skins, seeds, etc.

If you can prove to me, that the *value* of these things is not dependent upon labor, I will agree that it is useless to protect them.

But if I can prove to you that there is as much labor put upon a hundred francs worth of wool, as upon a hundred francs worth of cloth, you ought to acknowledge that protection is the right as much of the one, as of the other.

I ask you then why this bag of wool is worth a hundred francs? Is it not because this is its price of production? And what is the price of production, but the sum which has been distributed in wages for labor, payment of skill, and interest on money, among the various laborers and capitalists, who have assisted in the production of the article?

The Petitioners.—It is true that with regard to wool you may be right; but a bag of corn, a bar of iron, a hundred weight of coal, are these the produce of labor? Is it not nature which *creates* them?

Mr. de St. Cricq.—Without doubt, nature *creates* these substances, but it is labor which gives them their *value.* I have myself, in saying that labor *creates* material objects, used a false expression, which has led me into many farther errors. No man can *create.* No man can bring any thing from nothing; and if *production* is used as a synonym for *creation*, then indeed our labor must all be useless.

The agriculturist does not pretend that he has *created* the corn; but he has given it its *value.* He has by his own labor, and by that of his servants, his laborers, and his reapers, transformed into corn substances which were entirely dissimilar from it. What more is effected by the miller who converts it into flour, or by the baker who makes it into bread?

In order that a man may be dressed in cloth, numerous operations are first necessary. Before the intervention of any human labor, the real *primary materials* of this article are air, water, heat, gas, light, and the various salts which enter into its composition. These are indeed *untouched by human labor*, for they have no *value*, and I have never dreamed of their needing protection. But a first *labor* converts these substances into forage; a second into wool; a third into thread; a fourth into cloth; and a fifth into garments. Who can pretend to say, that all these contributions to the work, from the first furrow of the plough, to the last stitch of the needle, are not *labor?*

And because, for the sake of speed and greater perfection in the accomplishment of the final object, these various branches of labor are divided among as many classes of workmen, you, by an arbitrary distinction, determine that the order in which the various branches of labor follow each other shall regulate their importance, so that while the first is not allowed to merit the name of labor, the last shall receive all the favors of protection.

The Petitioners.—Yes, we begin to understand that neither wool nor corn are entirely *independent of human labor;* but certainly the agriculturist has not, like the manufacturer, had every thing to do by his own labor, and that of his workmen ; nature has assisted him ; and if there is some labor, at least all is not labor, in the production of corn.

Mr. de St. Cricq.—But it is the labor alone which gives it *value.* I grant that nature has assisted in the production of grain. I will even grant that it is exclusively her work ; but I must confess at least that I have constrained her to it by my labor. And remark, moreover, that when I sell my corn, it is not the *work of nature* which I make you pay for, but *my own.*

You will perceive, also, by following up your manner of arguing, that neither will manufactured articles be the production of labor. Does not the manufacturer also call upon nature to assist him? Does he not by the assistance of steam-machinery force into his service the weight of the atmosphere, as I, by the use of the plough, take advantage of its humidity? Is it the cloth-manufacturer who has created the laws of gravitation, transmission of forces and of affinities?

The Petitioners.—Well, well, we will give up wool, but assuredly coal is the work, the exclusive work, of nature. This, at least, is *independent of all human labor.*

Mr. de St. Cricq.—Yes, nature certainly has made coal; but *labor has made its value.* Where was the *value* of coal during the millions of years when it lay unknown and buried a hundred feet below the surface of the earth? It was necessary to seek it. Here was labor. It was necessary to transport it to a market. Again this was labor. The price which you pay for coal in the market is the remuneration given to these labors of digging and transportation.*

We see that, so far, all the advantage is on the side of Mr. de St. Cricq, and that the *value* of unmanufactured as of manufactured articles, represents always the expense, or what is the same thing, the *labor* of production; that it is impossible to conceive of an article bearing a *value, independent of*

* I do not, for many reasons, make explicit mention of such portion of the remuneration as belongs to the contractor, capitalist, etc. Firstly: because, if the subject be closely looked into, it will be seen that it is always either the reimbursing in advance, or the payment of anterior *labor.* Secondly: because, under the general labor, I include not only the salary of the workmen, but the legitimate payment of all co-operation in the work of production. Thirdly: finally, and above all, because the production of the manufactured articles is, like that of the raw material, burdened with interests and remunerations, entirely independent of *manual labor;* and that the objection, in itself, might be equally applied to the finest manufacture and to the roughest agricultural process.

human labor; that the distinction made by the petitioners is futile in theory, and, as the basis of an unequal division of favors, would be iniquitous in practice; for it would thence result that the one-third of the French occupied in manufactures, would receive all the benefits of monopoly, because they produce *by labor;* while the two other thirds, formed by the agricultural population, would be left to struggle against competition, under pretense that they produce *without labor.*

It will, I know, be insisted that it is advantageous to a nation to import the raw material, whether or not it be the result of labor; and to export manufactured articles. This is a very generally received opinion.

"In proportion," says the petition of Bordeaux, "as raw material is abundant, manufactures will increase and flourish."

"The abundance of raw material," it elsewhere says, "gives an unlimited scope to labor in those countries where it prevails."

"Raw material," says the petition from Havre, "being the element of labor, should be *regulated on a different system,* and ought to be admitted *immediately* and at the *lowest rate.*"

The same petition asks, that the protection of manufactured articles should be reduced, not *immediately,* but at some indeterminate time, not to the *lowest rate* of entrance, but to twenty per cent.

"Among other articles," says the petition of Lyons, "of which the low price and the abundance are necessary, the manufacturers name all *raw material.*"

All this is based upon error.

All *value* is, we have seen, the representative of labor. Now it is undoubtedly true that manufacturing labor increases ten-fold, a hundred-fold, the value of raw material, thus dispensing ten, a hundred-fold increased profits throughout the nation; and from this fact is deduced the following argument: The production of a hundred weight of iron, is the gain of only fifteen francs to the various workers therein engaged. This hundred weight of iron, converted into watch-springs, is increased in value by this process, ten thousand francs. Who can pretend that the nation is not more interested in securing the ten thousand francs, than the fifteen francs worth of labor?

In this reasoning it is forgotten, that international exchanges are, no more than individual exchanges, effected through weight and measure. The exchange is not between a hundred weight of unmanufactured iron, and a hundred weight of watch-springs, nor between a pound of wool just shorn, and a pound of wool just manufactured into cashmere, but between a fixed value in one of these articles, and a fixed equal value in another. To exchange equal value with. equal value, is to exchange equal labor with equal labor, and it is therefore not true that the nation which sells its hundred francs worth of cloth or of watch-springs, gains more than the one which furnishes its hundred francs worth of wool or of iron.

In a country where no law can be passed, no contribution imposed without the consent of the governed, the public can be robbed, only after it has first been cheated. Our own ignorance is the primary, the *raw material* of every act of extortion to which we are subjected, and it may safely be predicted of every *Sophism*, that it is the forerunner of an act of Spoliation. Good Public, whenever therefore you detect a Sophism in a petition, let me advise you, put your hand upon your pocket, for be assured, it is that which is particularly the point of attack.

Let us then examine what is the secret design which the ship-owners of Bordeaux and Havre, and the manufacturers of Lyons, would smuggle in upon us by this distinction between agricultural produce and manufactured produce.

"It is," say the petitioners of Bordeaux, "principally in this first class (that which comprehends raw material, *untouched by human labor*) that we find *the principal encouragement of our merchant vessels*. . . . . . A wise system of political economy would require that this class should not be taxed. . . . . . . The second class (articles which have received some preparation) may be considered as taxable. The third (articles which have received from labor all the finish of which they are capable) we regard as *most proper for taxation.*"

"Considering," say the petitioners of Hâvre, "that it is indispensable to reduce *immediately* and to the *lowest rate*, the raw material, in order that manufacturing industry may give employment to our merchant vessels, which furnish its first and indispensable means of labor."

The manufacturers could not allow themselves to be behindhand in civilities towards the ship-owners, and accordingly the petition of Lyons demands the free introduction of raw material, "in order to prove," it remarks, "that the interests of manufacturing towns are not opposed to those of maritime cities."

This may be true enough; but it must be confessed that both, taken in the sense of the petitioners, are terribly adverse to the interest of agriculture and of consumers.

This, then, gentlemen, is the aim of all your subtle distinctions! You wish the law to oppose the maritime transportation of *manufactured* articles, in order that the much more expensive transportation of the raw material should, by its larger bulk, in its rough, dirty and unimproved condition, furnish a more extensive business to your *merchant vessels.* And this is what you call a *wise system of political economy!*

Why not also petition for a law requiring that fir-trees, imported from Russia, should not be admitted without their branches, bark, and roots; that Mexican gold should be imported in the state of ore, and Buenos Ayres leathers only allowed an entrance into our ports, while still hanging to the dead bones and putrefying bodies to which they belong?

The stockholders of railroads, if they can obtain a majority in the Chambers, will no doubt soon favor us with a law forbidding the manufacture, at Cognac, of the brandy used in Paris. For, surely, they would consider it a wise law, which would, by forcing the transportation of ten casks of wine instead of one of brandy, thus furnish to Parisian industry an *indispensable encouragement to its labor*, and, at the same time, give employment to railroad locomotives!

Until when will we persist in shutting our eyes upon the following simple truth?

Labor and industry, in their general object, have but one legitimate aim, and this is the public good. To create useless industrial pursuits, to favor superfluous transportation, to maintain a superfluous labor, not for the good of the public, but at the expense of the public, is to act upon a *petitio principii*. For it is the result of labor, and not labor itself, which is a desirable object. All labor, without a result, is clear loss. To pay sailors for transporting rough dirt and filthy refuse across the ocean, is about as reasonable as it would be to engage their services, and pay them for pelting the water with pebbles. Thus we arrive at the conclusion that *political Sophisms*, notwithstanding their infinite variety, have one point in common, which is the constant confounding of the *means* with the *end*, and the development of the former at the expense of the latter.

XXII.

METAPHORS.

A Sophism will sometimes expand and extend itself through the whole tissue of a long and tedious theory. Oftener it contracts into a principle, and hides itself in one word.

"Heaven preserve us," said Paul Louis, "from the Devil and from the spirit of metaphor!" And, truly, it might be difficult to determine which of the two sheds the most noxious influence over our planet. The Devil, you will say, because it is he who implants in our hearts the spirit of spoliation. Aye; but he leaves the capacity for checking abuses, by the resistance of those who suffer. It is the genius of Sophism which paralyzes this resistance. The sword which the spirit of evil places in the hands of the aggressor, would fall powerless, if the shield of him who is attacked were not shattered in his grasp by the spirit of Sophism. Malbranche has, with great truth, inscribed upon the frontispiece of his book this sentence: *Error is the cause of human misery.*

Let us notice what passes in the world. Ambitious hypocrites may take a sinister interest in spreading, for instance, the germ of national enmities. The noxious seed may, in its developments, lead to a general conflagration, check civilization, spill torrents of blood, and draw upon the country that most terrible of scourges, *invasion.* Such hateful sentiments cannot fail to degrade, in the opinion of other nations, the people among whom they prevail, and force those who retain some love of justice to blush for their country. These are fearful evils, and it would be enough that the public should have a clear view of them, to induce them to secure themselves against the plotting of those who would expose them to such heavy chances. How, then, are they kept in darkness? How, but by metaphors? The meaning of three or four words is forced, changed, and depraved—and all is said.

Such is the use made, for instance, of the word *invasion.*

A master of French iron-works, exclaims: Save us from the *invasion* of English iron. An English landholder cries; Let us oppose the *invasion* of French corn. And forthwith all their efforts are bent upon raising barriers between these two nations. Thence follows isolation; isolation leads to hatred; hatred to war; and war to *invasion.* What matters it? say the two *Sophists;* is it not better to expose ourselves to a possible *invasion*, than to meet a certain one? And the people believe; and the barriers are kept up.

And yet what analogy can exist between an exchange and an invasion? What resemblance can possibly be discovered between a man-of-war, vomiting fire, death, and desolation over our cities—and a merchant vessel, which comes to offer in free and peaceable exchange, produce for produce?

Much in the same way has the word *inundation* been abused. This word is generally taken in a bad sense; and it is certainly of frequent occurrence for inundations to ruin fields and sweep away harvests. But if, as is the case in the inundations of the Nile, they were to leave upon the soil a superior value to that which they carried away, we ought, like the Egyptians, to bless and deify them. Would it not be well, before declaiming against the *inundations* of foreign produce, and checking them with expensive and embarrassing obstacles, to certify ourselves whether these inundations are of the number which desolate, or of those which fertilize a country? What would we think of Mehemet

Ali, if, instead of constructing, at great expense, dams across the Nile to increase the extent of its inundations, he were to scatter his piasters in attempts to deepen its bed, that he might rescue Egypt from the defilement of the *foreign* mud which is swept down upon it from the mountains of the Moon? Exactly such a degree of wisdom do we exhibit, when at the expense of millions, we strive to preserve our country .... From what? From the blessings with which Nature has gifted other climates.

Among the *metaphors* which sometimes conceal, each in itself, a whole theory of evil, there is none more common than that which is presented under the words *tribute* and *tributary.*

These words are so frequently employed as synonyms of *purchase* and *purchaser*, that the terms are now used almost indifferently. And yet there is as distinct a difference between a *tribute*, and a *purchase*, as between a *robbery* and an *exchange.* It appears to me that it would be quite as correct to say, Cartouche has broken open my strong box, and has *bought* a thousand crowns from me, as to state, as I have heard done to our honorable deputies, We have paid in *tribute* to Germany the value of a thousand horses which she has sold us.

The action of Cartouche was not a *purchase*, because he did not put, and with my consent, into my strong box an equivalent value to that which he took out. Neither could the purchase-money paid to Germany be *tribute*, because it was not on our part a forced payment, gratuitously received on hers, but a willing compensation from us for a thousand horses, which we ourselves judged to be worth 500,000 francs.

Is it necessary then seriously to criticise such abuses of language? Yes, for very seriously are they put forth in our books and journals. Nor can we flatter ourselves that they are the careless expressions of uneducated writers, ignorant even of the terms of their own language. They are current with a vast majority, and among the most distinguished of our writers. We find them in the mouths of our d'Argouts, Dupins, Villèles; of peers, deputies and ministers; men whose words become laws, and whose influence might establish the most revolting Sophisms, as the basis of the administration of their country.

A celebrated modern Philosopher has added to the categories of Aristotle the Sophism which consists in expressing in one word a *petitio principii.* He cites several examples, and might have added the word *tributary* to his nomenclature. For instance, the question is to determine whether foreign purchases are useful or hurtful. You answer, hurtful. And why? Because they render us *tributary* to foreigners. Truly here is a word, which begs the question at once.

How has this delusive figure of speech introduced itself into the rhetoric of monopolists?

Money is *withdrawn from the country* to satisfy the rapacity of a victorious enemy: money is also *withdrawn from the country* to pay for merchandise. The analogy is established between the two cases, calculating only the point of resemblance and abstracting that by which they differ.

And yet it is certainly true, that the non-reimbursement in the first case, and the reimbursement freely agreed upon in the second, establishes between them so decided a difference, as to render it impossible to class them under the same category. To be obliged, with a dagger at your throat, to give a hundred francs, or to give them willingly in order to obtain a desired object,—truly these are cases in which we can perceive little similarity. It might just as correctly be said, that it is a matter of indifference whether we eat our bread, or have it thrown into the water, because in both cases it is destroyed. We here draw a false conclusion, as in the case of the word *tribute*, by a vicious manner of reasoning, which supposes an entire similitude between two cases, their resemblance only being noticed and their difference suppressed.

CONCLUSION.

All the Sophisms which I have so far combated, relate to the restrictive policy; and some even on this subject, and those of the most remarkable, I have, in pity to the reader, passed over: *acquired rights; unsuitableness; exhaustion of money, etc., etc.*

But Social economy is not confined within this narrow circle. Fourierism, Saint Simonism, Commonism, agrarianism, anti-rentism, mysticism, sentimentalism, false philanthropy, affected aspirations for a chimerical equality and fraternity; questions relative to luxury, wages, machinery; to the pretended tyranny of capital; to colonies, outlets, population; to emigration, association, imposts, and loans, have encumbered the field of Science with a crowd of parasitical arguments,—*Sophisms*, whose rank growth calls for the spade and the weeding-hoe.

I am perfectly sensible of the defect of my plan, or rather absence of plan. By attacking as I do, one by one, so many incoherent Sophisms, which clash, and then again often mingle with each other, I am conscious that I condemn myself to a disorderly and capricious struggle, and am exposed to perpetual repetitions.

I should certainly much prefer to state simply how things *are*, without troubling myself to contemplate the thousand aspects under which ignorance *supposes* them to be.... To lay down at once the laws under which society prospers or perishes, would be *virtually* to destroy at once all Sophisms. When Laplace described what, up to his time, was known of the movements of celestial bodies, he dissipated, without even naming them, all the astrological reveries of the Egyptians, Greeks, and Hindoos, much more certainly than he could have done by attempting to refute them directly, through innumerable volumes. Truth is one, and the work which expounds it is an imposing and durable edifice. Error is multiple, and of ephemereal nature. The work which combats it, cannot bear in itself a principle of greatness or of durability.

But if power, and perhaps opportunity, have been wanting to me, to enable me to proceed in the manner of Laplace and of Say, I still cannot but believe that the mode adopted by me has also its modest usefulness. It appears to me likewise to be well suited to the wants of the age, and to the broken moments which it is now the habit to snatch for study.

A treatise has without doubt an incontestable superiority. But it requires to be read, meditated, and understood. It addresses itself to the select few. Its mission is first to fix attention, and then to enlarge the circle of acquired knowledge.

A work which undertakes the refutation of vulgar prejudices, cannot have so high an aim. It aspires only to clear the way for the steps of Truth; to prepare the minds of men to receive her; to rectify public opinion, and to snatch from unworthy hands dangerous weapons which they misuse.

It is above all, in social economy, that this hand-to-hand struggle, this ever-reviving combat with popular errors, has a true practical utility.

Sciences might be arranged in two categories. Those of the first class whose application belongs only to particular professions, can be understood only by the learned; but the most ignorant may profit by their fruits. We may enjoy the comforts of a watch; we may be transported by locomotives or steamboats, although knowing nothing of mechanism and astronomy. We walk according to the laws of equilibrium, while entirely ignorant of them.

But there are sciences whose influence upon the public is proportioned only to the information of that public itself, and whose efficacy consists not in the accumulated knowledge of some few learned heads, but in that which has diffused itself into the reason of man in the aggregate. Such are morals, hygiene, social economy, and (in countries where men belong to themselves) political economy. Of these sciences Bentham might above all have said: "It is better to circulate, than to advance them." What does it profit us that a great man, even a God, should promulgate moral laws, if the minds of men, steeped in error, will constantly mistake vice for virtue, and virtue for vice? What does it benefit us that Smith, Say, and, according to Mr. de St. Chamans, political economists of *every school*, should have proclaimed the superiority in all commercial transactions, of *liberty* above *restraint*, if those who make laws, and for whom laws are made, are convinced of the contrary?

These sciences, which have very properly been named *social*, are again peculiar in this, that they, being of common application, no one will confess himself ignorant of them. If the object be to determine a question in chemistry or geometry, nobody pretends to have an innate knowledge of the science, or is ashamed to consult Mr. Thénard, or to seek information from the pages of Legendre or Bezout. But in the social sciences authorities are rarely acknowledged. As each individual daily acts upon his own notions whether right or wrong, of morals, hygiene, and economy; of politics, whether reasonable or absurd, each one thinks he has a right to prose, comment, decide, and dictate in these matters. Are you sick? There is not a good old woman in the country who is not ready to tell you the cause and the remedy of your sufferings. "It is from humors in the blood," says she, "you must be purged." But what are these humors, or are there any humors at all? On this subject she troubles herself but little. This good old woman comes into my mind, whenever I hear an attempt made to account for all the maladies of the social body, by some trivial form of words. It is superabundance of produce, tyranny of capital, industrial plethora, or other such nonsense, of which, it would be fortunate if we could say: *Verba et voces prœtereaque nihil*, for these are errors from which fatal consequences follow.

From what precedes, the two following results may be deduced: 1st. That the social sciences, more than others, necessarily abound in *Sophisms*, because in their application, each individual consults only his own judgment and his own instincts. 2d. That in these sciences *Sophisms* are especially injurious, because they mislead opinion on a subject in which opinion is power—is law.

Two kinds of books then are necessary in these sciences, those which teach, and those which circulate; those which expound the truth, and those which combat error.

I believe that the inherent defect of this little work, *repetition*, is what is likely to be the cause of its principal utility. Among the Sophisms which it has discussed, each has undoubtedly its own formula and tendency, but all have a common root;

and this is, the *forgetfulness of the interests of men, considered as consumers.* By showing that a thousand mistaken roads all lead to this great *generative* Sophism, I may perhaps teach the public to recognize, to know, and to mistrust it, under all circumstances.

After all, I am less at forcing convictions, than at waking doubts.

I have no hope that the reader as he lays down my book will exclaim, *I know.* My aspirations will be fully satisfied, if he can but sincerely say, *I doubt.*

"I doubt, for I begin to fear that there may be something illusory in the supposed blessings of scarcity." (Sophism I.)

"I am not so certain of the beneficial effect of obstacles." (Sophism II.)

"*Effort without result*, no longer appears to me so desirable as *result without effort.*" (Sophism III.)

"I understand that the more an article has been labored upon, the more is its *value.* But in trade, do two *equal* values cease to be equal, because one comes from the plough, and the other from the workshop?" (Sophism XXI.)

"I confess that I begin to think it singular that mankind should be the better of hindrances and obstacles, or should grow rich upon taxes; and truly I would be relieved from some anxiety, would be really happy to see the proof of the fact, as stated by the author of "the Sophisms," that there is no incompatibility between prosperity and justice, between peace and liberty, between the extension of labor and the advance of intelligence." (Sophisms XIV and XX.)

"Without, then, giving up entirely to arguments, which I am yet in doubt whether to look upon as fairly reasoned, or as paradoxical, I will at least seek enlightenment from the masters of the science."

I will now terminate this sketch by a last and important recapitulation.

The world is not sufficiently conscious of the influence exercised over it by *Sophistry.*

When *might ceases to be right*, and the government of mere *strength* is dethroned, *Sophistry* transfers the empire to *cunning and subtilty.* It would be difficult to determine which of the two tyrannies is most injurious to mankind.

Men have an immoderate love for pleasure, influence, consideration, power—in a word, for riches; and they are, by an almost unconquerable inclination, pushed to procure these, at the expense of others.

But these *others*, who form the public, have a no less strong inclination to keep what they have acquired; and this they will do, if they have the *strength* and the *knowledge* to effect it.

Spoliation, which plays so important a part in the

affairs of this world, has then two agents; *Force* and *Cunning*. She has also two checks; *Courage* and *Knowledge*.

Force applied to spoliation, furnishes the great material for the annals of men. To retrace its history would be to present almost the entire history of every nation: Assyrians, Babylonians, Medes, Persians, Greeks, Romans, Goths, Franks, Huns, Turks, Arabs, Tartars, without counting the more recent expeditions of the English in India, the French in Africa, the Russians in Asia, etc., etc.

But among civilized nations surely the producers of riches are now become sufficiently numerous and strong to defend themselves.

Does this mean that they are no longer robbed? They are as much so as ever, and moreover they rob one another.

The only difference is that Spoliation has changed her agent. She acts no longer by *Force*, but by *Cunning*.

To rob the public, it is necessary to deceive them. To deceive them, it is necessary to persuade them that they are robbed for their own advantage, and to induce them to accept in exchange for their property, imaginary services, and often worse. Hence spring *Sophisms* in all their varieties. Then, since Force is held in check, *Sophistry* is no longer only an evil; it is the genius of evil, and requires a check in its turn. This check must be the enlightenment of the public, which must be rendered more *subtle* than the subtle, as it is already *stronger* than the strong.

GOOD PUBLIC! I now dedicate to you this first essay; though it must be confessed that the Preface is strangely transposed, and the Dedication a little tardy.

PART II.

SOPHISMS OF PROTECTION.

SECOND SERIES.

"The request of Industry to the government is as modest as that of Diogenes to Alexander: "Stand out of my sunshine."—BENTHAM.

I.

NATURAL HISTORY OF SPOLIATION.

WHY do I give myself up to that dry science, political economy?

The question is a proper one. All labor is so repugnant in its nature that one has the right to ask of what use it is.

Let us examine and see.

I do not address myself to those philosophers who, if not in their own names, at least in the name of humanity, profess to adore poverty.

I speak to those who hold wealth in esteem—and understand by this word, not the opulence of the few, but the comfort, the well-being, the security, the independence, the instruction, the dignity of all.

There are only two ways by which the means essential to the preservation, the adornment and the perfection of life may be obtained—production and spoliation. Some persons may say: "Spoliation is an accident, a local and transient abuse, denounced by morality, punished by the law, and unworthy the attention of political economy."

Still, however benevolent or optimistic one may be, he is compelled to admit that spoliation is practiced on so vast a scale in this world, and is so generally connected with all great human events, that no social science, and, least of all, political economy, can refuse to consider it.

I go farther. That which prevents the perfection of the social system (at least in so far as it is capable of perfection) is the constant effort of its members to live and prosper at the expense of each other. So that, if spoliation did not exist, society being perfect, the social sciences would be without an object.

I go still farther. When spoliation becomes a means of subsistence for a body of men united by social ties, in course of time they make a law which sanctions it, a morality which glorifies it.

It is enough to name some of the best defined

forms of spoliation to indicate the position it occupies in human affairs.

First comes war. Among savages the conqueror kills the conquered, to obtain an uncontested, if not incontestable, right to game.

Next slavery. When man learns that he can make the earth fruitful by labor, he makes this division with his brother: "You work and I eat."

Then comes superstition. "According as you give or refuse me that which is yours, I will open to you the gates of heaven or of hell."

Finally, monopoly appears. Its distinguishing characteristic is to allow the existence of the grand social law—*service for service*—while it brings the element of force into the discussion, and thus alters the just proportion between *service received* and *service rendered.*

Spoliation always bears within itself the germ of its own destruction. Very rarely the many despoil the few. In such a case the latter soon become so reduced that they can no longer satisfy the cupidity of the former, and spoliation ceases for want of sustenance.

Almost always the few oppress the many, and in that case spoliation is none the less undermined, for, if it has force as an agent, as in war and slavery, it is natural that force in the end should be on the side of the greater number. And if deception is the agent, as with superstition and monopoly, it is natural that the many should ultimately become enlightened.

Another law of Providence wars against spoliation. It is this:

Spoliation not only displaces wealth, but always destroys a portion.

War annihilates values.

Slavery paralyzes the faculties.

Monopoly transfers wealth from one pocket to another, but it always occasions the loss of a portion in the transfer.

This is an admirable law. Without it, provided the strength of oppressors and oppressed were equal, spoliation would have no end.

A moment comes when the destruction of wealth is such that the despoiler is poorer than he would have been if he had remained honest.

So it is with a people when a war costs more than the booty is worth; with a master who pays more for slave labor than for free labor; with a priesthood which has so stupefied the people and destroyed its energy that nothing more can be gotten out of it; with a monopoly which increases its attempts at absorption as there is less to absorb, just as the difficulty of milking increases with the emptiness of the udder.

Monopoly is a species of the genus spoliation. It has many varieties, among them sinecure, privilege, and restriction upon trade.

Some of the forms it assumes are simple and *naive*, like feudal rights. Under this *regime* the masses are despoiled, and know it.

Other forms are more complicated. Often the masses are plundered, and do not know it. It may even happen that they believe that they owe every thing to spoliation, not only what is left them but what is taken from them, and what is lost in the operation. I also assert that, in the course of time, thanks to the ingenious machinery of habit, many people become spoilers without knowing it or wishing it. Monopolies of this kind are begotten by fraud and nurtured by error. They vanish only before the light.

I have said enough to indicate that political economy has a manifest practical use. It is the torch which, unveiling deceit and dissipating error, destroys that social disorder called spoliation. Some one, a woman I believe, has correctly defined it as "the safety-lock upon the property of the people."

COMMENTARY.

If this little book were destined to live three or four thousand years, to be read and re-read, pondered and studied, phrase by phrase, word by word, and letter by letter, from generation to generation, like a new Koran; if it were to fill the libraries of the world with avalanches of annotations, explanations and paraphrases, I might leave to their fate, in their rather obscure conciseness, the thoughts which precede. But since they need a commentary, it seems wise to me to furnish it myself.

The true and equitable law of humanity is the *free exchange of service for service.* Spoliation consists in destroying by force or by trickery the freedom of exchange, in order to receive a service without rendering one.

Forcible spoliation is exercised thus: Wait till a man has produced something; then take it from him by violence.

It is solemnly condemned by the Decalogue: *Thou shalt not steal.*

When practiced by one individual on another, it is called robbery, and leads to the prison; when practiced among nations, it takes the name of conquest, and leads to glory.

Why this difference? It is worth while to search for the cause. It will reveal to us an irresistible power, public opinion, which, like the atmosphere, envelopes us so completely that we do not notice it. Rousseau never said a truer thing than this: "A great deal of philosophy is needed to understand the facts which are very near to us."

The robber, for the reason that he acts alone, has public opinion against him. He terrifies all who are about him. Yet, if he has companions, he plumes himself before them on his exploits, and here we may begin to notice the power of public opinion, for the approbation of his band serves to obliterate all consciousness of his turpitude, and even to make him proud of it. The warrior lives in a different atmosphere. The public opinion which would rebuke him is among the vanquished. He does not feel its influence. But the opinion of those by whom he is surrounded approves his acts and sustains him. He and his comrades are vividly conscious of the common interest which unites them. The country which has created enemies and dangers, needs to stimulate the courage of its children. To the most daring, to those who have enlarged the frontiers, and gathered the spoils of war, are given honors, reputation, glory. Poets sing their exploits. Fair women weave garlands for them. And such is the power of public opinion that it separates the idea of injustice from spoliation, and even rids the despoiler of the consciousness of his wrong-doing.

The public opinion which reacts against military spoliation, (as it exists among the conquered and not among the conquering people), has very little influence. But it is not entirely powerless. It gains in strength as nations come together and understand one another better. Thus, it can be seen that the study of languages and the free communication of peoples tend to bring about the supremacy of an opinion opposed to this sort of spoliation.

Unfortunately, it often happens that the nations adjacent to a plundering people are themselves spoilers when opportunity offers, and hence are imbued with the same prejudices.

Then there is only one remedy—time. It is necessary that nations learn by harsh experience the enormous disadvantage of despoiling each other.

You say there is another restraint—moral influences. But moral influences have for their object the increase of virtuous actions. How can they restrain these acts of spoliation when these very acts are raised by public opinion to the level of the highest virtues? Is there a more potent moral influence than religion? Has there ever been a religion more favorable to peace or more universally received than Christianity? And yet what has been witnessed during eighteen centuries? Men have gone out to battle, not merely in spite of religion, but in the very name of religion.

A conquering nation does not always wage offensive war. Its soldiers are obliged to protect the hearthstones, the property, the families, the independence and liberty of their native land. At such a time war assumes a character of sanctity and grandeur. The flag, blessed by the ministers of the God of Peace, represents all that is sacred on earth; the people rally to it as the living image of their country and their honor; the warlike virtues are exalted above all others. When the danger is over, the opinion remains, and by a natural reaction of that spirit of vengeance which confounds itself with patriotism, they love to bear the cherished flag from capital to capital. It seems that nature has thus prepared the punishment of the aggressor.

It is the fear of this punishment, and not the progress of philosophy, which keeps arms in the arsenals, for it cannot be denied that those people who are most advanced in civilization make war, and bother themselves very little with justice when they have no reprisals to fear. Witness the Himalayas, the Atlas, and the Caucasus.

If religion has been impotent, if philosophy is powerless, how is war to cease?

Political economy demonstrates that even if the victors alone are considered, war is always begun in the interest of the few, and at the expense of the many. All that is needed, then, is that the masses should clearly perceive this truth. The weight of public opinion, which is yet divided, would then be cast entirely on the side of peace.

Forcible spoliation also takes another form. Without waiting for a man to produce something in order to rob him, they take possession of the man himself, deprive him of his freedom, and force him to work. They do not say to him, "If you will do this for me, I will do that for you," but they say to him, "You take all the troubles; we all the enjoyments." This is slavery.

Now it is important to inquire whether it is not in the nature of uncontrolled power always to abuse itself.

For my part I have no doubt of it, and should as soon expect to see the power that could arrest a stone in falling proceed from the stone itself, as to trust force within any defined limits.

I should like to be shown a country where slavery has been abolished by the voluntary action of the masters.

Slavery furnishes a second striking example of the impotence of philosophical and religious sentiments in a conflict with the energetic activity of self-interest.

This may seem sad to some modern schools which seek the reformation of society in self-denial. Let them begin by reforming the nature of man.

In the Antilles the masters, from father to son, have, since slavery was established, professed the Christian religion. Many times a day they repeat these words: "All men are brothers. Love thy neighbor as thyself; in this are the law and the prophets fulfilled." Yet they hold slaves, and nothing seems to them more legitimate or natural. Do modern reformers hope that their moral creed will ever be as universally accepted, as popular, as authoritative, or as often on all lips as the Gospel? If *that* has not passed from the lips to the heart, over or through the great barrier of self-interest, how can they hope that their system will work this miracle?

Well, then, is slavery invulnerable? No; self-interest, which founded it, will one day destroy it, provided the special interests which have created it do not stifle those general interests which tend to overthrow it.

Another truth demonstrated by political economy is, that free labor is progressive, and slave labor stationary. Hence the triumph of the first over the second is inevitable. What has become of the cultivation of indigo by the blacks?

Free labor, applied to the production of sugar, is constantly causing a reduction in the price. Slave property is becoming proportionately less valuable to the master. Slavery will soon die out in America unless the price of sugar is artificially raised by legislation. Accordingly we see to-day the masters, their creditors and representatives, making vigorous efforts to maintain these laws, which are the pillars of the edifice.

Unfortunately they still have the sympathy of people among whom slavery has disappeared, from which circumstance the sovereignty of public opinion may again be observed. If public opinion is sovereign in the domain of force, it is much more so in the domain of fraud. Fraud is its proper sphere. Stratagem is the abuse of intelligence. Imposture on the part of the despoiler implies credulity on the part of the despoiled, and the natural antidote of credulity is truth. It follows that to enlighten the mind is to deprive this species of spoliation of its support.

I will briefly pass in review a few of the different kinds of spoliation which are practiced on an exceedingly large scale. The first which presents itself is spoliation through the avenue of superstition. In what does it consist? In the exchange of food, clothing, luxury, distinction, influence, power—substantial services for fictitious services. If I tell a man: "I will render you an immediate service," I am obliged to keep my word, or he would soon know what to depend upon, and my trickery would be unmasked.

But if I should tell him, "In exchange for your services I will do you immense service, not in this world but in another; after this life you may be eternally happy or miserable, and that happiness or misery depends upon me; I am a vicar between God and man, and can open to you the gates of heaven or of hell;" if that man believes me he is at my mercy.

This method of imposture has been very extensively practiced since the beginning of the world, and it is well known to what omnipotence the Egyptian priests attained by such means.

It is easy to see how impostors proceed. It is enough to ask one's self what he would do in their place.

If I, entertaining views of this kind, had arrived in the midst of an ignorant population, and were to succeed by some extraordinary act or marvelous appearance in passing myself off as a supernatural being, I would claim to be a messenger from God, having an absolute control over the future destinies of men.

Then I would forbid all examination of my claims. I would go still further, and, as reason would be my most dangerous enemy, I would interdict the use of reason—at least as applied to this dangerous subject. I would *taboo*, as the savages say, this question, and all those connected with it. To agitate them, discuss them, or even think of them, should be an unpardonable crime.

Certainly it would be the acme of art thus to put the barrier of the *taboo* upon all intellectual avenues which might lead to the discovery of my imposture. What better guarantee of its perpetuity than to make even doubt sacrilege?

However, I would add accessory guarantees to this fundamental one. For instance, in order that knowledge might never be disseminated among the masses, I would appropriate to myself and my accomplices the monopoly of the sciences. I would hide them under the veil of a dead language and hieroglyphic writing; and, in order that no danger might take me unawares, I would be careful to invent some ceremony which day by day would give me access to the privacy of all consciences.

It would not be amiss for me to supply some of the real wants of my people, especially if by doing so I could add to my influence and authority. For instance, men need education and moral teaching, and I would be the source of both. Thus I would guide as I pleased the minds and hearts of my people. I would join morality to my authority by an indissoluble chain, and I would proclaim that one could not exist without the other, so that if any audacious individual attempted to meddle with a *tabooed* question, society, which cannot exist without morality, would feel the very earth tremble under its feet, and would turn its wrath upon the rash innovator.

When things have come to this pass, it is plain that these people are more mine than if they were my slaves. The slave curses his chain, but my people will bless theirs, and I shall succeed in stamping, not on their foreheads, but in the very centre of their consciences, the seal of slavery.

Public opinion alone can overturn such a structure of iniquity; but where can it begin, if each stone is *tabooed?* It is the work of time and the printing press.

God forbid that I should seek to disturb those consoling beliefs which link this life of sorrows to a life of felicity. But, that the irresistible longing which attracts us toward religion has been abused, no one, not even the Head of Christianity, can deny. There is, it seems to me, one sign by which you can know whether the people are or are not dupes.

Examine religion and the priest, and see whether the priest is the instrument of religion, or religion the instrument of the priest.

If the priest is the instrument of religion, if his only thought is to disseminate its morality and its benefits on the earth, he will be gentle, tolerant, humble, charitable, and full of zeal; his life will reflect that of his divine model; he will preach liberty and equality among men, and peace and fraternity among nations; he will repel the allurements of temporal power, and will not ally himself with that which, of all things in this world, has the most need of restraint; he will be the man of the people, the man of good advice and tender consolations, the man of public opinion, the man of the Evangelist.

If, on the contrary, religion is the instrument of the priest, he will treat it as one does an instrument which is changed, bent and twisted in all ways so as to get out of it the greatest possible advantage for one's self. He will multiply *tabooed* questions; his morality will be as flexible as seasons, men, and circumstances. He will seek to impose on humanity by gesticulations and studied attitudes; an hundred times a day he will mumble over words whose sense has evaporated and which have become empty conventionalities. He will traffic in holy things, but just enough not to shake faith in their sanctity, and he will take care that the more intelligent the people are, the less open shall the traffic be. He will take part in the intrigues of the world, and he will always side with the powerful, on the simple condition that they side with him. In a word, it will be easy to see in all his actions that he does not desire to advance religion by the clergy, but the clergy by religion, and as so many efforts indicate an object, and as this object, according to the hypothesis, can be only power and wealth, the decisive proof that the people are dupes is when the priest is rich and powerful.

It is very plain that a true religion can be abused as well as a false one. The higher its authority the greater the fear that it may be severely tested. But there is much difference in the results. Abuse always stirs up to revolt the sound, enlightened, intelligent portion of a people. This inevitably weakens faith, and the weakening of a true religion is far more lamentable than of a false one. This kind of spoliation, and popular enlightenment, are always in an inverse ratio to one another, for it is in the nature of abuses to go as far as possible. Not that pure and devoted priests cannot be found in the midst of the most ignorant population, but how can the knave be prevented from donning the cassock and nursing the ambitious hope of wearing the mitre? Despoilers obey the Malthusian law; they multiply with the means of existence, and the means of existence of knaves is the credulity of their dupes. Turn whichever way you please, you always find the need of an enlightened public opinion. There is no other cure-all.

Another species of spoliation is *commercial fraud*, a term which seems to me too limited because the tradesman who changes his weights and measures is not alone culpable, but also the physician who receives a fee for evil counsel, the lawyer who provokes litigation, etc. In the exchange of two services one may be of less value than the other, but when the service received is that which has been agreed upon, it is evident that spoliation of that nature will diminish with the increase of public intelligence.

The next in order is the abuse in the *public service*—an immense field of spoliation, so immense that we can give it but partial consideration.

If God had made man a solitary animal, every one would labor for himself. Individual wealth would be in proportion to the services each one rendered to himself. But since *man is a social animal, one service is exchanged for another.* A proposition which you can transpose if it suits you.

In society there are certain requirements so general, so universal in their nature, that provision has been made for them in the organizing of the public service. Among these is the necessity of security. Society agrees to compensate in services of a different nature those who render it the service of guarding the public safety. In this there is nothing contrary to the principles of political economy. *Do this for me, I will do that for you.* The principle of the transaction is the same, although the process is different, but the circumstance has great significance.

In private transactions each individual remains the judge both of the service which he renders and of that which he receives. He can always decline an exchange, or negotiate elsewhere. There is no necessity of an interchange of services, except by previous voluntary agreement. Such is not the case with the State, especially before the establishment of representative government. Whether or not we require its services, whether they are good or bad, we are obliged to accept such as are offered and to pay the price.

It is the tendency of all men to magnify their own services and to disparage services rendered them, and private matters would be poorly regulated if there was not some standard of value. This guarantee we have not, (or we hardly have it,) in public affairs. But still society, composed of men, however strongly the contrary may be insinuated, obeys the universal tendency. The government wishes to serve us a great deal, much more than we desire, and forces us to acknowledge as a real service that which sometimes is widely different, and this is done for the purpose of demanding contributions from us in return.

The State is also subject to the law of Malthus. It is continually living beyond its means, it increases in proportion to its means, and draws its support solely from the substance of the people. Woe to the people who are incapable of limiting the sphere of action of the State. Liberty, private activity, riches, well-being, independence, dignity, depend upon this.

There is one circumstance which must be noticed: Chief among the services which we ask of the State is *security*. That it may guarantee this to us it must control a force capable of overcoming all individual or collective domestic or foreign forces which might endanger it. Combined with that fatal disposition among men to live at the expense of each other, which we have before noticed, this fact suggests a danger patent to all.

You will accordingly observe on what an immense scale spoliation, by the abuses and excesses of the government, has been practiced.

If one should ask what service has been rendered the public, and what return has been made therefor, by such governments as Assyria, Babylon, Egypt, Rome, Persia, Turkey, China, Russia, England, Spain and France, he would be astonished at the enormous disparity.

At last representative government was invented, and, *a priori*, one might have believed that the disorder would have ceased as if by enchantment.

The principle of these governments is this:

"The people themselves, by their representatives, shall decide as to the nature and extent of the public service and the remuneration for those services."

The tendency to appropriate the property of another, and the desire to defend one's own, are thus brought in contact. One might suppose that the latter would overcome the former. Assuredly I am convinced that the latter will finally prevail, but we must concede that thus far it has not.

Why? For a very simple reason. Governments have had too much sagacity; people too little.

Governments are skillful. They act methodically, consecutively, on a well concerted plan, which is constantly improved by tradition and experience. They study men and their passions. If they perceive, for instance, that they have warlike instincts, they incite and inflame this fatal propensity. They surround the nation with dangers through the conduct of diplomats, and then naturally ask for soldiers, sailors, arsenals and fortifications. Often they have but the trouble of accepting them. Then they have pensions, places, and promotions to offer. All this calls for money. Hence loans and taxes.

If the nation is generous, the government proposes to cure all the ills of humanity. It promises to increase commerce, to make agriculture prosperous, to develop manufactures, to encourage letters and arts, to banish misery, etc. All that is necessary is to create offices and to pay public functionaries.

In other words, their tactics consist in presenting as actual services things which are but hindrances; then the nation pays, not for being served, but for being subservient. Governments assuming gigantic proportions end by absorbing half of all the revenues. The people are astonished that while marvelous labor-saving inventions, destined to infinitely multiply productions, are ever increasing in number, they are obliged to toil on as painfully as ever, and remain as poor as before.

This happens because, while the government manifests so much ability, the people show so little. Thus, when they are called upon to choose their agents, those who are to determine the sphere of, and compensation for, governmental action, whom do they choose? The agents of the government. They entrust the executive power with the determination of the limit of its activity and its requirements. They are like the *Bourgeois Gentilhomme*, who referred the selection and number of his suits of clothes to his tailor.

However, things go from bad to worse, and at last the people open their eyes, not to the remedy, for there is none as yet, but to the evil.

Governing is so pleasant a trade that everybody desires to engage in it. Thus the advisers of the people do not cease to say: "We see your sufferings, and we weep over them. It would be otherwise if *we* governed you."

This period, which usually lasts for some time, is one of rebellions and insurrections. When the people are conquered, the expenses of the war are added to their burdens. When they conquer, there is a change of those who govern, and the abuses remain.

This lasts until the people learn to know and defend their true interests. Thus we always come back to this: there is no remedy but in the progress of public intelligence.

Certain nations seem remarkably inclined to become the prey of governmental spoliation. They are those where men, not considering their own dignity and energy, would believe themselves lost, if they were not governed and administered upon in all things. Without having traveled much, I have seen countries where they think agriculture can make no progress unless the State keeps up experimental farms; that there will presently be no horses if the State has no stables; and that fathers will not have their children educated, or will teach them only immoralities, if the State does not decide what it is proper to learn. In such a country revolutions may rapidly succeed one another, and one set of rulers after another be overturned. But the governed are none the less governed at the caprice and mercy of their rulers, until the people see that it is better to leave the greatest possible number of services in the category of those which the parties interested exchange after a fair discussion of the price.

We have seen that society is an exchange of services, and should be but an exchange of good and honest ones. But we have also proven that men have a great interest in exaggerating the relative value of the services they render one another. I cannot, indeed, see any other limit to these claims than the free acceptance or free refusal of those to whom these services are offered.

Hence it comes that certain men resort to the law to curtail the natural prerogatives of this liberty. This kind of spoliation is called privilege or monopoly. We will carefully indicate its origin and character.

Every one knows that the services which he offers in the general market are the more valued and better paid for, the scarcer they are. Each one, then, will ask for the enactment of a law to keep out of the market all who offer services similar to his.

This variety of spoliation being the chief subject of this volume, I will say little of it here, and will restrict myself to one remark:

When the monopoly is an isolated fact, it never fails to enrich the person to whom the law has granted it. It may then happen that each class of workmen, instead of seeking the overthrow of this monopoly, claim a similar one for themselves. This kind of spoliation, thus reduced to a system, becomes then the most ridiculous of mystifications for every one, and the definite result is that each one believes that he gains more from a general market impoverished by all.

It is not necessary to add that this singular *regime* also brings about an universal antagonism between all classes, all professions, and all peoples; that it requires the constant but always uncertain interference of government; that it swarms with the abuses which have been the subject of the preceding paragraph; that it places all industrial pursuits in hopeless insecurity; and that it accustoms men to place upon the law, and not upon themselves, the responsibility for their very existence. It would be difficult to imagine a more active cause of social disturbance.

JUSTIFICATION.

It may be asked, "Why this ugly word—spoliation? It is not only coarse, but it wounds and irritates; it turns calm and moderate men against you, and embitters the controversy."

I earnestly declare that I respect individuals; I believe in the sincerity of almost all the friends of Protection, and I do not claim that I have any right to suspect the personal honesty, delicacy of feeling, or philanthropy of any one. I also repeat that Protection is the work, the fatal work, of a common error, of which all, or nearly all, are at once victims and accomplices. But I cannot prevent things being what they are.

Just imagine some Diogenes putting his head out of his tub and saying, "Athenians, you are served by slaves. Have you never thought that you practice on your brothers the most iniquitous spoliation?" Or a tribune speaking in the forum, "Romans! you have laid the foundation of all your greatness on the pillage of other nations."

They would state only undeniable truths. But must we conclude from this that Athens and Rome were inhabited only by dishonest persons? that Socrates and Plato, Cato and Cincinnatus were despicable characters?

Who could harbor such a thought? But these great men lived amidst surroundings that relieved their consciences of the sense of this injustice. Even Aristotle could not conceive the idea of a society existing without slavery. In modern times slavery has continued to our own day without causing many scruples among the planters. Armies have served as the instruments of grand conquests —that is to say, of grand spoliations. Is this saying that they are not composed of officers and men as sensitive of their honor, even more so, perhaps, than men in ordinary industrial pursuits—men who would blush at the very thought of theft, and who would face a thousand deaths rather than stoop to a base action?

It is not individuals who are to blame, but the general movement of opinion which deludes and deceives them—a movement for which society in general is culpable.

Thus is it with monopoly. I accuse the system, and not individuals; society as a mass, and not this or that one of its members. If the greatest philosophers have been able to deceive themselves as to the iniquity of slavery, how much easier is it for farmers and manufacturers to deceive themselves as to the nature and effects of the protective system.

II.

TWO SYSTEMS OF MORALS.

ARRIVED at the end of the preceding chapter, if he gets so far, I imagine I hear the reader say:

"Well, now, was I wrong in accusing political economists of being dry and cold? What a picture of humanity! Spoliation is a fatal power, almost normal, assuming every form, practiced under every pretext, against law and according to law, abusing the most sacred things, alternately playing upon the feebleness and the credulity of the masses, and ever growing by what it feeds on. Could a more mournful picture of the world be imagined than this?"

The problem is, not to find whether the picture is mournful, but whether it is true. And for that we have the testimony of history.

It is singular that those who decry political economy, because it investigates men and the world as it finds them, are more gloomy than political economy itself, at least as regards the past and the present. Look into their books and their journals. What do you find? Bitterness and hatred of society. The very word *civilization* is for them a synonym for injustice, disorder and anarchy. They have even come to curse *liberty*, so little confidence have they in the development of the human race, the result of its natural organization. Liberty, according to them, is something which will bring humanity nearer and nearer to destruction.

It is true that they are optimists as regards the future. For, although humanity, in itself incapable, for six thousand years has gone astray, a revelation has come, which has pointed out to men the way of safety, and, if the flock are docile and obedient to the shepherd's call, will lead them to the promised land, where well-being may be attained without effort, where order, security and prosperity are the easy reward of improvidence.

To this end humanity, as Rousseau said, has only to allow these reformers to change the physical and moral constitution of man.

Political economy has not taken upon itself the mission of finding out the probable condition of society had it pleased God to make men different from what they are. It may be unfortunate that Providence, at the beginning, neglected to call to his counsels a few of our modern reformers. And, as the celestial mechanism would have been entirely different had the Creator consulted *Alphonso the Wise*, society, also, had He not neglected the advice of Fourier, would have been very different from that in which we are compelled to live, and move, and breathe. But, since we are here, our duty is to study and to understand His laws, especially if the amelioration of our condition essentially depends upon such knowledge.

We cannot prevent the existence of unsatisfied desires in the hearts of men.

We cannot satisfy these desires except by labor.

We cannot deny the fact that man has as much repugnance for labor as he has satisfaction with its results.

Since man has such characteristics, we cannot prevent the existence of a constant tendency among men to obtain their part of the enjoyments of life while throwing upon others, by force or by trickery, the burdens of labor. It is not for us to belie universal history, to silence the voice of the past, which attests that this has been the condition of things since the beginning of the world. We cannot deny that war, slavery, superstition, the abuses of government, privileges, frauds of every nature, and monopolies, have been the incontestable and terrible manifestations of these two sentiments united in the heart of man: *desire for enjoyment; repugnance to labor.*

"In the sweat of thy face shalt thou eat bread!" But every one wants as much bread and as little sweat as possible. This is the conclusion of history.

Thank Heaven, history also teaches that the division of blessings and burdens tends to a more exact equality among men. Unless one is prepared to deny the light of the sun, it must be admitted that, in this respect at least, society has made some progress.

If this be true, there exists in society a natural and providential force, a law which causes iniquity gradually to cease, and makes justice more and more a reality.

We say that this force exists in society, and that God has placed it there. If it did not exist we should be compelled, with the socialists, to search for it in those artificial means, in those arrangements which require a fundamental change in the physical and moral constitution of man, or rather we should consider that search idle and vain, for the reason that we could not comprehend the action of a lever without a place of support.

Let us, then, endeavor to indicate that beneficent force which tends progressively to overcome the maleficent force to which we have given the name spoliation, and the existence of which is only too well explained by reason and proved by experience.

Every maleficent act necessarily has two terms—the point of beginning and the point of ending; the man who performs the act and the man upon whom it is performed; or, in the language of the schools, the active and the passive agent. There are, then, two means by which the maleficent act can be prevented: by the voluntary absence of the active, or by the resistance of the passive agent. Whence two systems of morals arise, not antagonistic but concurrent; religious or philosophical morality, and the morality to which I permit myself to apply the name economical (utilitarian).

Religious morality, to abolish and extirpate the maleficent act, appeals to its author, to man in his capacity of active agent. It says to him: "Reform yourself; purify yourself; cease to do evil; learn to do well; conquer your passions; sacrifice your interests; do not oppress your neighbor, to succor and relieve whom is your duty; be first just, then generous." This morality will always be the most beautiful, the most touching, that which will exhibit the human race in all its majesty; which will the best lend itself to the offices of eloquence, and will most excite the sympathy and admiration of mankind.

Utilitarian morality works to the same end, but especially addresses itself to man in his capacity of passive agent. It points out to him the consequences of human actions, and, by this simple exhibition, stimulates him to struggle against those which injure, and to honor those which are useful to him. It aims to extend among the oppressed masses enough good sense, enlightenment and just defiance, to render oppression both difficult and dangerous.

It may also be remarked that utilitarian morality is not without its influence upon the oppressor. An act of spoliation causes good and evil—evil for him who suffers it, good for him in whose favor it is exercised—else the act would not have been performed. But the good by no means compensates the evil. The evil always, and necessarily, predominates over the good, because the very fact of oppression occasions a loss of force, creates dangers, provokes reprisals, and requires costly precautions. The simple exhibition of these effects is not then limited to retaliation of the oppressed; it places all, whose hearts are not perverted, on the side of justice, and alarms the security of the oppressors themselves.

But it is easy to understand that this morality which is simply a scientific demonstration, and would even lose its efficiency if it changed its character; which addresses itself not to the heart but to the intelligence; which seeks not to persuade but to convince; which gives proofs not counsels; whose mission is not to move but to enlighten, and which obtains over vice no other victory than to deprive it of its booty—it is easy to understand, I say, how this morality has been accused of being dry and prosaic. The reproach is true without being just. It is equivalent to saying that political economy is not everything, does not comprehend everything, is not the universal solvent. But who has ever made such an exorbitant pretension in its name? The accusation would not be well founded unless political economy presented its processes as final, and denied to philosophy and religion the use of their direct and proper means of elevating humanity. Look at the concurrent action of morality, properly so called, and of political economy—the one inveighing against spoliation by an exposure of its moral ugliness, the other bringing it into discredit in our judgment, by showing its evil consequences. Concede that the triumph of the religious moralist, when realized, is more beautiful, more consoling and more radical; at the same time it is not easy to deny that the triumph of economical science is more facile and more certain.

In a few lines, more valuable than many volumes, J. B. Say has already remarked that there are two ways of removing the disorder introduced by hypocrisy into an honorable family; to reform Tartuffe, or sharpen the wits of Orgon. Moliere, that great painter of human life, seems constantly to have had in view the second process as the more efficient.

Such is the case on the world's stage. Tell me what Cæsar did, and I will tell you what were the Romans of his day.

Tell me what modern diplomacy has accomplished, and I will describe the moral condition of the nations.

We should not pay two milliards of taxes if we did not appoint those who consume them to vote them.

We should not have so much trouble, difficulty and expense with the African question if we were as well convinced that two and two make four in political economy as in arithmetic.

M. Guizot would never have had occasion to say: "France is rich enough to pay for her glory," if France had never conceived a false idea of glory.

The same statesman never would have said: "*Liberty is too precious for France to traffic in it,*" if France had well understood that *liberty* and a *large budget* are incompatible.

Let religious morality then, if it can, touch the heart of the Tartuffes, the Cæsars, the conquerors of Algeria, the sinecurists, the monopolists, etc. The mission of political economy is to enlighten their dupes. Of these two processes, which is the more efficient aid to social progress? I believe it is the second. I believe that humanity cannot escape the necessity of first learning a *defensive morality.* I have read, observed, and made diligent inquiry, and have been unable to find any abuse, practiced to any considerable extent, that has perished by voluntary renunciation on the part of those who profited by it. On the contrary, I have seen many that have yielded to the manly resistance of those who suffered by them.

To describe the consequences of abuses, is the most efficient way of destroying the abuses themselves. And this is true particularly in regard to abuses which, like the protective system, while inflicting real evil upon the masses, are to those who seem to profit by them only an illusion and a deception.

Well, then, does this species of morality realize all the social perfection which the sympathetic nature of the human heart and its noblest faculties cause us to hope for? This I by no means pretend. Admit the general diffusion of this defensive morality—which, after all, is only a knowledge that the best understood interests are in accord with general utility and justice. A society, although very well regulated, might not be very attractive, where there were no knaves, only because there were no fools; where vice, always latent, and, so to speak, overcome by famine, would only stand in need of available plunder in order to be restored to vigor; where the prudence of the individual would be guarded by the vigilance of the mass, and, finally, where reforms, regulating external acts, would not have penetrated to the consciences of men. Such a state of society we sometimes see typified in one of those exact, rigorous and just men who is ever ready to resent the slightest infringement of his rights, and shrewd in avoiding impositions. You esteem him—possibly you admire him. You may make him your deputy, but you would not necessarily choose him for a friend.

Let, then, the two moral systems, instead of criminating each other, act in concert, and attack vice at its opposite poles. While the economists perform their task in uprooting prejudice, stimulating just and necessary opposition, studying and exposing the real nature of actions and things, let the religious moralist, on his part, perform his more attractive, but more difficult, labor; let him attack the very body of iniquity, follow it to its most vital parts, paint the charms of beneficence, self-denial and devotion, open the fountains of virtue where we can only choke the sources of vice—this is his duty. It is noble and beautiful. But why does he dispute the utility of that which belongs to us?

In a society which, though not superlatively virtuous, should nevertheless be regulated by the influences of *economical morality* (which is the knowledge of the economy of society), would there not be a field for the progress of religious morality ?

Habit, it has been said, is a second nature. A country where the individual had become unaccustomed to injustice, simply by the force of an enlightened public opinion, might, indeed, be pitiable; but it seems to me it would be well prepared to receive an education more elevated and more pure. To be disaccustomed to evil is a great step towards becoming good. Men cannot remain stationary. Turned aside from the paths of vice which would lead only to infamy, they appreciate better the attractions of virtue. Possibly it may be necessary for society to pass through this prosaic state, where men practice virtue by calculation, to be thence elevated to that more poetic region where they will no longer have need of such an exercise.

III.

THE TWO HATCHETS.

Petition of Jacques Bonhomme, Carpenter, to M. Cunin-Gridaine, Minister of Commerce.

MR. MANUFACTURER-MINISTER: I am a carpenter, as was Jesus; I handle the hatchet and the plane to serve you.

In chopping and splitting from morning until night in the domain of my lord, the King, the idea has occurred to me that my labor was as much *national* as yours.

And accordingly I don't understand why protection should not visit my shop as well as your manufactory.

For indeed, if you make cloths, I make roofs. Both by different means protect our patrons from cold and rain. But I have to run after customers while business seeks you. You know how to manage this by obtaining a monopoly, while my business is open to any one who chooses to engage in it.

What is there astonishing in this? Mr. Cunin, the Cabinet Minister, has not forgotten Mr. Cunin, the manufacturer, as was very natural. But unfortunately, my humble occupation has not given a Minister to France, although it has given a Saviour to the world.

And this Saviour, in the immortal code which he bequeathed to men, did not utter the smallest word by virtue of which carpenters might feel authorized to enrich themselves as you do at the expense of others.

Look, then, at my position. I earn thirty cents every day, excepts Sundays and holidays. If I apply to you for work at the same time with a Flemish workman, you give him the preference.

But I need clothing. If a Belgian weaver puts his cloth beside yours, you drive both him and his cloth out of the country. Consequently, forced to buy at your shop, where it is dearest, my poor thirty cents are really worth only twenty-eight.

What did I say? They are worth only twenty-six. For, instead of driving the Belgian weaver away at *your own expense* (which would be the least you could do) you compel me to pay those who, in your interest, force him out of the market.

And since a large number of your fellow-legislators, with whom you seem to have an excellent understanding, take away from me a cent or two each, under pretext of protecting somebody's coal, or oil, or wheat, when the balance is struck, I find that of my thirty cents I have only fifteen left from the pillage.

Possibly, you may answer that those few pennies which pass thus, without compensation, from my pocket to yours, support a number of people about your *chateau*, and at the same time assist you in keeping up your establishment. To which, if you would permit me, I would reply, they would likewise support a number of persons in my cottage.

However this may be, Hon. Minister-Manufacturer, knowing that I should meet with a cold reception were I to ask you to renounce the restriction imposed upon your customers, as I have a right to, I prefer to follow the fashion, and to demand for myself, also, a little morsel of *protection*.

To this, doubtless you will interpose some objections. "Friend," you will say, "I would be glad to protect you and your colleagues; but how can I confer such favors upon the labor of carpenters? Shall I prohibit the importation of houses by land and by sea?"

This would seem sufficiently ridiculous, but by giving much thought to the subject, I have discovered a way to protect the children of St. Joseph, and you will, I trust, the more readily grant it since it differs in no respect from the privilege which you vote for yourself every year. This wonderful way is to prohibit the use of sharp hatchets in France.

I say that this restriction would be neither more illogical nor arbitrary than that which you subject us to in regard to your cloth.

Why do you drive away the Belgians? Because they sell cheaper than you do. And why do they sell cheaper than you do? Because they are in some way or another your superiors as manufacturers.

Between you and the Belgians, then, there is exactly the same difference that there is between a dull hatchet and a sharp one. And you compel me, a carpenter, to buy the workmanship of your dull hatchet!

Consider France a laborer, obliged to live by his daily toil, and desiring, among other things, to purchase cloth. There are two means of doing this. The first is to card the wool and weave the cloth himself; the second is to manufacture clocks, or wines, or wall-paper, or something of the sort, and exchange them in Belgium for cloth.

The process which gives the larger result may be represented by the sharp hatchet; the other process by the dull one.

You will not deny that at the present day in France it is more difficult to manufacture cloth than to cultivate the vine—the former is the dull hatchet, the latter the sharp one—on the contrary, you make this greater difficulty the very reason why you recommend to us the worst of the two hatchets.

Now, then, be consistent, if you will not be just, and treat the poor carpenters as well as you treat yourself. Make a law which shall read: "It is forbidden to use beams or shingles which have not been fashioned by dull hatchets."

And you will immediately perceive the result.

Where we now strike an hundred blows with the ax, we shall be obliged to give three hundred. What a powerful encouragement to industry! Apprentices, journeymen and masters, we should suffer no more. We should be greatly sought after, and go away well paid. Whoever wishes to enjoy a roof must leave us to make his tariff, just as buyers of cloth are now obliged to submit to you.

As for those free-trade theorists, should they ever venture to call the utility of this system in question we should know where to go for an unanswerable argument. Your investigation of 1834 is at our service. We should fight them with that, for there you have admirably pleaded the cause of prohibition, and of dull hatchets, which are both the same.

IV.

INFERIOR COUNCIL OF LABOR.

"What! You have the assurance to demand for every citizen the right to buy, sell, trade, exchange, and to render service for service according to his own discretion, on the sole condition that he will conduct himself honestly, and not defraud the revenue? Would you rob the workingman of his labor, his wages and his bread?"

This is what is said to us. I know what the general opinion is; but I have desired to know what the laborers themselves think. I have had an excellent opportunity of finding out.

It was not one of those *Superior Councils of Industry* (Committee on the Revision of the Tariff), where large manufacturers, who style themselves laborers, influential ship-builders who imagine themselves seamen, and wealthy bondholders who think themselves workmen, meet and legislate in behalf of that philanthropy with whose nature we are so well acquainted.

No, they were workmen "to the manor born," real, practical laborers, such as joiners, carpenters, masons, tailors, shoemakers, blacksmiths, grocers, etc., etc., who had established in my village a *Mutual Aid Society.* Upon my own private authority I transformed it into an *Inferior Council of Labor* (People's Committee for Revising the Tariff), and I obtained a report which is as good as any other, although unencumbered by figures, and not distended to the proportions of a quarto volume and printed at the expense of the State.

The subject of my inquiry was the real or supposed influence of the protective system upon these poor people. The President, indeed, informed me that the institution of such an inquiry was somewhat in contravention of the principles of the society. For, in France, the land of liberty, those who desire to form associations must renounce political discussions—that is to say, the discussion of their common interests. However, after much hesitation, he made the question the order of the day.

The assembly was divided into as many sub-committees as there were different trades represented. A blank was handed to each sub-committee, which, after fifteen days' discussion, was to be filled and returned.

On the appointed day the venerable President took the chair (official style, for it was only a stool) and found upon the table (official style, again, for it was a deal plank across a barrel) a dozen reports, which he read in succession.

The first presented was that of the tailors. Here it is, as accurately as if it had been photographed:

RESULTS OF PROTECTION—REPORT OF THE TAILORS.

Disadvantages.	*Advantages.*
1. On account of the protective tariff, we pay more for our own bread, meat, sugar, thread, etc., which is equivalent to a considerable diminution of our wages.	None.
2. On account of the protective tariff, our patrons are also obliged to pay more for everything, and have less to spend for clothes, consequently we have less work and smaller profits.	1. We have examined the question in every light, and have been unable to perceive a single point in regard to which the protective system is advantageous to our trade.
3. On account of the protective tariff, clothes are expensive, and people make them wear longer, which results in a loss of work, and compels us to offer our services at greatly reduced rates.	

Here is another report:

EFFECTS OF PROTECTION—REPORT OF THE BLACKSMITHS.

Disadvantages.	*Advantages.*
1. The protective system imposes a tax (which does not get into the Treasury) every time we eat, drink, warm, or clothe ourselves. 2. It imposes a similar tax upon our neighbors, and hence, having less money, most of them use wooden pegs, instead of buying nails, which deprives us of labor. 3. It keeps the price of iron so high that it can no longer be used in the country for plows, or gates, or house fixtures, and our trade, which might give work to so many who have none, does not even give ourselves enough to do. 4. The deficit occasioned in the Treasury by those goods *which do not enter* is made up by taxes on our salt.	None.

The other reports, with which I will not trouble the reader, told the same story. Gardeners, carpenters, shoemakers, boatmen, all complained of the same grievances.

I am sorry there were no day laborers in our association. Their report would certainly have been exceedingly instructive. But, unfortunately, the poor laborers of our province, all *protected* as they are, have not a cent, and, after having taken care of their cattle, cannot go themselves to the *Mutual Aid Society*. The pretended favors of protection do not prevent them from being the pariahs of modern society.

What I would especially remark is the good sense with which our villagers have perceived not only the direct evil results of protection, but also the indirect evil which, affecting their patrons, reacts upon themselves.

This is a fact, it seems to me, which the economists of the school of the *Moniteur Industriel* do not understand.

And possibly some men, who are fascinated by a very little protection, the agriculturists, for instance, would voluntarily renounce it if they noticed this side of the question. Possibly, they might say to themselves: "It is better to support one's self surrounded by well-to-do neighbors, than to be protected in the midst of poverty." For to seek to encourage every branch of industry by successively creating a void around them, is as vain as to attempt to jump away from one's shadow.

V.

DEARNESS — CHEAPNESS.

I CONSIDER it my duty to say a few words in regard to the delusion caused by the words *dear* and *cheap*. At the first glance, I am aware, you may be disposed to find these remarks somewhat subtile, but whether subtile or not, the question is whether they are true. For my part I consider them perfectly true, and particularly well adapted to cause reflection among a large number of those who cherish a sincere faith in the efficacy of protection.

Whether advocates of free trade or defenders of protection, we are all obliged to make use of the expression *dearness* and *cheapness.* The former take sides in behalf of *cheapness*, having in view the interests of consumers. The latter pronounce themselves in favor of *dearness*, preoccupying themselves solely with the interests of the producer. Others intervene, saying, *producer and consumer are one and the same*, which leaves wholly undecided the question whether cheapness or dearness ought to be the object of legislation.

In this conflict of opinion it seems to me that there is only one position for the law to take—to allow prices to regulate themselves naturally. But the principle of "let alone" has obstinate enemies. They insist upon legislation without even knowing the desired objects of legislation. It would seem, however, to be the duty of those who wish to create high or low prices artificially, to state, and to substantiate, the reasons of their preference. The burden of proof is upon them. Liberty is always considered beneficial until the contrary is proved, and to allow prices naturally to regulate themselves is liberty. But the *roles* have been changed. The partisans of high prices have obtained a triumph for their system, and it has fallen to defenders of natural prices to prove the advantages of their system. The argument on both sides is conducted with two words. It is very essential, then, to understand their meaning.

It must be granted at the outset that a series of events have happened well calculated to disconcert both sides.

In order to produce *high prices* the protectionists have obtained high tariffs, and still low prices have come to disappoint their expectations.

In order to produce *low prices*, free traders have sometimes carried their point, and, to their great astonishment, the result in some instances has been an increase instead of a reduction in prices.

For instance, in France, to protect farmers, a law was passed imposing a duty of twenty-two per cent. upon imported wools, and the result has been that native wools have been sold for much lower prices than before the passage of the law.

In England a law in behalf of the consumers was passed, exempting foreign wools from duty, and the consequence has been that native wools have sold higher than ever before.

And this is not an isolated fact, for the price of wool has no special or peculiar nature which takes it out of the general law governing prices. The same fact has been reproduced under analogous circumstances. Contrary to all expectation, protection has frequently resulted in low prices, and free trade in high prices. Hence there has been a deal of perplexity in the discussion, the protectionists saying to their adversaries: "These low prices that you talk about so much are the result of our system;" and the free traders replying: "Those high prices which you find so profitable are the consequence of free trade."

There evidently is a misunderstanding, an illusion, which must be dispelled. This I will endeavor to do.

Suppose two isolated nations, each composed of a million inhabitants; admit that, other things being equal, one nation had exactly twice as much of everything as the other—twice as much wheat, wine, iron, fuel, books, clothing, furniture, etc. It will be conceded that one will have twice as much wealth as the other.

There is, however, no reason for the statement that the *absolute prices* are different in the two nations. They possibly may be higher in the wealthiest nation. It may happen that in the United States everything is nominally dearer than in Poland, and that, nevertheless, the people there are less generally supplied with everything; by which it may be seen that the abundance of products, and not the absolute price, constitutes wealth. In order, then, accurately to compare free trade and protection the inquiry should not be which of the two causes high prices or low prices, but which of the two produces abundance or scarcity.

For observe this: Products are exchanged, the one for the other, and a relative scarcity and a relative abundance leave the absolute price exactly at the same point, but not so the condition of men.

Let us look into the subject a little further.

Since the increase and the reduction of duties have been accompanied by results so different from what had been expected, a fall of prices frequently succeeding the increase of the tariff, and a rise sometimes following a reduction of duties, it has become necessary for political economy to attempt the explanation of a phenomenon which so overthrows received ideas; for, whatever may be said, science is simply a faithful exposition and a true explanation of facts.

This phenomenon may be easily explained by one circumstance which should never be lost sight of.

It is that there are *two causes* for high prices, and not one merely.

The same is true of low prices. One of the best established principles of political economy is that price is determined by the law of supply and demand.

The price is then affected by two conditions—the demand and the supply. These conditions are necessarily subject to variation. The relations of demand to supply may be exactly counterbalanced, or may be greatly disproportionate, and the variations of price are almost interminable.

Prices rise either on account of augmented demand or diminished supply.

They fall by reason of an augmentation of the supply or a diminution of the demand.

Consequently there are two kinds of *dearness* and two kinds of *cheapness.* There is a bad dearness, which results from a diminution of the supply; for this implies scarcity and privation. There is a good dearness—that which results from an increase of demand; for this indicates the augmentation of the general wealth.

There is also a good cheapness, resulting from abundance. And there is a baneful cheapness—such as results from the cessation of demand, the inability of consumers to purchase.

And observe this: Prohibition causes at the same time both the dearness and the cheapness which are of a bad nature; a bad dearness, resulting from a diminution of the supply (this indeed is its avowed object), and a bad cheapness, resulting from a diminution of the demand, because it gives a false direction to capital and labor, and overwhelms consumers with taxes and restrictions.

So that, *as regards the price*, these two tendencies neutralize each other; and for this reason, the protective system, restricting the supply and the demand at the same time, does not realize the high prices which are its object.

But with respect to the condition of the people, these two tendencies do not neutralize each other; on the contrary, they unite in impoverishing them.

The effect of free trade is exactly the opposite. Possibly it does not cause the cheapness which it promises; for it also has two tendencies, the one towards that desirable form of cheapness resulting from the increase of supply, or from abundance; the other towards that dearness consequent upon the increased demand and the development of the general wealth. These two tendencies neutralize themselves as regards the *mere price;* but they concur in their tendency to ameliorate the condition of mankind. In a word, under the protective system men recede towards a condition of feebleness as regards both supply and demand; under the free-trade system, they advance towards a condition where development is gradual without any necessary increase in the absolute prices of things.

Price is not a good criterion of wealth. It might continue the same when society had relapsed into the most abject misery, or had advanced to a high state of prosperity.

Let me make application of this doctrine in a few words: A farmer in the south of France supposes himself as rich as Crœsus, because he is protected by law from foreign competition. He is as poor as

Job—no matter, he will none the less suppose that this protection will sooner or later make him rich. Under these circumstances, if the question was propounded to him, as it was by the committee of the Legislature, in these terms: "Do you want to be subject to foreign competition? yes or no," his first answer would be "No," and the committee would record his reply with great enthusiasm.

We should go, however, to the bottom of things. Doubtless foreign competition, and competition of any kind, is always inopportune; and, if any trade could be permanently rid of it, business, for a time, would be prosperous.

But protection is not an isolated favor. It is a system. If, in order to protect the farmer, it occasions a scarcity of wheat and of beef, in behalf of other industries it produces a scarcity of iron, cloth, fuel, tools, etc.—in short, a scarcity of everything.

If, then, the scarcity of wheat has a tendency to increase the price by reason of the diminution of the supply, the scarcity of all other products for which wheat is exchanged has likewise a tendency to depreciate the value of wheat on account of a falling off of the demand; so that it is by no means certain that wheat will be a mill dearer under a protective tariff than under a system of free trade. This alone is certain, that inasmuch as there is a smaller amount of everything in the country, each individual will be more poorly provided with everything.

The farmer would do well to consider whether it would not be more desirable for him to allow the importation of wheat and beef, and, as a consequence, to be surrounded by a well-to-do community, able to consume and to pay for every agricultural product.

There is a certain province where the men are covered with rags, dwell in hovels, and subsist on chestnuts. How can agriculture flourish there? What can they make the earth produce, with the expectation of profit? Meat? They eat none. Milk? They drink only the water of springs. Butter? It is an article of luxury far beyond them. Wool? They get along without it as much as possible. Can any one imagine that all these objects of consumption can be thus left untouched by the masses, without lowering prices?

That which we say of a farmer, we can say of a manufacturer. Cloth-makers assert that foreign competition will lower prices owing to the increased quantity offered. Very well, but are not these prices raised by the increase of the demand? Is the consumption of cloth a fixed and invariable quantity? Is each one as well provided with it as he might and should be? And if the general wealth were developed by the abolition of all these taxes and hindrances, would not the first use made of it by the population be to clothe themselves better?

Therefore the question, the eternal question, is

not whether protection favors this or that special branch of industry, but whether, all things considered, restriction is, in its nature, more profitable than freedom?

Now, no person can maintain that proposition. And just this explains the admission which our opponents continually make to us: "You are right on principle."

If that is true, if restriction aids each special industry only through a greater injury to the general prosperity, let us understand, then, that the price itself, considering that alone, expresses a relation between each special industry and the general industry, between the supply and the demand, and that, reasoning from these premises, this *remunerative price* (the object of protection) is more hindered than favored by it.

APPENDIX.

We published an article entitled *Dearness-Cheapness*, which gained for us the two following letters. We publish them, with the answers:

"DEAR MR. EDITOR:—You upset all my ideas. I preached in favor of free trade, and found it very convenient to put prominently forward the idea of *cheapness.* I went everywhere, saying, "With free trade, bread, meat, woolens, linen, iron and coal will fall in price." This displeased those who sold, but delighted those who bought. Now, you raise a doubt as to whether *cheapness* is the result of free trade. But if not, of what use is it? What will the people gain, if foreign competition, which may interfere with them in their sales, does not favor them in their purchases?"

My Dear Free Trader:—Allow us to say that you have but half read the article which provoked your letter. We said that free trade acted precisely like roads, canals and railways, like everything which facilitates communications, and like everything which destroys obstacles. Its first tendency is to increase the quantity of the article which is relieved from duties, and consequently to lower its price. But by increasing, at the same time, the quantity of all the things for which this article is exchanged, it increases the *demand*, and consequently the price rises. You ask us what the people will gain. Suppose they have a balance with certain scales, in each one of which they have for their use a certain quantity of the articles which you have enumerated. If a little grain is put in one scale it will gradually sink, but if an equal quantity of cloth, iron and coal is added in the others, the equilibrium will be maintained. Looking at the beam above, there will be no change. Looking at the people, we shall see them better fed, clothed and warmed.

"Dear Mr. Editor:—I am a cloth manufacturer, and a protectionist. I confess that your article on *dearness* and *cheapness* has led me to reflect. It has something specious about it, and if well proven, would work my conversion."

My Dear Protectionist:—We say that the end and aim of your restrictive measures is a wrongful one—*artificial dearness.* But we do not say that they always realize the hopes of those who initiate them. It is certain that they inflict on the consumer all the evils of dearness. It is not certain that the producer gets the profit. Why? Because if they diminish the supply they also diminish the *demand.*

This proves that in the economical arrangement of this world there is a moral force, a *vis medicatrix*, which in the long run causes inordinate ambition to become the prey of a delusion.

Pray, notice, sir, that one of the elements of the prosperity of each special branch of industry is the general prosperity. The rent of a house is not merely in proportion to what it has cost, but also to the number and means of the tenants. Do two houses which are precisely alike necessarily rent for the same sum? Certainly not, if one is in Paris and the other in Lower Brittany. Let us never speak of a price without regarding the *conditions*, and let us understand that there is nothing more futile than to try to build the prosperity of the parts on the ruin of the whole. This is the attempt of the restrictive system.

Competition always has been, and always will be, disagreeable to those who are affected by it. Thus we see that in all times and in all places men try to get rid of it. We know, and you too, perhaps, a municipal council where the resident merchants make a furious war on the foreign ones. Their projectiles are import duties, fines, etc., etc.

Now, just think what would have become of Paris, for instance, if this war had been carried on there with success.

Suppose that the first shoemaker who settled there had succeeded in keeping out all others, and that the first tailor, the first mason, the first printer, the first watchmaker, the first hair-dresser, the first physician, the first baker, had been equally fortunate. Paris would still be a village, with twelve or fifteen hundred inhabitants. But it was not thus. Each one, except those whom you still keep away, came to make money in this market, and that is precisely what has built it up. It has been a long series of collisions for the enemies of competition, and from one collision after another, Paris has become a city of a million inhabitants. The general prosperity has gained by this, doubtless, but have the shoemakers and tailors, individually, lost anything by it? For you, this is the question. As competitors came, you said: The price of boots will fail. Has it been so? No, for if the *supply* has increased, the *demand* has increased also.

Thus will it be with cloth; therefore let it come in. It is true that you will have more competitors, but you will also have more customers, and richer ones. Did you never think of this when seeing nine-tenths of your countrymen deprived during the winter of that superior cloth that you make?

This is not a very long lesson to learn. If you wish to prosper, let your customers do the same.

When this is once known, each one will seek his welfare in the general welfare. Then, jealousies between individuals, cities, provinces and nations, will no longer vex the world.

VI.

TO ARTISANS AND LABORERS.

MANY papers have attacked me before you. Will you not read my defense?

I am not mistrustful. When a man writes or speaks, I believe that he thinks what he says.

What is the question? To ascertain which is the more advantageous for you, restriction or liberty.

I believe that it is liberty; they believe it is restriction; it is for each one to prove his case.

Was it necessary to insinuate that we are the agents of England?

You will see how easy recrimination would be on this ground.

We are, they say, agents of the English, because

some of us have used the English words *meeting*, *free trader!*

And do not they use the English words *drawback* and *budget?*

We imitate Cobden and the English democracy!

Do not they parody Bentinck and the British aristocracy?

We borrow from perfidious Albion the doctrine of liberty.

Do not they borrow from her the sophisms of protection?

We follow the commercial impulse of Bordeaux and the South.

Do not they serve the greed of Lille, and the manufacturing North?

We favor the secret designs of the ministry, which desires to turn public attention away from the protective policy.

Do not they favor the views of the Custom House officers, who gain more than anybody else by this protective *regime?*

So you see that if we did not ignore this war of epithets, we should not be without weapons.

But that is not the point in issue.

The question which I shall not lose sight of is this:

Which is better for the working-classes, to be free or not to be free to purchase from abroad?

Workmen, they say to you, "If you are free to

buy from abroad these things which you now make yourselves, you will no longer make them. You will be without work, without wage,s and without bread. It is then for your own good that your liberty be restricted."

This objection recurs in all forms. They say, for instance, "If we clothe ourselves with English cloth, if we make our plowshares with English iron, if we cut our bread with English knives, if we wipe our hands with English napkins, what will become of the French workmen—what will become of the *national labor?*"

Tell me, workmen, if a man stood on the pier at Boulogne, and said to every Englishman who landed: If you will give me those English boots, I will give you this French hat; or, if you will let me have this English horse, I will let you have this French carriage; or, Are you willing to exchange this Birmingham machine for this Paris clock? or, again, Does it suit you to barter your Newcastle coal for this Champagne wine? I ask you whether, supposing this man makes his proposals with average judgment, it can be said that our *national labor*, taken as a whole, would be harmed by it?

Would it be more so if there were twenty of these people offering to exchange services at Boulogne instead of one; if a million barters were made instead of four; and if the intervention of merchants and money was called on to facilitate them and multiply them indefinitely?

Now, let one country buy of another at wholesale to sell again at retail, or at retail to sell again at wholesale, it will always be found, if the matter is followed out to the end, that *commerce consists of mutual barter of products for products, of services for services.* If, then, *one barter* does not injure the *national labor*, since it implies as much *national labor given* as *foreign labor received*, a hundred million of them cannot hurt the country.

But, you will say, where is the advantage? The advantage consists in making a better use of the resources of each country, so that the same amount of labor gives more satisfaction and well-being everywhere.

There are some who employ singular tactics against you. They begin by admitting the superiority of freedom over the prohibitive system, doubtless in order that they may not have to defend themselves on that ground.

Next they remark that in going from one system to another there will be some *displacement* of labor.

Then they dilate upon the sufferings which, according to themselves, this *displacement* must cause. They exaggerate and amplify them; they make of them the principal subject of discussion; they present them as the exclusive and definite result of reform, and thus try to enlist you under the standard of monopoly.

These tactics have been employed in the service

of all abuses, and I must frankly admit one thing, that it always embarrasses even the friends of those reforms which are most useful to the people. You will understand why.

When an abuse exists, everything arranges itself upon it.

Human existences connect themselves with it, others with these, then still others, and this forms a great edifice.

Do you raise your hand against it? Each one protests; and notice this particularly, those persons who protest always seem at the first glance to be right, because it is easier to show the disorder which must accompany the reform than the order which will follow it.

The friends of the abuse cite particular instances; they name the persons and their workmen who will be disturbed, while the poor devil of a reformer can only refer to the *general good*, which must insensibly diffuse itself among the masses. This does not have the effect which the other has.

Thus, supposing it is a question of abolishing slavery. "Unhappy people," they say to the colored men, "who will feed you? The master distributes floggings, but he also distributes rations."

It is not seen that it is not the master who feeds the slave, but his own labor which feeds both himself and master.

When the convents of Spain were reformed, they

said to the beggars, "Where will you find broth and clothing? The Abbot is your providence. Is it not very convenient to apply to him?"

And the beggars said: "That is true. If the Abbot goes, we see what we lose, but we do not see what will come in its place."

They do not notice that if the convents gave alms they lived on alms, so that the people had to give them more than they could receive back.

Thus, workmen, a monopoly imperceptibly puts taxes on your shoulders, and then furnishes you work with the proceeds.

Your false friends say to you: If there was no monopoly, who would furnish you work?

You answer: This is true, this is true. The labor which the monopolists procure us is certain. The promises of liberty are uncertain.

For you do not see that they first take money from you, and then give you back a *part* of it for your labor.

Do you ask who will furnish you work? Why, you will give each other work. With the money which will no longer be taken from you, the shoemaker will dress better, and will make work for the tailor. The tailor will have new shoes oftener, and keep the shoemaker employed. So it will be with all occupations.

They say that with freedom there will be fewer workmen in the mines and the mills.

I do not believe it. But if this does happen, it is *necessarily* because there will be more labor freely in the open air.

For if, as they say, these mines and spinning mills can be sustained only by the aid of taxes imposed on *everybody* for their benefit, these taxes once abolished, *everybody* will be more comfortably off, and it is the comfort of all which feeds the labor of each one.

Excuse me if I linger at this demonstration. I have so great a desire to see you on the side of liberty.

In France, capital invested in manufactures yields, I suppose, five per cent. profit. But here is Mondor, who has one hundred thousand francs invested in a manufactory, on which he loses five per cent. The difference between the loss and gain is ten thousand francs. What do they do? They assess upon you a little tax of ten thousand francs, which is given to Mondor, and you do not notice it, for it is very skillfully disguised. It is not the tax gatherer who comes to ask you your part of the tax, but you pay it to Mondor, the manufacturer, every time you buy your hatchets, your trowels, and your planes. Then they say to you: If you do not pay this tax, Mondor can work no longer, and his employes, John and James, will be without labor. If this tax was remitted, would you not get work yourselves, and on your own account too?

And, then, be easy, when Mondor has no longer this soft method of obtaining his profit by a tax, he will use his wits to turn his loss into a gain, and John and James will not be dismissed. Then all will be profit *for all.*

You will persist, perhaps, saying: "We understand that after the reform there will be in general more work than before, but in the meanwhile John and James will be on the street."

To which I answer:

First. When employment changes its place only to increase, the man who has two arms and a heart is not long on the street.

Second. There is nothing to hinder the State from reserving some of its funds to avoid stoppages of labor in the transition, which I do not myself believe will occur.

Third. Finally, if to get out of a rut and get into a condition which is better for all, and which is certainly more just, it is absolutely necessary to brave a few painful moments, the workmen are ready, or I know them ill. God grant that it may be the same with employers.

Well, because you are workmen, are you not intelligent and moral? It seems that your pretended friends forget it. It is surprising that they discuss such a subject before you, speaking of wages and interests, without once pronouncing the word *justice.* They know, however, full well that the situation is *unjust*. Why, then, have they not the courage to tell you so, and say, "Workmen, an iniquity prevails in the country, but it is of advantage to you and it must be sustained." Why? Because they know that you would answer, No.

But it is not true that this iniquity is profitable to you. Give me your attention for a few moments and judge for yourselves.

What do they protect in France? Articles made by great manufacturers in great establishments, iron, cloth and silks, and they tell you that this is done not in the interest of the employer, but in your interest, in order to insure you wages.

But every time that foreign labor presents itself in the market in such a form that it may hurt *you*, but not the great manufacturers, do they not allow it to come in?

Are there not in Paris thirty thousand Germans who make clothes and shoes? Why are they allowed to establish themselves at your side when cloth is driven away? Because the cloth is made in great mills owned by manufacturing legislators. But clothes are made by workmen in their rooms.

These gentlemen want no competition in the turning of wool into cloth, because that is *their* business; but when it comes to converting cloth into clothes, they admit competition, because that is *your* trade.

When they made railroads they excluded English

rails, but they imported English workmen to make them. Why? It is very simple; because English rails compete with the great rolling mills, and English muscles compete only with yours.

We do not ask them to keep out German tailors and English laborers. We ask that cloth and rails may be allowed to come in. We ask justice for all, equality before the law for all.

It is a mockery to tell us that these Custom House restrictions have *your* advantage in view. Tailors, shoemakers, carpenters, millers, masons, blacksmiths, merchants, grocers, jewelers, butchers, bakers and dressmakers, I challenge you to show me a single instance in which restriction profits you, and if you wish, I will point out four where it hurts you.

And after all, just see how much of the appearance of truth this self-denial, which your journals attribute to the monopolists, has.

I believe that we can call that the *natural rate of wages* which would establish itself *naturally* if there were freedom of trade. Then, when they tell you that restriction is for your benefit, it is as if they told you that it added a *surplus* to your *natural* wages. Now, an *extra natural* surplus of wages must be taken from somewhere; it does not fall from the moon; it must be taken from those who pay it.

You are then brought to this conclusion, that,

according to your pretended friends, the protective system has been created and brought into the world in order that capitalists might be sacrificed to laborers!

Tell me, is that probable?

Where is your place in the Chamber of Peers? When did you sit at the Palais Bourbon? Who has consulted you? Whence came this idea of establishing the protective system?

I hear your answer: *We* did not establish it. We are neither Peers nor Deputies, nor Counselors of State. The capitalists have done it.

By heavens, they were in a delectable mood that day. What! the capitalists made this law; *they* established the prohibitive system, so that you laborers should make profits at their expense!

But here is something stranger still.

How is it that your pretended friends who speak to you now of the goodness, generosity and self-denial of capitalists, constantly express regret that you do not enjoy your political rights? From their point of view, what could you do with them? The capitalists have the monopoly of legislation, it is true. Thanks to this monopoly, they have granted themselves the monopoly of iron, cloth, coal, wood and meat, which is also true. But now your pretended friends say that the capitalists, in acting thus, have stripped themselves, without being obliged to do it, to enrich you without your being entitled to it. Surely, if you were electors and deputies, you could not manage your affairs better; you would not even manage them as well.

If the industrial organization which rules us is made in your interest, it is a perfidy to demand political rights for you; for these democrats of a new species can never get out of this dilemma; the law, made by the present law-makers, gives you *more*, or gives you *less*, than your natural wages. If it gives you *less*, they deceive you in inviting you to support it. If it gives you *more*, they deceive you again by calling on you to claim political rights, when those who now exercise them, make sacrifices for you which you, in your honesty, could not yourselves vote.

Workingmen, God forbid that the effect of this article should be to cast in your hearts the germs of irritation against the rich. If mistaken *interests* still support monopoly, let us not forget that it has its root in *errors*, which are common to capitalists and workmen. Then, far from laboring to excite them against one another, let us strive to bring them together. What must be done to accomplish this? If it is true that the natural social tendencies aid in effacing inequality among men, all we have to do to let those tendencies act is to remove the artificial obstructions which interfere with their operation, and allow the relations of different classes to establish themselves on the principle of *justice*, which, to my mind, is the principle of FREEDOM.

VII.

A CHINESE STORY.

THEY exclaim against the greed and the selfishness of the age!

Open the thousand books, the thousand papers, the thousand pamphlets, which the Parisian presses throw out every day on the country; is not all this the work of little saints?

What spirit in the painting of the vices of the time! What touching tenderness for the masses! With what liberality they invite the rich to divide with the poor, or the poor to divide with the rich! How many plans of social reform, social improvement, and social organization! Does not even the weakest writer devote himself to the well-being of the laboring classes? All that is required is to advance them a little money to give them time to attend to their humanitarian pursuits.

There is nothing which does not assume to aid in the well-being and moral advancement of the people—nothing, not even the Custom House. You believe that it is a tax machine, like a duty or a toll at the end of a bridge? Not at all. It is an essentially civilizing, fraternizing and equalizing institution. What would you have? It is the fashion. It is necessary to put or affect to put feeling or sentimentality everywhere, even in the cure of all troubles.

But it must be admitted that the Custom House organization has a singular way of going to work to realize these philanthropic aspirations.

It puts on foot an army of collectors, assistant collectors, inspectors, assistant inspectors, cashiers, accountants, receivers, clerks, supernumeraries, tide-waiters, and all this in order to exercise on the industry of the people that negative action which is summed up in the word *to prevent.*

Observe that I do not say *to tax*, but really *to prevent.*

And *to prevent*, not acts reproved by morality, or opposed to public order, but transactions which are innocent, and which they have even admitted are favorable to the peace and harmony of nations.

However, humanity is so flexible and supple that, in one way or another, it always overcomes these attempts at prevention.

It is for the purpose of increasing labor. If people are kept from getting their food from abroad they produce it at home. It is more laborious, but they must live. If they are kept from passing along the valley, they must climb the mountains. It is longer, but the point of destination must be reached.

This is sad, but amusing. When the law has thus created a certain amount of obstacles, and when, to overcome them, humanity has diverted a corresponding amount of labor, you are no longer allowed to call for the reform of the law; for, if you point out the *obstacle*, they show you the labor which it brings into play; and if you say this is not labor created but *diverted*, they answer you as does the *Esprit Public*—"The impoverishing only is certain and immediate; as for the enriching, it is more than problematical."

This recalls to me a Chinese story, which I will tell you.

There were in China two great cities, Tchin and Tchan. A magnificent canal connected them. The Emperor thought fit to have immense masses of rock thrown into it, to make it useless.

Seeing this, Kouang, his first Mandarin, said to him: "Son of Heaven, you make a mistake." To which the Emperor replied: "Kouang, you are foolish."

You understand, of course, that I give but the substance of the dialogue.

At the end of three moons the Celestial Emperor had the Mandarin brought, and said to him: "Kouang, look."

And Kouang, opening his eyes, looked.

He saw at a certain distance from the canal a multitude of men *laboring*. Some excavated, some filled up, some leveled, and some laid pavement, and the Mandarin, who was very learned, thought to himself: They are making a road.

At the end of three more moons, the Emperor, having called Kouang, said to him: "Look."

And Kouang looked.

And he saw that the road was made; and he noticed that at various points, inns were building. A medley of foot passengers, carriages and palanquins went and came, and innumerable Chinese, oppressed by fatigue, carried back and forth heavy burdens from Tchin to Tchan, and from Tchan to Tchin, and Kouang said: It is the destruction of the canal which has given labor to these poor people. But it did not occur to him that this labor was *diverted* from other employments.

Then more moons passed, and the Emperor said to Kouang: "Look."

And Kouang looked.

He saw that the inns were always full of travelers, and that they being hungry, there had sprung up, near by, the shops of butchers, bakers, charcoal dealers, and bird's nest sellers. Since these worthy men could not go naked, tailors, shoemakers and umbrella and fan dealers had settled there, and as they do not sleep in the open air, even in the Celestial Empire, carpenters, masons and thatchers congregated there. Then came police officers, judges and fakirs; in a word, around each stopping place there grew up a city with its suburbs.

Said the Emperor to Kouang: "What do you think of this?"

And Kouang replied: "I could never have believed that the destruction of a canal could create so much labor for the people." For he did not think that it was not labor created, but *diverted;* that travelers ate when they went by the canal just as much as they did when they were forced to go by the road.

However, to the great astonishment of the Chinese, the Emperor died, and this Son of Heaven was committed to earth.

His successor sent for Kouang, and said to him: "Clean out the canal."

And Kouang said to the new Emperor: "Son of Heaven, you are doing wrong."

And the Emperor replied: "Kouang, you are foolish."

But Kouang persisted and said: "My Lord, what is your object?"

"My object," said the Emperor, "is to facilitate the movement of men and things between Tchin and Tchan; to make transportation less expensive, so that the people may have tea and clothes more cheaply."

But Kouang was in readiness. He had received, the evening before, some numbers of the *Moniteur*

Industriel, a Chinese paper. Knowing his lesson by heart, he asked permission to answer, and, having obtained it, after striking his forehead nine times against the floor, he said: "My Lord, you try, by facilitating transportation, to reduce the price of articles of consumption, in order to bring them within the reach of the people; and to do this you begin by making them lose all the labor which was created by the destruction of the canal. Sire, in political economy, absolute cheapness"—

The Emperor. "I believe that you are reciting something."

Kouang. "That is true, and it would be more convenient for me to read."

Having unfolded the *Esprit Public*, he read: "In political economy the absolute cheapness of articles of consumption is but a secondary question. The problem lies in the equilibrium of the price of labor and that of the articles necessary to existence. The abundance of labor is the wealth of nations, and the best economic system is that which furnishes them the greatest possible amount of labor. Do not ask whether it is better to pay four or eight cents cash for a cup of tea, or five or ten shillings for a shirt. These are puerilities unworthy of a serious mind. No one denies your proposition. The question is, whether it is better to pay more for an article, and to have, through the abundance and price of labor, more means of acquiring it, or whether it is better to impoverish the sources of labor, to diminish the mass of national production, and to transport articles of consumption by canals, more cheaply it is true, but, at the same time, to deprive a portion of our laborers of the power to buy them, even at these reduced prices."

The Emperor not being altogether convinced, Kouang said to him: "My Lord, be pleased to wait. I have the *Moniteur Industriel* to quote from."

But the Emperor said: "I do not need your Chinese newspapers to tell me that to create *obstacles* is to turn labor in that direction. Yet that is not my mission. Come, let us clear out the canal, and then we will reform the tariff."

Kouang went away plucking out his beard, and crying: Oh, Fo! Oh, Pe! Oh, Le! and all the monosyllabic and circumflex gods of Cathay, take pity on your people; for there has come to us an Emperor of the *English school*, and I see very plainly that, in a little while, we shall be in want of everything, since it will not be necessary for us to do anything!

VIII.

POST HOC, ERGO PROPTER HOC.

"AFTER this, therefore on account of this." The most common and the most false of arguments.

Real suffering exists in England.

This occurrence follows two others:

First. The reduction of the tariff.

Second. The loss of two consecutive harvests.

To which of these last two circumstances is the first to be attributed?

The protectionists do not fail to exclaim: "It is this cursed freedom which does all the mischief. It promised us wonders and marvels; we welcomed it, and now the manufactories stop and the people suffer."

Commercial freedom distributes, in the most uniform and equitable manner, the fruits which Providence grants to the labor of man. If these fruits are partially destroyed by any misfortune, it none the less looks after the fair distribution of what remains. Men are not as well provided for, of course, but shall we blame freedom or the bad harvest?

Freedom rests on the same principle as insurance. When a loss happens, it divides, among a great many people, and a great number of years, evils which without it would accumulate on one nation and one season. But have they ever thought of saying that fire was no longer a scourge, since there were insurance companies?

In 1842, '43 and '44, the reduction of taxes began in England. At the same time the harvests were very abundant, and we can justly believe that these two circumstances had much to do with the wonderful prosperity shown by that country during that period.

In 1845 the harvest was bad, and in 1846 it was still worse. Breadstuffs grew dear, the people spent their money for food, and used less of other articles. There was a diminished demand for clothing; the manufactories were not so busy, and wages showed a declining tendency. Happily, in the same year, the restrictive barriers were again lowered, and an enormous quantity of food was enabled to reach the English market. If it had not been for this, it is almost certain that a terrible revolution would now fill Great Britain with blood.

Yet they make freedom chargeable with disasters, which it prevents and remedies, at least in part.

A poor leper lived in solitude. No one would touch what he had contaminated. Compelled to do everything for himself, he dragged out a miserable existence. A great physician cured him. Here was our hermit in full possession of the *freedom of exchange*. What a beautiful prospect opened before him! He took pleasure in calculating the advantages, which, thanks to his connection with other men, he could draw from his vigorous arms. Unluckily, he broke both of them. Alas! his fate was most miserable. The journalists of that country, witnessing his misfortune, said: "See to what misery this ability to exchange has reduced him! Really, he was less to be pitied when he lived alone."

"What!" said the physician; "do not you consider his two broken arms? Do not they form a part of his sad destiny? His misfortune is to have lost his arms, and not to have been cured of leprosy. He would be much more to be pitied if he was both maimed and a leper."

Post hoc, ergo propter hoc; do not trust this sophism.

IX.

ROBBERY BY BOUNTIES.

THEY find my little book of *Sophisms* too theoretical, scientific, and metaphysical. Very well. Let us try a trivial, commonplace, and, if necessary, coarse style. Convinced that the public is *duped* in the matter of protection, I have desired to prove it. But the public wishes to be shouted at. Then let us cry out:

"Midas, King Midas, has asses' ears!"

An outburst of frankness often accomplishes more than the politest circumlocution.

To tell the truth, my good people, *they are robbing you.* It is harsh, but it is true.

The words *robbery, to rob, robber,* will seem in very bad taste to many people. I say to them as Harpagon did to Elise, Is it the *word* or the *thing* that alarms you?

Whover has fraudulently taken that which does not belong to him, is guilty of robbery. (*Penal Code, Art.* 379.)

To rob: To take furtively, or by force. (*Dictionary of the Academy.*)

Robber: He who takes more than his due. (*The same.*)

Now, does not the monopolist, who, by a law of his own making, obliges me to pay him twenty francs for an article which I can get elsewhere for fifteen, take from me fraudulently five francs, which belong to me?

Does he not take it furtively, or by force?

Does he not require of me more than his due?

He carries off, he takes, he demands, they will say, but not *furtively* or *by force,* which are the characteristics of robbery.

When our tax levy is burdened with five francs for the bounty which this monopolist carries off, takes, or demands, what can be more *furtive*, since so few of us suspect it? And for those who are not deceived, what can be more *forced*, since, at the first refusal to pay, the officer is at our doors?

Still, let the monopolists reassure themselves. These robberies, by means of bounties or tariffs, even if they do violate equity as much as robbery, do not break the law; on the contrary, they are perpetrated through the law. They are all the worse for this, but they have nothing to do with *criminal justice*.

Besides, willy-nilly, we are all *robbers* and *robbed* in the business. Though the author of this book cries *stop thief*, when he buys, others can cry the same after him, when he sells. If he differs from many of his countrymen, it is only in this: he knows that he loses by this game more than he gains, and they do not; if they did know it, the game would soon cease.

Nor do I boast of having first given this thing its true name. More than sixty years ago, Adam Smith said:

"When manufacturers meet it may be expected that a conspiracy will be planned against the pockets of the public." Can we be astonished at this when the public pay no attention to it?

An assembly of manufacturers deliberate officially under the name of *Industrial League.* What goes on there, and what is decided upon?

I give a very brief summary of the proceedings of one meeting:

"A Ship-builder. Our mercantile marine is at the last gasp (warlike digression). It is not surprising. I cannot build without iron. I can get it at ten francs *in the world's market;* but, through the law, the managers of the French forges compel me to pay them fifteen francs. Thus they take five francs from me. I ask freedom to buy where I please.

"An Iron Manufacturer. *In the world's market* I can obtain transportation for twenty francs. The ship-builder, through the law, requires thirty. Thus he *takes* ten francs from me. He plunders me; I plunder him. It is all for the best.

"A Public Official. The conclusion of the ship-builder's argument is highly imprudent. Oh, let us cultivate the touching union which makes our strength; if we relax an iota from the theory of protection, good-bye to the whole of it.

"The Ship-builder. But, for us, protection is a failure. I repeat that the shipping is nearly gone.

"A Sailor. Very well, let us raise the discriminating duties against goods imported in foreign bottoms, and let the ship-builder, who now takes thirty francs from the public, hereafter take forty.

"A Minister. The government will push to its

extreme limits the admirable mechanism of these discriminating duties, but I fear that it will not answer the purpose.

"A Government Employe. You seem to be bothered about a very little matter. Is there any safety but in the bounty? If the consumer is willing, the tax-payer is no less so. Let us pile on the taxes, and let the ship-builder be satisfied. I propose a bounty of five francs, to be taken from the public revenues, to be paid to the ship-builder for each quintal of iron that he uses.

"Several Voices. Seconded, seconded.

"A Farmer. I want a bounty of three francs for each bushel of wheat.

"A Weaver. And I two francs for each yard of cloth.

"The Presiding Officer. That is understood. Our meeting will have originated the system of *drawbacks*, and it will be its eternal glory. What branch of manufacturing can lose hereafter, when we have two so simple means of turning losses into gains—the *tariff* and *drawbacks*. The meeting is adjourned."

Some supernatural vision must have shown me in a dream the coming appearance of the *bounty* (who knows if I did not suggest the thought to M. Dupin?), when some months ago I wrote the following words:

"It seems evident to me that protection, without

changing its nature or effects, might take the form of a direct tax levied by the State, and distributed in indemnifying bounties to privileged manufacturers."

And after having compared protective duties with the bounty:

"I frankly avow my preference for the latter system; it seems to me more just, more economical, and more truthful. More just, because if society wishes to give gratuities to some of its members, all should contribute; more economical, because it would save much of the expense of collection, and do away with many obstacles; and, finally, more truthful, because the public could see the operation plainly, and would know what was done."

Since the opportunity is so kindly offered us, let us study this *robbery by bounties.* What is said of it will also apply to *robbery by tariff*, and as it is a little better disguised, the direct will enable us to understand the indirect, cheating. Thus the mind proceeds from the simple to the complex.

But is there no simpler variety of robbery? Certainly, there is *highway robbery*, and all it needs is to be legalized, or, as they say now-a-days, *organized.*

I once read the following in somebody's travels:

"When we reached the Kingdom of A—— we found all industrial pursuits suffering. Agriculture groaned, manufactures complained, commerce murmured, the navy growled, and the government did not know whom to listen to. At first it thought of taxing all the discontented, and of dividing among them the proceeds of these taxes after having taken its share; which would have been like the method of managing lotteries in our dear Spain. There are a thousand of you; the State takes a dollar from each one, cunningly steals two hundred and fifty, and then divides up seven hundred and fifty, in greater or smaller sums, among the players. The worthy Hidalgo, who has received three-quarters of a dollar, forgetting that he has spent a whole one, is wild with joy, and runs to spend his shillings at the tavern. Something like this once happened in France. Barbarous as the country of A—— was, however, the government did not trust the stupidity of the inhabitants enough to make them accept such singular protection, and hence this was what it devised:

"The country was intersected with roads. The government had them measured, exactly, and then said to the farmers, 'All that you can steal from travelers between these boundaries is yours; let it serve you as a *bounty*, a protection, and an encouragement.' It afterwards assigned to each manufacturer and each ship-builder, a bit of road to work up, according to this formula:

Dono tibi et concedo,
Virtutem et puissantiam,
Robbandi,

Pillageandi,
Stealandi,
Cheatandi,
Et Swindlandi,
Impune per totam istam,
Viam.

"Now it has come to pass that the natives of the Kingdom of A—— are so familiarized with this regime, and so accustomed to think only of what they steal, and not of what is stolen from them, so habituated to look at pillage but from the pillager's point of view, that they consider the sum of all these private robberies as a *national profit*, and refuse to give up a system of protection without which, they say, no branch of industry can live."

Do you say, it is not possible that an entire nation could see an *increase of riches* where the inhabitants plundered one another?

Why not? We have this belief in France, and every day we organize and practice *reciprocal robbery* under the name of bounties and protective tariffs.

Let us exaggerate nothing, however; let us concede that as far as the *mode of collection*, and the collateral circumstances, are concerned, the system in the Kingdom of A—— may be worse than ours; but let us say, also, that as far as principles and necessary results are concerned, there is not an atom of difference between these two kinds of robbery legally organized to eke out the profits of industry.

Observe, that if *highway robbery* presents some difficulties of execution, it has also certain advantages which are not found in the *tariff robbery.*

For instance: An equitable division can be made between all the plunderers. It is not thus with tariffs. They are by nature impotent to protect certain classes of society, such as artizans, merchants, literary men, lawyers, soldiers, etc., etc.

It is true that *bounty robbery* allows of infinite subdivisions, and in this respect does not yield in perfection to *highway robbery,* but on the other hand it often leads to results which are so odd and foolish, that the natives of the Kingdom of A—— may laugh at it with great reason.

That which the plundered party loses in highway robbery is gained by the robber. The article stolen remains, at least, in the country. But under the dominion of *bounty robbery,* that which the duty takes from the French is often given to the Chinese, the Hottentots, Caffirs, and Algonquins, as follows:

A piece of cloth is worth a *hundred francs* at Bordeaux. It is impossible to sell it below that without loss. It is impossible to sell it for more than that, for the *competition* between merchants forbids. Under these circumstances, if a Frenchman desires to buy the cloth, he must pay a *hundred francs,* or do without it. But if an Englishman comes, the government interferes, and says to the merchant: "Sell your cloth, and I will make the tax-payers give you *twenty francs* (through the operation of the *drawback*). The merchant, who wants, and can get, but one hundred francs for his cloth, delivers it to the Englishman for eighty francs. This sum added to the twenty francs, the product of the *bounty robbery*, makes up his price. It is then precisely as if the tax-payers had given twenty francs to the Englishman, on condition that he would buy French cloth at twenty francs below the cost of manufacture,—at twenty francs below what it costs us. Then bounty robbery has this peculiarity, that the *robbed* are inhabitants of the country which allows it, and the *robbers* are spread over the face of the globe.

It is truly wonderful that they should persist in holding this proposition to have been demonstrated: *All that the individual robs from the mass is a general gain.* Perpetual motion, the philosopher's stone, and the squaring of the circle, are sunk in oblivion; but the theory of *progress by robbery* is still held in honor. *A priori*, however, one might have supposed that it would be the shortest lived of all these follies.

Some say to us: You are, then, partisans of the *let alone* policy? economists of the superannuated school of the Smiths and the Says? You do not desire the *organization of labor?* Why, gentlemen, organize labor as much as you please, but we will watch to see that you do not organize *robbery*.

Others say, *bounties*, *tariffs*, all these things may have been overdone. We must use, without abusing them. A wise liberty, combined with moderate protection, is what *serious* and practical men claim. Let us beware of *absolute principles*. This is exactly what they said in the Kingdom of A——, according to the Spanish traveler. "Highway robbery," said the wise men, "is neither good nor bad in itself; it depends on circumstances. Perhaps too much freedom of pillage has been given; perhaps not enough. Let us see; let us examine; let us balance the accounts of each robber. To those who do not make enough, we will give a little more road to work up. As for those who make too much, we will reduce their share."

Those who spoke thus acquired great fame for moderation, prudence, and wisdom. They never failed to attain the highest offices of the State.

As for those who said, "Let us repress injustice altogether; let us allow neither *robbery*, nor *half robbery*, nor *quarter robbery*," they passed for theorists, dreamers, bores—always parroting the same thing. The people also found their reasoning too easy to understand. How can that be true which is so very simple?

X.

THE TAX COLLECTOR.

JACQUES BONHOMME, Vine-grower.
M. LASOUCHE, Tax Collector.

L. You have secured twenty hogsheads of wine?

J. Yes, with much care and sweat.

—Be so kind as to give me six of the best.

—Six hogsheads out of twenty! Good heavens! You want to ruin me. If you please, what do you propose to do with them?

—The first will be given to the creditors of the State. When one has debts, the least one can do is to pay the interest.

—Where did the principal go?

—It would take too long to tell. A part of it was once upon a time put in cartridges, which made the finest smoke in the world; with another part men were hired who were maimed on foreign ground, after having ravaged it. Then, when these expenses brought the enemy upon us, he would not leave without taking money with him, which we had to borrow.

—What good do I get from it now?

—The satisfaction of saying:

> How proud am I of being a Frenchman
> When I behold the triumphal column,

And the humiliation of leaving to my heirs an estate burdened with a perpetual rent. Still one must pay what he owes, no matter how foolish a use may have been made of the money. That accounts for one hogshead, but the five others?

—One is required to pay for public services, the civil list, the judges who decree the restitution of the bit of land your neighbor wants to appropriate, the policemen who drive away robbers while you sleep, the men who repair the road leading to the city, the priest who baptizes your children, the teacher who educates them, and myself, your servant, who does not work for nothing.

—Certainly, service for service. There is nothing to say against that. I had rather make a bargain directly with my priest, but I do not insist on this. So much for the second hogshead. This leaves four, however.

—Do you believe that two would be too much for your share of the army and navy expenses?

—Alas, it is little compared with what they have cost me already. They have taken from me two sons whom I tenderly loved.

—The balance of power in Europe must be maintained.

—Well, my God! the balance of power would be the same if these forces were everywhere reduced a half or three-quarters. We should save our children and our money. All that is needed is to understand it.

—Yes, but they do not understand it.

—That is what amazes me. For every one suffers from it.

—You wished it so, Jacques Bonhomme.

—You are jesting, my dear Mr. Collector; have I a vote in the legislative halls?

—Whom did you support for Deputy?

—An excellent General, who will be a Marshal presently, if God spares his life.

—On what does this excellent General live?

—My hogsheads, I presume.

—And what would happen were he to vote for a reduction of the army and your military establishment?

—Instead of being made a Marshal, he would be retired.

—Do you now understand that yourself?

—Let us pass to the fifth hogshead, I beg of you.

—That goes to Algeria.

—To Algeria! And they tell me that all Mussulmans are temperance people, the barbarians! What services will they give me in exchange for this ambrosia, which has cost me so much labor?

—None at all; it is not intended for Mussulmans, but for good Christians who spend their days in Barbary.

—What can they do there which will be of service to me?

—Undertake and undergo raids; kill and be

killed; get dysenteries and come home to be doctored; dig harbors, make roads, build villages and people them with Maltese, Italians, Spaniards and Swiss, who live on your hogshead, and many others which I shall come in the future to ask of you.

—Mercy! This is too much, and I flatly refuse you my hogshead. They would send a wine-grower who did such foolish acts to the mad-house. Make roads in the Atlas Mountains, when I cannot get out of my own house! Dig ports in Barbary when the Garonne fills up with sand every day! Take from me my children whom I love, in order to torment Arabs! Make me pay for the houses, grain and horses, given to the Greeks and Maltese, when there are so many poor around us!

—The poor! Exactly; they free the country of this *superfluity*.

—Oh, yes, by sending after them to Algeria the money which would enable them to live here.

—But then you lay the basis of a *great empire*, you carry *civilization* into Africa, and you crown your country with immortal glory.

—You are a poet, my dear Collector; but I am a vine-grower, and I refuse.

—Think that in a few thousand years you will get back your advances a hundred fold. All those who have charge of the enterprise say so.

—At first they asked me for one barrel of wine

to meet expenses, then two, then three, and now I am taxed a hogshead. I persist in my refusal.

—It is too late. Your *representative* has agreed that you shall give a hogshead.

—That is but too true. Cursed weakness! It seems to me that I was unwise in making him my agent; for what is there in common between the General of an army and the poor owner of a vineyard?

—You see well that there is something in common between you, were it only the wine you make, and which, in your name, he votes to himself.

—Laugh at me; I deserve it, my dear Collector. But be reasonable, and leave me the sixth hogshead at least. The interest of the debt is paid, the civil list provided for, the public service assured, and the war in Africa perpetuated. What more do you want?

—The bargain is not made with me. You must tell your desires to the General. *He* has disposed of your vintage.

—But what do you propose to do with this poor hogshead, the flower of my flock? Come, taste this wine. How mellow, delicate, velvety it is!

—Excellent, delicious! It will suit D——, the cloth manufacturer, admirably.

—D——, the manufacturer! What do you mean?

—That he will make a good bargain out of it.

—How? What is that? I do not understand you.

—Do you not know that D—— has started a magnificent establishment very useful to the country, but which loses much money every year?

—I am very sorry. But what can I do to help him?

—The Legislature saw that if things went on thus, D—— would either have to do a better business or close his manufactory.

—But what connection is there between D——'s bad speculations and my hogshead?

—The Chamber thought that if it gave D—— a little wine from your cellar, a few bushels of grain taken from your neighbors, and a few pennies cut from the wages of the workingmen, his losses would change into profits.

—This recipe is as infallible as it is ingenious. But it is shockingly unjust. What! is D—— to cover his losses by taking my wine?

—Not exactly the wine, but the proceeds of it. That is what we call a *bounty for encouragement*. But you look amazed! Do not you see what a great service you render to the country?

—You mean to say to D——?

—To the country. D—— asserts that, thanks to this arrangement, his business prospers, and thus it is, says he, that the country grows rich. That is what he recently said in the Chamber of which he is a member.

—It is a damnable fraud! What! A fool goes

into a silly enterprise, he spends his money, and if he extorts from me wine or grain enough to make good his losses, and even to make him a profit, he calls it a general gain!

—Your *representative* having come to that conclusion, all you have to do is to give me the six hogsheads of wine, and sell the fourteen that I leave you for as much as possible.

—That is my business.

—For, you see, it would be very annoying if you did not get a good price for them

—I will think of it.

—For there are many things which the money you receive must procure.

—I know it, sir. I know it.

—In the first place, if you buy iron to renew your spades and plowshares, a law declares that you must pay the iron-master twice what it was worth.

—Ah, yes; does not the same thing happen in the Black Forest?

—Then, if you need oil, meat, cloth, coal, wool and sugar, each one by the law will cost you twice what it is worth.

—But this is horrible, frightful, abominable.

—What is the use of these hard words? You yourself, through your *authorized* agent——

—Leave me alone with my authorized agent. I made a very strange disposition of my vote, it is true. But they shall deceive me no more, and I will be represented by some good and honest countryman.

—Bah, you will re-elect the worthy General.

—I? I re-elect the General to give away my wine to Africans and manufacturers?

—You will re-elect him, I say.

—That is a little *too much.* I will not re-elect him, if I do not want to.

—But you will want to, and you will re-elect him.

—Let him come here and try. He will see who he will have to settle with.

—We shall see. Good bye. I take away your six hogsheads, and will proceed to divide them as the General has directed.

XI.

UTOPIAN IDEAS.

If I were His Majesty's Minister!

—Well, what would you do?

—I should begin by—by—upon my word, by being very much embarrassed. For I should be Minister only because I had the majority, and I should have that only because I had made it, and I could only have made it, honestly at least, by governing according to its ideas. So if I undertake to carry out my ideas and to run counter to its ideas, I shall not have the majority, and if I do not, I cannot be His Majesty's Minister.

—Just imagine that you are so, and that consequently the majority is not opposed to you, what would you do?

—I would look to see on which side *justice* is.

—And then?

—I would seek to find where *utility* was.

—What next?

—I would see whether they agreed, or were in conflict with one another.

—And if you found they did not agree?

—I would say to the King, take back your portfolio.

—But suppose you see that *justice* and *utility* are one?

—Then I will go straight ahead.

—Very well, but to realize utility by justice, a third thing is necessary.

—What is that?

—Possibility.

—You conceded that.

—When?

—Just now

—How?

—By giving me the majority.

—It seems to me that the concession was rather hazardous, for it implies that the majority clearly sees what is just, clearly sees what is useful, and clearly sees that these things are in perfect accord.

—And if it sees this clearly, the good will, so to speak, do itself.

—This is the point to which you are constantly bringing me—to see a possibility of reform only in the progress of the general intelligence.

—By this progress all reform is infallible.

—Certainly. But this preliminary progress takes time. Let us suppose it accomplished. What will you do? for I am eager to see you at work, doing, practicing.

—I should begin by reducing letter postage to ten centimes.

—I heard you speak of five, once.

—Yes; but as I have other reforms in view, I must move with prudence, to avoid a deficit in the revenues.

—Prudence? This leaves you with a deficit of thirty millions.

—Then I will reduce the salt tax to ten francs.

—Good! Here is another deficit of thirty millions. Doubtless you have invented some new tax.

—Heaven forbid! Besides, I do not flatter myself that I have an inventive mind.

—It is necessary, however. Oh, I have it. What

was I thinking of? You are simply going to diminish the expense. I did not think of that.

—You are not the only one. I shall come to that; but I do not count on it at present.

—What! you diminish the receipts, without lessening expenses, and you avoid a deficit?

—Yes, by diminishing other taxes at the same time.

(Here the interlocutor, putting the index finger of his right hand on his forehead, shook his head, which may be translated thus: He is rambling terribly.)

—Well, upon my word, this is ingenious. I pay the Treasury a hundred francs; you relieve me of five francs on salt, five on postage; and in order that the Treasury may nevertheless receive one hundred francs, you relieve me of ten on some other tax?

—Precisely; you understand me.

—How can it be true? I am not even sure that I have heard you.

—I repeat that I balance one remission of taxes by another.

—I have a little time to give, and I should like to hear you expound this paradox.

—Here is the whole mystery: I know a tax which costs you twenty francs, not a sou of which gets to the Treasury. I relieve you of half of it, and make the other half take its proper destination.

—You are an unequaled financier. There is but one difficulty. What tax, if you please, do I pay, which does not go to the Treasury?

—How much does this suit of clothes cost you?

—A hundred francs.

—How much would it have cost you if you had gotten the cloth from Belgium?

—Eighty francs.

—Then why did you not get it there?

—Because it is prohibited.

—Why?

—So that the suit may cost me one hundred francs instead of eighty.

—This denial, then, costs you twenty francs?

—Undoubtedly.

—And where do these twenty francs go?

—Where do they go? To the manufacturer of the cloth.

—Well, give me ten francs for the Treasury, and I will remove the restriction, and you will gain ten francs.

—Oh, I begin to see. The treasury account shows that it loses five francs on postage and five on salt, and gains ten on cloth. That is even.

—Your account is—you gain five francs on salt, five on postage, and ten on cloth.

—Total, twenty francs. This is satisfactory enough. But what becomes of the poor cloth manufacturer?

—Oh, I have thought of him. I have secured compensation for him by means of the tax reductions which are so profitable to the Treasury. What I have done for you as regards cloth, I do for him in regard to wool, coal, machinery, etc., so that he can lower his price without loss.

—But are you sure that will be an equivalent?

—The balance will be in his favor. The twenty francs that you gain on the cloth will be multiplied by those which I will save for you on grain, meat, fuel, etc. This will amount to a large sum, and each one of your 35,000,000 fellow-citizens will save the same way. There will be enough to consume the cloths of both Belgium and France. The nation will be better clothed; that is all.

—I will think on this, for it is somewhat confused in my head.

—After all, as far as clothes go, the main thing is to be clothed. Your limbs are your own, and not the manufacturer's. To shield them from cold is your business and not his. If the law takes sides for him against you, the law is unjust, and you allowed me to reason on the hypothesis that what is unjust is hurtful.

—Perhaps I admitted too much; but go on and explain your financial plan.

—Then I will make a tariff.

—In two folio volumes?

—No, in two sections.

—Then they will no longer say that this famous axiom "No one is supposed to be ignorant of the law" is a fiction. Let us see your tariff.

—Here it is: Section First. All imports shall pay an *ad valorem* tax of five per cent.

—Even *raw materials?*

—Unless they are *worthless.*

—But they all have value, much or little.

—Then they will pay much or little.

—How can our manufactories compete with foreign ones which have these *raw materials* free?

—The expenses of the State being certain, if we close this source of revenue, we must open another; this will not diminish the relative inferiority of our manufactories, and there will be one bureau more to organize and pay.

—That is true; I reasoned as if the tax was to be annulled, not changed. I will reflect on this. What is your second section?

—Section Second. All exports shall pay an *ad valorem* tax of five per cent.

—Merciful Heavens, Mr. Utopist! You will certainly be stoned, and, if it comes to that, I will throw the first one.

—We agreed that the majority were enlightened.

—Enlightened! Can you claim that an export duty is not onerous?

—All taxes are onerous, but this is less so than others.

—The carnival justifies many eccentricities. Be so kind as to make this new paradox appear specious, if you can.

—How much did you pay for this wine?

—A franc per quart.

—How much would you have paid outside the city gates?

—Fifty centimes.

—Why this difference?

—Ask the *octroi** which added ten sous to it.

—Who established the *octroi*?

—The municipality of Paris, in order to pave and light the streets.

—This is, then, an import duty. But if the neighboring country districts had established this *octroi* for their profit, what would happen?

—I should none the less pay a franc for wine worth only fifty centimes, and the other fifty centimes would pave and light Montmartre and the Batignolles.

—So that really it is the consumer who pays the tax?

—There is no doubt of that.

—Then by taxing exports you make foreigners help pay your expenses.†

* The entrance duty levied at the gates of French towns.

† I understand M. Bastiat to mean merely that export duties are not necessarily more onerous than import duties. The statement that all taxes are paid by the consumer, is liable to important modifications. An export duty may be laid in such way, and on such articles, that it will be paid

—I find you at fault, this is not *justice.*

—Why not? In order to secure the production of any one thing, there must be instruction, security, roads, and other costly things in the country. Why shall not the foreigner who is to consume this product, bear the charges its production necessitates?

—This is contrary to received ideas.

—Not the least in the world. The last purchaser must repay all the direct and indirect expenses of production.

—No matter what you say, it is plain that such a measure would paralyze commerce, and cut off all exports.

—That is an illusion. If you were to pay this tax besides all the others, you would be right. But, if the hundred millions raised in this way, relieve you of other taxes to the same amount, you go into foreign markets with all your advantages, and even with more, if this duty has occasioned less embarrassment and expense.

—I will reflect on this. So now the salt, postage and customs are regulated. Is all ended there?

—I am just beginning.

—Pray, initiate me in your Utopian ideas.

—I have lost sixty millions on salt and postage. I shall regain them through the customs; which also gives me something more precious.

wholly by the foreign consumer, without loss to the producing country, but it is only when the additional cost does not lessen the demand, or induce the foreigner to produce the same article. *Translator.*

—What, pray?

—International relations founded on justice, and a probability of peace which is equivalent to a certainty. I will disband the army.

—The whole army?

—Except special branches, which will be voluntarily recruited, like all other professions. You see, conscription is abolished.

—Sir, you should say recruiting.

—Ah, I forgot, I cannot help admiring the ease with which, in certain countries, the most unpopular things are perpetuated by giving them other names.

—Like *consolidated duties*, which have become *indirect contributions.*

—And the *gendarmes*, who have taken the name of *municipal guards.*

—In short, trusting to Utopia, you disarm the country.

—I said that I would muster out the army, not that I would disarm the country. I intend, on the contrary, to give it invincible power.

—How do you harmonize this mass of contradictions?

—I call all the citizens to service.

—Is it worth while to relieve a portion from service in order to call out everybody?

—You did not make me Minister in order that I should leave things as they are. Thus, on my advent to power, I shall say with Richelieu, "the State maxims are changed." My first maxim, the one which will serve as a basis for my administration, is this: Every citizen must know two things —How to earn his own living, and defend his country.

—It seems to me, at the first glance, that there is a spark of good sense in this.

—Consequently, I base the national defense on a law consisting of two sections.

Section First. Every able-bodied citizen, without exception, shall be under arms for four years, from his twenty-first to his twenty-fifth year, in order to receive military instruction.—

—This is pretty economy! You send home four hundred thousand soldiers and call out ten millions.

—Listen to my second section:

SEC. 2. *Unless* he proves, at the age of twenty-one, that he knows the school of the soldier perfectly.

—I did not expect this turn. It is certain that to avoid four years' service, there will be a great emulation among our youth, to learn *by the right flank* and *double quick, march.* The idea is odd.

—It is better than that. For without grieving families and offending equality, does it not assure the country, in a simple and inexpensive manner, of ten million defenders, capable of defying a coalition of all the standing armies of the globe?

—Truly, if I were not on my guard, I should end in getting interested in your fancies.

The Utopist, getting excited: Thank Heaven, my estimates are relieved of a hundred millions! I suppress the *octroi.* I refund indirect contributions. I—

Getting more and more excited: I will proclaim religious freedom and free instruction. There shall be new resources. I will buy the railroads, pay off the public debt, and starve out the stock gamblers.

—My dear Utopist!

—Freed from too numerous cares, I will concentrate all the resources of the government on the repression of fraud, the administration of prompt and even-handed justice. I—

—My dear Utopist, you attempt too much. The nation will not follow you.

—You gave me the majority.

—I take it back.

—Very well; then I am no longer Minister; but my plans remain what they are—Utopian ideas.

XII.

SALT, POSTAGE, AND CUSTOMS.

[This chapter is an amusing dialogue relating principally to English Postal Reform. Being inapplicable to any condition of things existing in the United States, it is omitted.—*Translator.*]

XIII.

THE THREE ALDERMEN.

A DEMONSTRATION IN FOUR TABLEAUX.

First Tableau.

[The scene is in the hotel of Alderman Pierre. The window looks out on a fine park; three persons are seated near a good fire.]

Pierre. Upon my word, a fire is very comfortable when the stomach is satisfied. It must be agreed that it is a pleasant thing. But, alas! how many worthy people like the King of Yvetot,

> "Blow on their fingers for want of wood."

Unhappy creatures, Heaven inspires me with a charitable thought. You see these fine trees. I will cut them down and distribute the wood among the poor.

Paul and Jean. What! gratis?

Pierre. Not exactly. There would soon be an end of my good works if I scattered my property thus. I think that my park is worth twenty thousand livres; by cutting it down I shall get much more for it.

Paul. A mistake. Your wood as it stands is worth more than that in the neighboring forests, for it renders services which that cannot give, When cut down it will, like that, be good for burning only, and will not be worth a sou more per cord.

Pierre. Oh! Mr. Theorist, you forget that I am a practical man. I supposed that my reputation as a speculator was well enough established to put me above any charge of stupidity. Do you think that I shall amuse myself by selling my wood at the price of other wood?

Paul. You must.

Pierre. Simpleton! Suppose I prevent the bringing of any wood to Paris?

Paul. That will alter the case. But how will you manage it?

Pierre. This is the whole secret. You know that wood pays an entrance duty of ten sous per cord. To-morrow I will induce the Aldermen to raise this duty to one hundred, two hundred, or three hundred livres, so high as to keep out every fagot. Well, do you see? If the good people do not want to die of cold, they must come to my wood-yard. They will fight for my wood; I shall sell it for its weight in gold, and this well-regulated deed of charity will enable me to do others of the same sort.

Paul. This is a fine idea, and it suggests an equally good one to me.

Jean. Well, what is it?

Paul. How do you find this Normandy butter?

Jean. Excellent.

Paul. Well, it seemed passable a moment ago. But do you not think it is a little strong? I want to make a better article at Paris. I will have four or five hundred cows, and I will distribute milk, butter and cheese to the poor people.

Pierre and Jean. What! as a charity?

Paul. Bah, let us always put charity in the foreground. It is such a fine thing that its counterfeit even is an excellent card. I will give my butter to the people and they will give me their money. Is that called selling?

Jean. No, according to the *Bourgeois Gentilhomme;* but call it what you please, you ruin yourself. Can Paris compete with Normandy in raising cows?

Paul. I shall save the cost of transportation.

Jean. Very well; but the Normans are able to

beat the Parisians, even if they do have to pay for transportation.

Paul. Do you call it *beating* any one to furnish him things at a low price?

Jean. It is the time-honored word. You will always be beaten.

Paul. Yes; like Don Quixote. The blows will fall on Sancho. Jean, my friend, you forgot the *octroi.*

Jean. The *octroi!* What has that to do with your butter?

Paul. To-morrow I will demand *protection,* and I will induce the Council to prohibit the butter of Normandy and Brittany. The people must do without butter, or buy mine, and that at my price, too.

Jean. Gentlemen, your philanthrophy carries me along with it. "In time one learns to howl with the wolves." It shall not be said that I am an unworthy Alderman. Pierre, this sparkling fire has illumined your soul; Paul, this butter has given an impulse to your understanding, and I perceive that this piece of salt pork stimulates my intelligence. To-morrow I will vote myself, and make others vote, for the exclusion of hogs, dead or alive; this done, I will build superb stock-yards in the middle of Paris "for the unclean animal forbidden to the Hebrews." I will become swineherd and pork-seller, and we shall see how the good people of Lutetia can help getting their food at my shop.

Pierre. Gently, my friends; if you thus run up the price of butter and salt meat, you diminish the profit which I expected from my wood.

Paul. Nor is my speculation so wonderful, if you ruin me with your fuel and your hams.

Jean. What shall I gain by making you pay an extra price for my sausages, if you overcharge me for pastry and fagots?

Pierre. Do you not see that we are getting into a quarrel? Let us rather unite. Let us make *reciprocal concessions.* Besides, it is not well to listen only to miserable self-interest. *Humanity* is concerned, and must not the warming of the people be secured?

Paul. That it is true, and people must have butter to spread on their bread.

Jean. Certainly. And they must have a bit of pork for their soup.

All Together. Forward, charity! Long live philanthrophy! To-morrow, to-morrow, we will take the octroi by assault.

Pierre. Ah, I forgot. One word more which is important. My friends, in this selfish age people are suspicious, and the purest intentions are often misconstrued. Paul, you plead for *wood;* Jean, defend *butter;* and I will devote myself to domestic *swine.* It is best to head off invidious suspicions.

Paul and Jean (leaving). Upon my word, what a clever fellow!

SECOND TABLEAU.

The Common Council.

Paul. My dear colleagues, every day great quantities of wood come into Paris, and draw out of it large sums of money. If this goes on, we shall all be ruined in three years, and what will become of the poor people? [Bravo.] Let us prohibit foreign wood. I am not speaking for myself, for you could not make a tooth-pick out of all the wood I own. I am, therefore, perfectly disinterested. [Good, good.] But here is Pierre, who has a park, and he will keep our fellow-citizens from freezing. They will no longer be in a state of *dependence* on the charcoal dealers of the Yonne. Have you ever thought of the risk we run of dying of cold, if the proprietors of these foreign forests should take it into their heads not to bring any more wood to Paris? Let us, therefore, prohibit wood. By this means we shall stop the drain of specie, we shall start the wood-chopping business, and open to our workmen a new source of labor and wages. [Applause.]

Jean. I second the motion of the Honorable member—a proposition so philanthrophic and so disinterested, as he remarked. It is time that we should stop this intolerable *freedom of entry*, which has brought a ruinous competition upon our market, so that there is not a province tolerably well situated for producing some one article which does not inundate us with it, sell it to us at a low price, and depress Parisian labor. It is the business of the State to *equalize the conditions of production* by wisely graduated duties; to allow the entrance from without of whatever is dearer there than at Paris, and thus relieve us from an unequal *contest.* How, for instance, can they expect us to make milk and butter in Paris as against Brittany and Normandy? Think, gentlemen; the Bretons have land cheaper, feed more convenient, and labor more abundant. Does not common sense say that the conditions must be equalized by a protecting duty? I ask that the duty on milk and butter be raised to a thousand per cent., and more, if necessary. The breakfasts of the people will cost a little more, but wages will rise! We shall see the building of stables and dairies, a good trade in churns, and the foundation of new industries laid. I, myself, have not the least interest in this plan. I am not a cowherd, nor do I desire to become one. I am moved by the single desire to be useful to the laboring classes. [Expressions of approbation.]

Pierre. I am happy to see in this assembly statesmen so pure, enlightened, and devoted to the interests of the people. [Cheers.] I admire their self-denial, and cannot do better than follow such noble examples. I support their motion, and I also make one to exclude Poitou hogs. It is not that I want to become a swineherd or pork dealer, in which case my conscience would forbid my making this motion; but is it not shameful, gentlemen, that we should be paying tribute to these poor Poitevin peasants who have the audacity to come into our own market, take possession of a business that we could have carried on ourselves, and, after having inundated us with sausages and hams, take from us, perhaps, nothing in return? Anyhow, who says that the balance of trade is not in their favor, and that we are not compelled to pay them a tribute in money? Is it not plain that if this Poitevin industry were planted in Paris, it would open new fields to Parisian labor? Moreover, gentlemen, is it not very likely, as Mr. Lestiboudois said, that we buy these Poitevin salted meats, not with our income, but our capital? Where will this land us? Let us not allow greedy, avaricious and perfidious rivals to come here and sell things cheaply, thus making it impossible for us to produce them ourselves. Aldermen, Paris has given us its confidence, and we must show ourselves worthy of it. The people are without labor, and we must create it, and if salted meat costs them a little more, we shall, at least, have the consciousness that we have sacrificed our interests to those of the masses, as every good Alderman ought to do. [Thunders of applause.]

A Voice. I hear much said of the poor people; but, under the pretext of giving them labor, you begin by taking away from them that which is worth more than labor itself—wood, butter, and soup.

Pierre, Paul and Jean. Vote, vote. Away with your theorists and generalizers! Let us vote. [The three motions are carried.]

THIRD TABLEAU.

Twenty Years After.

Son. Father, decide; we must leave Paris. Work is slack, and everything is dear.

Father. My son, you do not know how hard it is to leave the place where we were born.

Son. The worst of all things is to die there of misery.

Father. Go, my son, and seek a more hospitable country. For myself, I will not leave the grave where your mother, sisters and brothers lie. I am eager to find, at last, near them, the rest which is denied me in this city of desolation.

Son. Courage, dear father, we will find work elsewhere — in Poitou, Normandy or Brittany. They say that the industry of Paris is gradually transferring itself to those distant countries.

Father. It is very natural. Unable to sell us wood and food, they stopped producing more than they needed for themselves, and they devoted their spare time and capital to making those things which we formerly furnished them.

Son. Just as at Paris, they quit making handsome furniture and fine clothes, in order to plant trees, and raise hogs and cows. Though quite young, I have seen vast storehouses, sumptuous buildings, and quays thronged with life on those banks of the Seine which are now given up to meadows and forests.

Father. While the provinces are filling up with cities, Paris becomes country. What a frightful revolution! Three mistaken Aldermen, aided by public ignorance, have brought down on us this terrible calamity.

Son. Tell me this story, my father.

Father. It is very simple. Under the pretext of establishing three new trades at Paris, and of thus supplying labor to the workmen, these men secured the prohibition of wood, butter, and meats. They assumed the right of supplying their fellow-citizens with them. These articles rose immediately to an exorbitant price. Nobody made enough to buy them, and the few who could procure them by using up all they made were unable to buy anything else; consequently all branches of industry stopped at once—all the more so because the provinces no longer offered a market. Misery, death, and emigration began to depopulate Paris.

Son. When will this stop?

Father. When Paris has become a meadow and a forest.

Son. The three Aldermen must have made a great fortune.

Father. At first they made immense profits, but at length they were involved in the common misery.

Son. How was that possible?

Father. You see this ruin; it was a magnificent house, surrounded by a fine park. If Paris had kept on advancing, Master Pierre would have got more rent from it annually than the whole thing is now worth to him.

Son. How can that be, since he got rid of competition?

Father. Competition in selling has disappeared; but competition in buying also disappears every day, and will keep on disappearing until Paris is an open field, and Master Pierre's woodland will be worth no more than an equal number of acres in the forest of Bondy. Thus, a monopoly, like every species of injustice, brings its own punishment upon itself.

Son. This does not seem very plain to me, but the decay of Paris is undeniable. Is there, then, no means of repealing this unjust measure that Pierre and his colleagues adopted twenty years ago?

Father. I will confide my secret to you. I will

remain at Paris for this purpose; I will call the people to my aid. It depends on them whether they will replace the *octroi* on its old basis, and dismiss from it this fatal principle, which is grafted on it, and has grown there like a parasite fungus.

Son. You ought to succeed on the very first day.

Father. No; on the contrary, the work is a difficult and laborious one. Pierre, Paul and Jean understand one another perfectly. They are ready to do anything rather than allow the entrance of wood, butter and meat into Paris. They even have on their side the people, who clearly see the labor which these three protected branches of business give, who know how many wood-choppers and cow-drivers it gives employment to, but who cannot obtain so clear an idea of the labor that would spring up in the free air of liberty.

Son. If this is all that is needed, you will enlighten them.

Father. My child, at your age, one doubts at nothing. If I wrote, the people would not read; for all their time is occupied in supporting a wretched existence. If I speak, the Aldermen will shut my mouth. The people will, therefore, remain long in their fatal error; political parties, which build their hopes on their passions, attempt to play upon their prejudices, rather than to dispel them. I shall then have to deal with the powers that be—

the people and the parties. I see that a storm will burst on the head of the audacious person who dares to rise against an iniquity which is so firmly rooted in the country.

Son. You will have justice and truth on your side.

Father. And they will have force and calumny. If I were only young! But age and suffering have exhausted my strength.

Son. Well, father, devote all that you have left to the service of the country. Begin this work of emancipation, and leave to me for an inheritance the task of finishing it.

FOURTH TABLEAU.

The Agitation.

Jacques Bonhomme. Parisians, let us demand the reform of the *octroi;* let it be put back to what it was. Let every citizen be FREE to buy wood, butter and meat where it seems good to him.

The People. Hurrah for LIBERTY!

Pierre. Parisians, do not allow yourselves to be seduced by these words. Of what avail is the freedom of purchasing, if you have not the means? and how can you have the means, if labor is wanting? Can Paris produce wood as cheaply as the forest of Bondy, or meat at as low price as Poitou, or butter as easily as Normandy? If you open the doors to these rival products, what will become of the wood cutters, pork dealers, and cattle drivers? They cannot do without protection.

The People. Hurrah for PROTECTION!

Jacques. Protection! But do they protect you, workmen? Do not you compete with one another? Let the wood dealers then suffer competition in their turn. They have no right to raise the price of their wood by law, unless they, also, by law, raise wages. Do you not still love equality?

The People. Hurrah for EQUALITY!

Pierre. Do not listen to this factious fellow. We have raised the price of wood, meat, and butter, it is true; but it is in order that we may give good wages to the workmen. We are moved by charity.

The People. Hurrah for CHARITY!

Jacques. Use the *octroi*, if you can, to raise wages, or do not use it to raise the price of commodities. The Parisians do not ask for charity, but justice.

The People. Hurrah for JUSTICE!

Pierre. It is precisely the dearness of products which will, by reflex action, raise wages.

The People. Hurrah for DEARNESS!

Jacques. If butter is dear, it is not because you pay workmen well; it is not even that you may make great profits; it is only because Paris is ill situated for this business, and because you desired that they should do in the city what ought to be done in the country, and in the country what was done in the city. The people have no *more* labor, only they labor at something else. They get no *more* wages, but they do not buy things as cheaply.

The People. Hurrah for CHEAPNESS!

Pierre. This person seduces you with his fine words. Let us state the question plainly. Is it not true that if we admit butter, wood, and meat, we shall be inundated with them, and die of a plethora? There is, then, no other way in which we can preserve ourselves from this new inundation, than to shut the door, and we can keep up the price of things only by causing scarcity artificially.

A Very Few Voices. Hurrah for SCARCITY!

Jacques. Let us state the question as it is. Among all the Parisians we can divide only what is in Paris; the less wood, butter and meat there is, the smaller each one's share will be. There will be less if we exclude than if we admit. Parisians, individual abundance can exist only where there is general abundance.

The People. Hurrah for ABUNDANCE!

Pierre. No matter what this man says, he cannot prove to you that it is to your interest to submit to unbridled competition.

The People. Down with COMPETITION!

Jacques. Despite all this man's declamation, he cannot make you *enjoy* the sweets of restriction.

The People. Down with RESTRICTION!

Pierre. I declare to you that if the poor dealers in cattle and hogs are deprived of their livelihood, if they are sacrificed to theories, I will not be answerable for public order. Workmen, distrust this man. He is an agent of perfidious Normandy; he is under the pay of foreigners. He is a traitor, and must be hanged. [The people keep silent.]

Jacques. Parisians, all that I say now, I said to you twenty years ago, when it occurred to Pierre to use the *octroi* for his gain and your loss. I am not an agent of Normandy. Hang me if you will, but this will not prevent oppression from being oppression. Friends, you must kill neither Jacques nor Pierre, but liberty if it frightens you, or restriction if it hurts you.

The People. Let us hang nobody, but let us emancipate everybody.

XIV.

SOMETHING ELSE.

—WHAT is restriction?

—A partial prohibition.

—What is prohibition?

—An absolute restriction.

—So that what is said of one is true of the other?

—Yes, comparatively. They bear the same relation to each other that the arc of the circle does to the circle.

—Then if prohibition is bad, restriction cannot be good.

—No more than the arc can be straight if the circle is curved.

—What is the common name for restriction and prohibition?

—Protection.

—What is the definite effect of protection?

—To require from men *harder labor for the same result.*

—Why are men so attached to the protective system?

—Because, since liberty would accomplish the same result *with less labor*, this apparent diminution of labor frightens them.

—Why do you say *apparent?*

—Because all labor economized can be devoted to *something else.*

—What?

—That cannot and need not be determined.

—Why?

—Because, if the total of the comforts of France could be gained with a diminution of one-tenth on the total of its labor, no one could determine what comforts it would procure with the labor remaining at its disposal. One person would prefer to be better clothed, another better fed, another better taught, and another more amused.

—Explain the workings and effect of protection.

—It is not an easy matter. Before taking hold of a complicated instance, it must be studied in the simplest one.

—Take the simplest you choose.

—Do you recollect how Robinson Crusoe, having no saw, set to work to make a plank?

—Yes. He cut down a tree, and then with his ax hewed the trunk on both sides until he got it down to the thickness of a board.

—And that gave him an abundance of work?

—Fifteen full days.

—What did he live on during this time?

—His provisions.

—What happened to the ax?

—It was all blunted.

—Very good; but there is one thing which, perhaps, you do not know. At the moment that Robinson gave the first blow with his ax, he saw a plank which the waves had cast up on the shore.

—Oh, the lucky accident! He ran to pick it up?

—It was his first impulse; but he checked himself, reasoning thus:

"If I go after this plank, it will cost me but the labor of carrying it and the time spent in going to and returning from the shore.

"But if I make a plank with my ax, I shall in the first place obtain work for fifteen days, then I shall wear out my ax, which will give me an opportunity of repairing it, and I shall consume my provisions, which will be a third source of labor, since they must be replaced. Now, *labor is wealth*. It is plain that I will ruin myself if I pick up this stranded board. It is important to protect my *personal labor*, and now that I think of it, I can create myself additional labor by kicking this board back into the sea."

—But this reasoning was absurd!

—Certainly. Nevertheless it is that adopted by every nation which *protects* itself by prohibition. It rejects the plank which is offered it in exchange for a little labor, in order to give itself more labor. It sees a gain even in the labor of the custom house officer. This answers to the trouble which Robinson took to give back to the waves the present they wished to make him. Consider the nation a collective being, and you will not find an atom of difference between its reasoning and that of Robinson.

—Did not Robinson see that he could use the time saved in doing *something else?*

—What '*something else*'?

—So long as one has wants and time, one has always *something* to do. I am not bound to specify the labor that he could undertake.

—I can specify very easily that which he would have avoided.

—I assert, that Robinson, with incredible blindness, confounded labor with its result, the end with the means, and I will prove it to you.

—It is not necessary. But this is the restrictive or prohibitory system in its simplest form. If it appears absurd to you, thus stated, it is because the two qualities of producer and consumer are here united in the same person.

—Let us pass, then, to a more complicated instance.

—Willingly. Some time after all this, Robinson having met Friday, they united, and began to work in common. They hunted for six hours each morning and brought home four hampers of game. They worked in the garden for six hours each afternoon, and obtained four baskets of vegetables.

One day a canoe touched at the Island of Despair. A good-looking stranger landed, and was allowed to dine with our two hermits. He tasted, and praised the products of the garden, and before taking leave of his hosts, said to them:

"Generous Islanders, I dwell in a country much richer in game than this, but where horticulture is unknown. It would be easy for me to bring you every evening four hampers of game if you would give me only two baskets of vegetables."

At these words Robinson and Friday stepped on one side, to have a consultation, and the debate which followed is too interesting not to be given *in extenso:*

Friday. Friend, what do you think of it?

Robinson. If we accept we are ruined.

Friday. Is that certain? Calculate!

Robinson. It is all calculated. Hunting, crushed out by competition, will be a lost branch of industry for us.

Friday. What difference does that make, if we have the game?

Robinson. Theory! It will not be the product of our labor.

Friday. Yes, it will, since we will have to give vegetables to get it.

Robinson. Then what shall we make?

Friday. The four hampers of game cost us six hours' labor. The stranger gives them to us for two baskets of vegetables, which take us but three hours. Thus three hours remain at our disposal.

Robinson. Say rather that they are taken from our activity. There is our loss. *Labor is wealth*, and if we lose a fourth of our time we are one-fourth poorer.

Friday. Friend, you make an enormous mistake. The same amount of game and vegetables and three free hours to boot make progress, or there is none in the world.

Robinson. Mere generalities. What will we do with these three hours?

Friday. We will do *something else.*

Robinson. Ah, now I have you. You can specify nothing. It is very easy to say *something else—something else.*

Friday. We will fish. We will adorn our houses. We will read the Bible.

Robinson. Utopia! Is it certain that we will do this rather than that?

Friday. Well, if we have no wants, we will rest. Is rest nothing?

Robinson. When one rests one dies of hunger.

Friday. Friend, you are in a vicious circle. I speak of a rest which diminishes neither our gains nor our vegetables. You always forget that by means of our commerce with this stranger, nine hours of labor will give us as much food as twelve now do.

Robinson. It is easy to see that you were not reared in Europe. Perhaps you have never read the *Moniteur Industriel?* It would have taught you this: "All time saved is a dear loss. Eating is not the important matter, but working. Nothing which we consume counts, if it is not the product of our labor. Do you wish to know whether you are rich? Do not look at your comforts, but at your trouble?" This is what the *Moniteur Industriel* would have taught you. I, who am not a theorist, see but the loss of our hunting.

Friday. What a strange perversion of ideas. But—

Robinson. No *buts.* Besides, there are political reasons for rejecting the interested offers of this perfidious stranger.

Friday. Political reasons!

Robinson. Yes. In the first place he makes these offers only because they are for his advantage.

Friday. So much the better, since they are for ours also.

Robinson. Then by these exchanges we shall become dependent on him.

Friday. And he on us. We need his game, he our vegetables, and we will live in good friendship.

Robinson. Fancy! Do you want I should leave you without an answer?

Friday. Let us see; I am still waiting a good reason.

Robinson. Supposing that the stranger learns to cultivate a garden, and that his island is more fertile than ours. Do you see the consequences?

Friday. Yes. Our relations with the stranger will stop. He will take no more vegetables from us, since he can get them at home with less trouble. He will bring us no more game, since we will have nothing to give in exchange, and we will be then just where you want us to be now.

Robinson. Short-sighted savage! You do not see that after having destroyed our hunting, by inundating us with game, he will kill our gardening by overwhelming us with vegetables.

Friday. But he will do that only so long as we give him *something else;* that is to say, so long as we find *something else* to produce, which will economize our labor.

Robinson. Something else—something else! You always come back to that. You are very vague, friend Friday; there is nothing practical in your views.

The contest lasted a long time, and, as often happens, left each one convinced that he was right. However, Robinson having great influence over Friday, his views prevailed, and when the stranger came for an answer, Robinson said to him:

"Stranger, in order that your proposition may be accepted, we must be quite sure of two things:

"The first is, that your island is not richer in game than ours, for we will struggle but with *equal arms.*

"The second is, that you will lose by the bargain.

For, as in every exchange there is necessarily a gainer and a loser, we would be cheated, if you were not. What have you to say?"

"Nothing, nothing," replied the stranger, who burst out laughing, and returned to his canoe.

—The story would not be bad if Robinson was not so foolish.

—He is no more so than the committee in Hauteville street.

—Oh, there is a great difference. You suppose one solitary man, or, what comes to the same thing, two men living together. This is not our world; the diversity of occupations, and the intervention of merchants and money, change the question materially.

—All this complicates transactions, but does not change their nature.

—What! Do you propose to compare modern commerce to mere exchanges?

—Commerce is but a multitude of exchanges; the real nature of the exchange is identical with the real nature of commerce, as small labor is of the same nature with great, and as the gravitation which impels an atom is of the same nature as that which attracts a world.

—Thus, according to you, these arguments, which in Robinson's mouth are so false, are no less so in the mouths of our protectionists?

—Yes; only error is hidden better under the complication of circumstances.

—Well, now, select some instance from what has actually occurred.

—Very well; in France, in view of custom and the exigencies of the climate, cloth is an useful article. Is it the essential thing *to make it, or to have it?*

—A pretty question! To have it, we must make it.

—That is not necessary. It is certain that to have it some one must make it; but it is not necessary that the person or country using it should make it. You did not produce that which clothes you so well, nor France the coffee it uses for breakfast.

—But I purchased my cloth, and France its coffee.

—Exactly, and with what?

—With specie.

—But you did not make the specie, nor did France.

—We bought it.

—With what?

—With our products which went to Peru.

—Then it is in reality your labor that you exchange for cloth, and French labor that is exchanged for coffee?

—Certainly.

—Then it is not absolutely necessary to make what one consumes?

—No, if one makes *something else*, and gives it in exchange.

—In other words, France has two ways of procuring a given quantity of cloth. The first is to make it, and the second is to make *something else*, and exchange *that something else* abroad for cloth. Of these two ways, which is the best?

—I do not know.

—Is it not that which, *for a fixed amount of labor, gives the greatest quantity of cloth?*

—It seems so.

—Which is best for a nation, to have the choice of these two ways, or to have the law forbid its using one of them at the risk of rejecting the best?

—It seems to me that it would be best for the nation to have the choice, since in these matters it always makes a good selection.

—The law which prohibits the introduction of foreign cloth, decides, then, that if France wants cloth, it must make it at home, and that it is forbidden to make that *something else* with which it could purchase foreign cloth?

—That is true.

—And as it is obliged to make cloth, and forbidden to make *something else*, just because the other thing would require less labor (without which France would have no occasion to do anything with it), the law virtually decrees, that for a certain amount of labor, France shall have but one yard of cloth, making it itself, when, for the same amount of labor, it could have had two yards, by making *something else.*

—But what other thing?

—No matter what. Being free to choose, it will make *something else* only so long as there is *something else* to make.

—That is possible; but I cannot rid myself of the idea that the foreigners may send us cloth and not take something else, in which case we shall be prettily caught. Under all circumstances, this is the objection, even from your own point of view. You admit that France will make this *something else,* which is to be exchanged for cloth, with less labor than if it had made the cloth itself?

—Doubtless.

—Then a certain quantity of its labor will become inert?

—Yes; but people will be no worse clothed—a little circumstance which causes the whole misunderstanding. Robinson lost sight of it, and our protectionists do not see it, or pretend not to. The stranded plank thus paralyzed for fifteen days Robinson's labor, so far as it was applied to the making of a plank, but it did not deprive him of it. Distinguish, then, between these two kinds of diminution of labor, one resulting in *privation,* and the other in *comfort.* These two things are very different, and if you assimilate them, you reason like Robinson. In the most complicated, as in the most simple instances, the sophism consists in this: *Judging of the utility of labor by its duration and intensity, and not by its results*, which leads to this economic policy, *a reduction of the results of labor, in order to increase its duration and intensity.*

XV.

THE LITTLE ARSENAL OF THE FREE TRADER.

—If they say to you: There are no absolute principles; prohibition may be bad, and restriction good—

Reply: Restriction *prohibits* all that it keeps from coming in.

—If they say to you: Agriculture is the nursing mother of the country—

Reply: That which feeds a country is not exactly agriculture, but *grain.*

—If they say to you: The basis of the sustenance of the people is agriculture—

Reply: The basis of the sustenance of the people is *grain.* Thus a law which causes *two* bushels of grain to be obtained by agricultural labor at the expense of four bushels, which the same labor would have produced but for it, far from being a law of sustenance, is a law of starvation.

—If they say to you: A restriction on the admission of foreign grain leads to more cultivation, and, consequently, to a greater home production—

Reply: It leads to sowing on the rocks of the mountains and the sands of the sea. To milk and steadily milk, a cow gives more milk; for who can tell the moment when not a drop more can be obtained? But the drop costs dear.

—If they say to you: Let bread be dear, and the wealthy farmer will enrich the artisans—

Reply: Bread is dear when there is little of it, a thing which can make but poor, or, if you please, rich people who are starving.

—If they insist on it, saying: When food is dear, wages rise—

Reply by showing that in April, 1847, five-sixths of the workingmen were beggars.

—If they say to you: The profits of the workingmen must rise with the dearness of food—

Reply: This is equivalent to saying that in an unprovisioned vessel everybody has the same number of biscuits whether he has any or not.

—If they say to you: A good price must be secured for those who sell grain—

Reply: Certainly; but good wages must be secured to those who buy it.

—If they say to you: The land owners, who make the law, have raised the price of food without troubling themselves about wages, because they know that when food becomes dear, wages *naturally* rise—

Reply: On this principle, when workingmen come to make the law, do not blame them if they fix a high rate of wages without troubling themselves to protect grain, for they know that if wages are raised, articles of food will *naturally* rise in price.

—If they say to you: What, then, is to be done?

Reply: Be just to everybody.

—If they say to you: It is essential that a great country should manufacture iron—

Reply: The most essential thing is that this great country *should have iron.*

—If they say to you: It is necessary that a great country should manufacture cloth.

Reply: It is more necessary that the citizens of this great country *should have cloth.*

—If they say to you: Labor is wealth—

Reply: It is false.

And, by way of developing this, add: A bleeding is not health, and the proof of it is, that it is done to restore health.

—If they say to you: To compel men to work over rocks and get an ounce of iron from a ton of ore, is to increase their labor, and, consequently, their wealth—

Reply: To compel men to dig wells, by denying them the use of river water, is to add to their *useless* labor, but not their wealth.

—If they say to you: The sun gives his heat and light without requiring remuneration—

Reply: So much the better for me, since it costs me nothing to see distinctly.

—And if they reply to you: Industry in general loses what you would have paid for lights—

Retort: No, for having paid nothing to the sun, I use that which it saves me in paying for clothes, furniture and candles.

—So, if they say to you: These English rascals have capital which pays them nothing—

Reply: So much the better for us; they will not make us pay interest.

—If they say to you: These perfidious Englishmen find iron and coal at the same spot—

Reply: So much the better for us; they will not make us pay anything for bringing them together.

—If they say to you: The Swiss have rich pastures which cost little—

Reply: The advantage is on our side, for they will ask for a lesser quantity of our labor to furnish our farmers oxen and our stomachs food.

—If they say to you: The lands in the Crimea are worth nothing, and pay no taxes—

Reply: The gain is on our side, since we buy grain free from those charges.

—If they say to you: The serfs of Poland work without wages—

Reply: The loss is theirs and the gain is ours, since their labor is deducted from the price of the grain which their masters sell us.

—Then, if they say to you: Other nations have many advantages over us—

Reply: By exchange, they are forced to let us share in them.

—If they say to you: With liberty we shall be swamped with bread, beef *a la mode*, coal, and coats—

Reply: We shall be neither cold nor hungry.

—If they say to you: With what shall we pay?

Reply: Do not be troubled about that. If we are to be inundated, it will be because we are able to pay. If we cannot pay we will not be inundated.

—If they say to you: I would allow free trade, if a stranger, in bringing us one thing, took away another; but he will carry off our specie—

Reply: Neither specie nor coffee grow in the fields of Beauce or come out of the manufactories of Elbeuf. For us to pay a foreigner with specie is like paying him with coffee.

—If they say to you: Eat meat—

Reply: Let it come in.

—If they say to you, like the *Presse:* When you have not the money to buy bread with, buy beef—

Reply: This advice is as wise as that of Vautour to his tenant, "If a person has not money to pay his rent with, he ought to have a house of his own."

—If they say to you, like the *Presse:* The State ought to teach the people why and how it should eat meat—

Reply: Only let the State allow the meat free entrance, and the most civilized people in the world are old enough to learn to eat it without any teacher.

—If they say to you: The State ought to know everything, and foresee everything, to guide the people, and the people have only to let themselves be guided—

Reply: Is there a State outside of the people, and a human foresight outside of humanity? Archimedes might have repeated all the days of his life, "With a lever and a fulcrum I will move the world," but he could not have moved it, for want of those two things. The fulcrum of the State is the nation, and nothing is madder than to build so many hopes on the State; that is to say, to assume a collective science and foresight, after having established individual folly and short-sightedness.

—If they say to you: My God! I ask no favors,

but only a duty on grain and meat, which may compensate for the heavy taxes to which France is subjected; a mere little duty, equal to what these taxes add to the cost of my grain—

Reply: A thousand pardons, but I, too, pay taxes. If, then, the protection which you vote yourself results in burdening for me, your grain with your proportion of the taxes, your insinuating demand aims at nothing less than the establishment between us of the following arrangement, thus worded by yourself: "Since the public burdens are heavy, I, who sell grain, will pay nothing at all; and you, my neighbor, the buyer, shall pay two parts, to wit, your share and mine." My neighbor, the grain dealer, you may have power on your side, but not reason.

—If they say to you: It is, however, very hard for me, a tax payer, to compete in my own market with foreigners who pay none—

Reply: First, This is not *your* market, but *our* market. I who live on grain, and pay for it, must be counted for something.

Secondly. Few foreigners at this time are free from taxes.

Thirdly. If the tax which you vote repays to you, in roads, canals and safety, more than it costs you, you are not justified in driving away, at my expense, the competition of foreigners who do not pay the tax but who do not have the safety, roads and canals. It is the same as saying: I want a compensating duty, because I have fine clothes, stronger horses and better plows than the Russian laborer.

Fourthly. If the tax does not repay what it costs, do not vote it.

Fifthly. If, after you have voted a tax, it is your pleasure to escape its operation, invent a system which will throw it on foreigners. But the tariff only throws your proportion on me, when I already have enough of my own.

—If they say to you: Freedom of commerce is necessary among the Russians *that they may exchange their products with advantage* (opinion of M. Thiers, April, 1847)—

Reply: This freedom is necessary everywhere, and for the same reason.

—If they say to you: Each country has its wants; it is according to that that *it must act* (M. Thiers)—

Reply: It is according to that that *it acts of itself* when no one hinders it.

—If they say to you: Since we have no sheet iron, its admission must be allowed (M. Thiers)—

Reply: Thank you, kindly.

—If they say to you: Our merchant marine must have freight; owing to the lack of return cargoes our vessels cannot compete with foreign ones—

Reply: When you want to do everything at home, you can have cargoes neither going nor coming. It is as absurd to wish for a navy under a prohibitory system as to wish for carts where all transportation is forbidden.

—If they say to you: Supposing that protection is unjust, everything is founded on it; there are moneys invested, and rights acquired, and it cannot be abandoned without suffering—

Reply: Every injustice profits some one (except, perhaps, restriction, which in the long run profits no one), and to use as an argument the disturbance which the cessation of the injustice causes to the person profiting by it, is to say that an injustice, only because it has existed for a moment, should be eternal.

XVI.

THE RIGHT AND THE LEFT HAND.

[*Report to the King.*]

SIRE—When we see these men of the *Libre Echange* audaciously disseminating their doctrines, and maintaining that the right of buying and selling is implied by that of ownership (a piece of insolence that M. Billault has criticised like a true lawyer), we may be allowed to entertain serious fears as to the destiny of *national labor;* for what will Frenchmen do with their arms and intelligences when they are free?

The Ministry which you have honored with your confidence has naturally paid great attention to so serious a subject, and has sought in its wisdom for a *protection* which might be substituted for that which appears compromised. It proposes to you to forbid your faithful subjects the use of the right hand.

Sire, do not wrong us so far as to think that we lightly adopted a measure which, at the first glance, may appear odd. Deep study of the *protective system* has revealed to us this syllogism, on which it entirely rests:

The more one labors, the richer one is.

The more difficulties one has to conquer, the more one labors.

Ergo, the more difficulties one has to conquer, the richer one is.

What is *protection*, really, but an ingenious application of this formal reasoning, which is so compact that it would resist the subtlety of M. Billault himself?

Let us personify the country. Let us look on it as a collective being, with thirty million mouths, and, consequently, sixty million arms. This being makes a clock, which he proposes to exchange in

Belgium for ten quintals of iron. "But," we say to him, "make the iron yourself." "I cannot," says he; "it would take me too much time, and I could not make five quintals while I can make one clock." "Utopist!" we reply; "for this very reason we forbid your making the clock, and order you to make the iron. Do not you see that we create you labor?"

Sire, it will not have escaped your sagacity, that it is just as if we said to the country, *Labor with the left hand, and not with the right.*

The creation of obstacles to furnish labor an opportunity to develop itself, is the principle of the *restriction* which is dying. It is also the principle of the *restriction* which is about to be created. Sire, to make such regulations is not to innovate, but to preserve.

The efficacy of the measure is incontestable. It is difficult—much more difficult than one thinks—to do with the left hand what one was accustomed to do with the right. You will convince yourself of it, Sire, if you will condescend to try our system on something which is familiar to you,—like shuffling cards, for instance. We can then flatter ourselves that we have opened an illimitable career to labor.

When workmen of all kinds are reduced to their left hands, consider, Sire, the immense number that will be required to meet the present consumption, supposing it to be invariable, which we always do when we compare differing systems of production. So prodigious a demand for manual labor cannot fail to bring about a considerable increase in wages; and pauperism will disappear from the country as if by enchantment.

Sire, your paternal heart will rejoice at the thought that the benefits of this regulation will extend over that interesting portion of the great family whose fate excites your liveliest solicitude.

What is the destiny of women in France? That sex which is the boldest and most hardened to fatigue, is, insensibly, driving them from all fields of labor.

Formerly they found a refuge in the lottery offices. These have been closed by a pitiless philanthropy; and under what pretext? "To save," said they, "the money of the poor." Alas! has a poor man ever obtained from a piece of money enjoyments as sweet and innocent as those which the mysterious urn of fortune contained for him? Cut off from all the sweets of life, how many delicious hours did he introduce into the bosom of his family when, every two weeks, he put the value of a day's labor on a *quatern*. Hope had always her place at the domestic hearth. The garret was peopled with illusions; the wife promised herself that she would eclipse her neighbors with the splendor of her attire; the son saw himself drum-major, and the daughter felt herself carried toward the altar in the arms of her betrothed. To have a beautiful dream is certainly something.

The lottery was the poetry of the poor, and we have allowed it to escape them.

The lottery dead, what means have we of providing for our *proteges?*—tobacco, and the postal service.

Tobacco, certainly; it progresses, thanks to Heaven, and the distinguished habits which august examples have been enabled to introduce among our elegant youth.

But the postal service! We will say nothing of that, but make it the subject of a special report.

Then what is left to your female subjects except tobacco? Nothing, except embroidery, knitting, and sewing, pitiful resources, which are more and more restricted by that barbarous science, mechanics.

But as soon as your ordinance has appeared, as soon as the right hands are cut off or tied up, everything will change face. Twenty, thirty times more embroiderers, washers and ironers, seamstresses and shirt-makers, would not meet the consumption (*honi soit qui mal y pense*) of the kingdom; always assuming that it is invariable, according to our way of reasoning.

It is true that this supposition might be denied by cold-blooded theorists, for dresses and shirts would be dearer. But they say the same thing of the iron which France gets from our mines, compared to the vintage it could get on our hillsides. This argument can, therefore, be no more entertained against *left-handedness* than against *protection;* for this very dearness is the result and the sign of the excess of efforts and of labors, which is precisely the basis on which, in one case, as in the other, we claim to found the prosperity of the working classes.

Yes, we make a touching picture of the prosperity of the sewing business. What movement! What activity! What life! Each dress will busy a hundred fingers instead of ten. No longer will there be an idle young girl, and we need not, Sire, point out to your perspicacity the moral results of this great revolution. Not only will there be more women employed, but each one of them will earn more, for they cannot meet the demand, and if competition still shows itself, it will no longer be among the workingwomen who make the dresses, but the beautiful ladies who wear them.

You see, Sire, that our proposition is not only conformable to the economic traditions of the government, but it is also essentially moral and democratic.

To appreciate its effect, let us suppose it realized; let us transport ourselves in thought into the future; let us imagine the system in action for twenty years. Idleness is banished from the country; ease and concord, contentment and morality, have entered all families together with labor; there is no more misery and no more prostitution. The left hand being very clumsy at its work, there is a superabundance of labor, and the pay is satisfactory. Everything is based on this, and, as a consequence, the workshops are filled. Is it not true, Sire, that if Utopians were to suddenly demand the freedom of the right hand, they would spread alarm throughout the country? Is it not true that this pretended reform would overthrow all existences? Then our system is good, since it cannot be overthrown without causing great distress.

However, we have a sad presentiment that some day (so great is the perversity of man) an association will be organized to secure the liberty of right hands.

It seems to us that we already hear these free-right-handers speak as follows in the Salle Montesquieu:

"People, you believe yourselves richer because they have taken from you one hand; you see but the increase of labor which results to you from it. But look also at the dearness it causes, and the forced decrease in the consumption of all articles. This measure has not made capital, which is the source of wages, more abundant. The waters which flow from this great reservoir are directed into other channels; the quantity is not increased, and the definite result is, for the nation, as a whole, a loss of comfort equal to the excess of the production of several millions of right hands, over several millions of left hands. Then let us form a league, and, at the expense of some inevitable disturbances, let us conquer the right of working with both hands."

Happily, Sire, there will be organized an *association for the defense of left-handed labor*, and the *Sinistrists* will have no trouble in reducing to nothing all these generalities and realities, suppositions and abstractions, reveries and Utopias. They need only to exhume the *Moniteur Industriel* of 1846, and they will find, ready-made, arguments against *free trade*, which destroy so admirably this *liberty of the right hand*, that all that is required is to substitute one word for another.

"The Parisian *Free Trade* League never doubted but that it would have the assistance of the workingmen. But the workingmen can no longer be led by the nose. They have their eyes open, and they know political economy better than our diplomaed professors. *Free trade*, they replied, will take from us our labor, and labor is our real, great, sovereign property; *with labor, with much labor, the price of articles of merchandise is never beyond reach.* But without labor, even if bread should cost but a penny a pound, the workingman is compelled to die of hunger. Now, your doctrines, instead of increasing the amount of labor in France, diminish it; that is to say, you reduce us to misery." (Number of October 13, 1846.)

"It is true, that when there are too many manufactured articles to sell, their price falls; but as wages decrease when these articles sink in value, the result is, that, instead of being able to buy them, we can buy nothing. Thus, when they are cheapest, the workingman is most unhappy." (Gauthier de Rumilly, *Moniteur Industriel* of November 17.)

It would not be ill for the Sinistrists to mingle some threats with their beautiful theories. This is a sample:

"What! to desire to substitute the labor of the right hand for that of the left, and thus to cause a forced reduction, if not an annihilation of wages, the sole resource of almost the entire nation!

"And this at the moment when poor harvests already impose painful sacrifices on the workingman, disquiet him as to his future, and make him more accessible to bad counsels and ready to abandon the wise course of conduct he had hitherto adhered to!"

We are confident, Sire, that thanks to such wise reasonings, if a struggle takes place, the left hand will come out of it victorious.

Perhaps, also, an association will be formed in order to ascertain whether the right and the left hand are not both wrong, and if there is not a third hand between them, in order to conciliate all.

After having described the *Dexterists* as seduced by the *apparent liberality of a principle, the correctness of which has not yet been verified by experience*, and the *Sinistrists* as encamping in the positions they have gained, it will say:

"And yet they deny that there is a third course to pursue in the midst of the conflict; and they do not see that the working classes have to defend themselves, at the same moment, against those who wish to change nothing in the present situation, because they find their advantage in it, and against those who dream of an economic revolution of which they have calculated neither the extent nor the significance." (*National* of October 16.)

We do not desire, however, to hide from your Majesty the fact that our plan has a vulnerable side. They may say to us: In twenty years all left hands will be as skilled as right ones are now, and you can no longer count on *left-handedness* to increase the national labor.

We reply to this, that, according to learned physicians, the left side of the body has a natural weakness, which is very reassuring for the future of labor.

Finally, Sire, consent to sign the law, and a great principle will have prevailed: *All wealth comes from the intensity of labor.* It will be easy for us to extend it, and vary its application. We will declare, for instance, that it shall be allowable to work only with the feet. This is no more impossible (for there have been instances) than to extract iron from the mud of the Seine. There have even been men who wrote with their backs. You see, Sire, that we do not lack means of increasing national labor. If they do begin to fail us, there remains the boundless resource of amputation.

If this report, Sire, was not intended for publication, we would call your attention to the great influence which systems analogous to the one we submit to you, are capable of giving to men in power. But this is a subject which we reserve for consideration in private counsel.

XVII.

SUPREMACY BY LABOR.

"As in a time of war, supremacy is attained by superiority in arms, can, in a time of peace, supremacy be secured by superiority in labor?"

This question is of the greatest interest at a time when no one seems to doubt that in the field of industry, as on that of battle, *the stronger crushes the weaker*.

This must result from the discovery of some sad and discouraging analogy between labor, which exercises itself on things, and violence, which exercises itself on men; for how could these two things be identical in their effects, if they were opposed in their nature?

And if it is true that in manufacturing as in war, supremacy is the necessary result of superiority, why need we occupy ourselves with progress or social economy, since we are in a world where all has been so arranged by Providence that one and the same result, oppression, necessarily flows from the most antagonistic principles?

Referring to the new policy toward which commercial freedom is drawing England, many persons make this objection, which, I admit, occupies the sincerest minds. "Is England doing anything more than pursuing the same end by different means? Does she not constantly aspire to universal supremacy? Sure of the superiority of her capital and labor, does she not call in free competition to stifle the industry of the continent, reign as a sovereign, and conquer the privilege of feeding and clothing the ruined peoples?"

It would be easy for me to demonstrate that these alarms are chimerical; that our pretended inferiority is greatly exaggerated; that all our great branches of industry not only resist foreign competition, but develop themselves under its influence, and that its infallible effect is to bring about an increase in general consumption capable of absorbing both foreign and domestic products.

To-day I desire to attack this objection directly, leaving it all its power and the advantage of the ground it has chosen. Putting English and French on one side, I will try to find out in a general way, if, even though by superiority in one branch of industry, one nation has crushed out similar iudustrial pursuits in another one, this nation has made a step toward supremacy, and that one toward dependence; in other words, if both do not gain by the operation, and if the conquered do not gain the most by it.

If we see in any product but a cause of labor, it is certain that the alarm of the protectionists is well founded. If we consider iron, for instance, only in connection with the masters of forges, it might be feared that the competition of a country where iron was a gratuitous gift of nature, would extinguish the furnaces of another country, where ore and fuel were scarce.

But is this a complete view of the subject? Are there relations only between iron and those who make it? Has it none with those who use it? Is its definite and only destination to be produced? And if it is useful, not on account of the labor which it causes, but on account of the qualities which it possesses, and the numerous services for which its hardness and malleability fit it, does it not follow that foreigners cannot reduce its price, even so far as to prevent its production among us, without doing us more good, under the last statement of the case, than it injures us, under the first?

Please consider well that there are many things which foreigners, owing to the natural advantages which surround them, hinder us from producing directly, and in regard to which we are placed, *in reality*, in the hypothetical position which we examined relative to iron. We produce at home neither tea, coffee, gold nor silver. Does it follow that our labor, as a whole, is thereby diminished? No; only to create the equivalent of these things, to acquire them by way of exchange, we detach from our general labor a *smaller* portion than we would require to produce them ourselves. More remains to us to use for other things. We are so much the richer and stronger. All that external rivalry can do, even in cases where it absolutely keeps us from any certain form of labor, is to encourage our labor, and increase our productive power. Is that the road to *supremacy*, for foreigners?

If a mine of gold were to be discovered in France, it does not follow that it would be for our interests to work it. It is even certain that the enterprise ought to be neglected, if each ounce of gold absorbed more of our labor than an ounce of gold bought in Mexico with cloth. In this case, it would be better to keep on seeing our mines in our manufactories. What is true of gold is true of iron.

The illusion comes from the fact that one thing is not seen. That is, that foreign superiority prevents national labor, only under some certain form, and makes it superfluous under this form, but by putting at our disposal the very result of the labor thus annihilated. If men lived in diving-bells, under the water, and had to provide themselves with air by the use of pumps, there would be an immense source of labor. To destroy this labor, *leaving men in this condition*, would be to do them a terrible injury. But if labor ceases, because the necessity for it has gone; because men are placed in another position, where air reaches their lungs without an effort, then the loss of this labor is not to be regretted, except in the eyes of those who appreciate in labor, only the labor itself.

It is exactly this sort of labor which machines, commercial freedom, and progress of all sorts, gradually annihilate; not useful labor, but labor which has become superfluous, supernumerary, objectless, and without result. On the other hand, protection restores it to activity; it replaces us under the water, so as to give us an opportunity of pumping; it forces us to ask for gold from the inaccessible national mine, rather than from our national manufactories. All its effect is summed up in this phrase—*loss of power.*

It must be understood that I speak here of general effects, and not of the temporary disturbances occasioned by the transition from a bad to a good system. A momentary disarrangement necessarily accompanies all progress. This may be a reason for making the transition a gentle one, but not for systematically interdicting all progress, and still less for misunderstanding it.

They represent industry to us as a conflict. This is not true; or is true only when you confine yourself to considering each branch of industry in its effects on some similar branch—in isolating both, in the mind, from the rest of humanity. But there is something else; there are its effects on consumption, and the general well-being.

This is the reason why it is not allowable to assimilate labor to war as they do.

In war, *the strongest overwhelms the weakest.*

In labor, *the strongest gives strength to the weakest.* This radically destroys the analogy.

Though the English are strong and skilled; possess immense invested capital, and have at their disposal the two great powers of production, iron and fire, all this is converted into the *cheapness* of the product; and who gains by the cheapness of the product?—he who buys it.

It is not in their power to absolutely annihilate any portion of our labor. All that they can do is to make it superfluous through some result acquired

—to give air at the same time that they suppress the pump; to increase thus the force at our disposal, and, which is a remarkable thing, to render their pretended supremacy more impossible, as thei: superiority becomes more undeniable.

Thus, by a rigorous and consoling demonstration, we reach this conclusion: That *labor* and *violence*, so opposed in their nature, are, whatever socialists and protectionists may say, no less so in their effects.

All we required, to do that, was to distinguish between *annihilated* labor and *economized* labor.

Having less iron *because* one works less, or having more iron *although* one works less, are things which are more than different,—they are opposites. The protectionists confound them; we do not. That is all.

Be convinced of one thing. If the English bring into play much activity, labor, capital, intelligence, and natural force, it is not for the love of us. It is to give themselves many comforts in exchange for their products. They certainly desire to receive at least as much as they give, and *they make at home the payment for that which they buy elsewhere.* If then, they inundate us with their products, it is because they expect to be inundated with ours. In this case, the best way to have much for ourselves is to be free to choose between these two methods of production: direct production or indirect production. All the British Machiavelism cannot lead us to make a bad choice.

Let us then stop assimilating industrial competition with war; a false assimilation, which is specious only when two rival branches of industry are isolated, in order to judge of the effects of competition. As soon as the effect produced on the general well-being is taken into consideration, the analogy disappears.

In a battle, he who is killed is thoroughly killed, and the army is weakened just that much. In manufactures, one manufactory succumbs only so far as the total of national labor replaces what it produced, *with an excess.* Imagine a state of affairs where for one man, stretched on the plain, two spring up full of force and vigor. If there is a planet where such things happen, it must be admitted that war is carried on there under conditions so different from those which obtain here below, that it does not even deserve that name.

Now, this is the distinguishing character of what they have so inappropriately called an *industrial war.*

Let the Belgians and English reduce the price of their iron, if they can, and keep on reducing it, until they bring it down to nothing. They may thereby put out one of our furnaces—kill one of our soldiers; but I defy them to hinder a thousand other industries, more profitable than the disabled one, immediately, and, as a necessary consequence of this very cheapness, resuscitating and developing themselves.

Let us decide that supremacy by labor is impossible and contradictory, since all superiority which manifests itself among a people is converted into cheapness, and results only in giving force to all others. Let us, then, banish from political economy all these expressions borrowed from the vocabulary cf battles: *to struggle with equal arms, to conquer, to crush out, to stifle, to be beaten, invasion, tribute.* What do these words mean? Squeeze them, and nothing comes out of them. We are mistaken; there come from them absurd errors and fatal prejudices. These are the words which stop the blending of peoples, their peaceful, universal, indissoluble alliance, and the progress of humanity.

PART III.

SPOLIATION AND LAW.*

To the Protectionists of the General Council of Manufactures:

GENTLEMEN—Let us for a few moments inter change moderate and friendly opinions.

You are not willing that political economy should believe and teach free trade.

This is as though you were to say, "We are not willing that political economy should occupy itself with society, exchange, value, law, justice, property.

* On the 27th of April, 1850, after a very curious discussion, which was reproduced in the *Moniteur*, the General Council of Agriculture, Manufactures and Commerce issued the following order:

"Political economy shall be taught by the government professors, not merely from the theoretical point of view of free trade, but also with special regard to the facts and legislation which control French industry."

It was in reply to this decree that Bastiat wrote the pamphlet *Spoliation and Law*, which first appeared in the *Journal des Economistes*, May 15, 1850.

We recognize only two principles—oppression and spoliation."

Can you possibly conceive of political economy without society? Or of society without exchange? Or of exchange without a relative value between the two articles, or the two services, exchanged? Can you possibly conceive the idea of *value*, except as the result of the *free* consent of the exchangers? Can you conceive of one product being *worth* another, if, in the barter, one of the parties is not *free?* Is it possible for you to conceive of the free consent of two parties without liberty? Can you possibly conceive that one of the contracting parties is deprived of his liberty unless he is oppressed by the other? Can you possibly conceive of an exchange between an oppressor and one oppressed, unless the equivalence of the services is altered, or unless, as a consequence, law, justice, and the rights of property have been violated?

What do you really want? Answer frankly.

You are not willing that trade should be free!

You desire, then, that it shall not be free? You desire, then, that trade shall be carried on under the influence of oppression? For if it is not carried on under the influence of oppression, it will be carried on under the influence of liberty, and that is what you do not desire.

Admit, then, that it is law and justice which embarrass you; that that which troubles you is property—not your own, to be sure, but another's. You are altogether unwilling to allow others to freely dispose of their own property (the essential condition of ownership); but you well understand how to dispose of your own—and of theirs.

And, accordingly, you ask the political economists to arrange this mass of absurdities and monstrosities in a definite and well-ordered system; to establish, in accordance with your practice, the theory of spoliation.

But they will never do it; for, in their eyes, spoliation is a principle of hatred and disorder, and the most particularly odious form which it can assume is *the legal form.*

And here, Mr. Benoit d' Azy, I take you to task. You are moderate, impartial, and generous. You are willing to sacrifice your interests and your fortune. This you constantly declare. Recently, in the General Council, you said: "If the rich had only to abandon their wealth to make the people rich we should all be ready to do it." [Hear, hear. It is true.] And yesterday, in the National Assembly, you said: "If I believed that it was in my power to give to the workingmen all the work they need, I would give all I possess to realize this blessing. Unfortunately, it is impossible."

Although it pains you that the sacrifice is so useless that it should not be made, and you exclaim, with Basile, "Money! money! I detest it—but I will keep it," assuredly no one will question a generosity so retentive, however barren. It is a virtue which loves to envelop itself in a veil of modesty, especially when it is purely latent and negative, As for you, you will lose no opportunity to proclaim it in the ears of all France from the tribune of the *Luxembourg* and the *Palais Legislatif.*

But no one desires you to abandon your fortune, and I admit that it would not solve the social problem.

You wish to be generous, but cannot. I only venture to ask that you will be just. Keep your fortune, but permit me also to keep mine. Respect my property as I respect yours. Is this too bold a request on my part?

Suppose we lived in a country under a free trade *regime*, where every one could dispose of his property and his labor at pleasure. Does this make your hair stand? Reassure yourself, this is only an hypothesis.

One would then be as free as the other. There would, indeed, be a law in the code, but this law, impartial and just, would not infringe our liberty, but would guarantee it, and it would take effect only when we sought to oppress each other. There would be officers of the law, magistrates and police; but they would only execute the law. Under such a state of affairs, suppose that you owned an iron foundry, and that I was a hatter. I should need iron for my business. Naturally I should seek to solve this problem: "How shall I best procure the iron necessary for my business with the least possible amount of labor?" Considering my situation, and my means of knowledge, I should discover that the best thing for me to do would be to make hats, and sell them to a Belgian who would give me iron in exchange.

But you, being the owner of an iron foundry, and considering my case, would say to yourself: "I shall be obliged to *compel* that fellow to come to my shop."

You, accordingly, take your sword and pistols, and, arming your numerous retinue, proceed to the frontier, and, at the moment I am engaged in making my trade, you cry out to me: "Stop that, or I will blow your brains out!" "But, my lord, I am in need of iron." "I have it to sell." "But, sir, you ask too much for it." "I have my reasons for that." "But, my good sir, I also have my reasons for preferring cheaper iron." "Well, we shall see who shall decide between your reasons and mine! Soldiers, advance!"

In short, you forbid the entry of the Belgian iron, and prevent the export of my hats.

Under the condition of things which we have supposed (that is, under a *regime* of liberty), you cannot deny that that would be, on your part, manifestly an act of oppression and spoliation.

Accordingly, I should resort to the law, the magistrate, and the power of the government. They would intervene. You would be tried, condemned, and justly punished.

But this circumstance would suggest to you a bright idea. You would say to yourself: "I have been very simple to give myself so much trouble. What! place myself in a position where I must kill some one, or be killed! degrade myself! put my domestics under arms! incur heavy expenses! give myself the character of a robber, and render myself liable to the laws of the country! And all this in order to compel a miserable hatter to come to my foundry to buy iron at my price! What if I should make the interest of the law, of the magistrate, of the public authorities, my interests? What if I could get them to perform the odious act on the frontier which I was about to do myself?"

Enchanted by this pleasing prospect, you secure a nomination to the Chambers, and obtain the passage of a law conceived in the following terms:

SECTION 1. There shall be a tax levied upon everybody (but especially upon that cursed hatmaker).

SEC. 2. The proceeds of this tax shall be applied to the payment of men to guard the frontier in the interest of iron-founders.

SEC. 3. It shall be their duty to prevent the exchange of hats or other articles of merchandise with the Belgians for iron.

SEC. 4. The ministers of the government, the prosecuting attorneys, jailers, customs officers, and all officials, are entrusted with the execution of this law.

I admit, sir, that in this form robbery would be far more lucrative, more agreeable, and less perilous than under the arrangements which you had at first determined upon. I admit that for you it would offer a very pleasant prospect. You could most assuredly laugh in your sleeve, for you would then have saddled all the expenses upon me.

But I affirm that you would have introduced into society a vicious principle, a principle of immorality, of disorder, of hatred, and of incessant revolutions; that you would have prepared the way for all the various schemes of socialism and communism.

You, doubtless, find my hypothesis a very bold one. Well, then, let us reverse the case. I consent for the sake of the demonstration.

Suppose that I am a laborer and you an iron-founder.

It would be a great advantage to me to buy hatchets cheap, and even to get them for nothing. And I know that there are hatchets and saws in your establishment. Accordingly, without any ceremony, I enter your warehouse and seize everything that I can lay my hands upon.

But, in the exercise of your legitimate right of

self-defense, you at first resist force with force; afterwards, invoking the power of the law, the magistrate, and the constables, you throw me into prison—and you do well.

Oh! ho! the thought suggests itself to me that I have been very awkward in this business. When a person wishes to enjoy the property of other people, he will, unless he is a fool, act *in accordance* with the law, and not *in violation* of it. Consequently, just as you have made yourself a protectionist, I will make myself a socialist. Since you have laid claim to the *right to profit*, I claim the *right to labor*, or to the instruments of labor.

For the rest, I read my Louis Blanc in prison, and I know by heart this doctrine: "In order to disenthrall themselves, the common people have need of tools to work with; it is the function of the government to provide them." And again: "If one admits that; in order to be really free, a man requires the ability to exercise and to develop his faculties, the result is that society owes each of its members instruction, without which the human mind is incapable of development, and the instruments of labor, without which human activities have no field for their exercise. But by what means can society give to each one of its members the necessary instruction and the necessary instruments of labor, except by the intervention of the State?" So that if it becomes necessary to revolutionize the country, I also will force my way into the halls of legislation. I also will pervert the law, and make it perform in my behalf and at your expense the very act for which it just now punished me.

My decree is modeled after yours:

SECTION 1. There shall be taxes levied upon every citizen, and especially upon iron founders.

SEC. 2. The proceeds of this tax shall be applied to the creation of armed corps, to which the title of the *fraternal constabulary* shall be given.

SEC. 3. It shall be the duty of the *fraternal constabulary* to make their way into the warehouses of hatchets, saws, etc., to take possession of these tools, and to distribute them to such workingmen as may desire them.

Thanks to this ingenious device, you see, my lord, that I shall no longer be obliged to bear the risks, the costs, the odium, or the scruples of robbery. The State will rob for me as it has for you. We shall both be playing the same game.

It remains to be seen what would be the condition of French society on the realization of my second hypothesis, or what, at least, is the condition of it after the almost complete realization of the first hypothesis. I do not desire to discuss here the economy of the question. It is generally believed that in advocating free trade we are exclusively influenced by the desire to allow capital and labor to take the direction most advantageous to them. This is an error. This consideration is merely secondary. That which wounds, afflicts, and is revolting to us in the protective system, is the denial of right, of justice, of property; it is the fact that the system turns the law against justice and against property, when it ought to protect them; it is that it undermines and perverts the very conditions of society. And to the question in this aspect I invite your most serious consideration.

What is law, or at least what ought it to be? What is its rational and moral mission? Is it not to hold the balance even between all rights, all liberties, and all property? Is it not to cause justice to rule among all? Is it not to prevent and to repress oppression and robbery wherever they are found?

And are you not shocked at the immense, radical, and deplorable innovation introduced into the world by compelling the law itself to commit the very crimes to punish which is its especial mission —by turning the law in principle and in fact against liberty and property?

You deplore the condition of modern society. You groan over the disorder which prevails in institutions and ideas. But is it not your system which has perverted everything, both institutions and ideas?

What! the law is no longer the refuge of the oppressed, but the arm of the oppressor! The law is no longer a shield, but a sword! The law no longer holds in her august hands a scale, but false weights and measures! And you wish to have society well regulated!

Your system has written over the entrance of the legislative halls these words: "Whoever acquires any influence here can obtain his share of the legalized pillage."

And what has been the result? All classes of society have become demoralized by shouting around the gates of the palace: "Gave me a share of the spoils."

After the revolution of February, when universal suffrage was proclaimed, I had for a moment hoped to have heard this sentiment: "No more pillage for any one, justice for all." And that would have been the real solution of the social problem. Such was not the case. The doctrine of protection had for generations too profoundly corrupted the age, public sentiments and ideas. No. In making inroads upon the National Assembly, each class, in accordance with your system, has endeavored to make the law an instrument of rapine. There have been demanded heavier imposts, gratuitous credit, the right to employment, the right to assistance, the guaranty of incomes and of minimum wages, gratuitous instruction, loans to industry, etc., etc.; in short, every one has endeavored to live and thrive at the expense of others. And upon what have these pretensions been based? Upon the authority of your precedents. What sophisms have been invoked? Those that you have propagated for two centuries. With you they have talked about *equalizing the conditions of labor.* With you they have declaimed against ruinous competition. With you they have ridiculed the *let alone* principle, that is to say, *liberty.* With you they have said that the law should not confine itself to being just, but should come to the aid of suffering industries, protect the feeble against the strong, secure profits to individuals at the expense of the community, etc., etc. In short, according to the expression of Mr. Charles Dupin, socialism has come to establish the theory of robbery. It has done what you have done, and that which you desire the professors of political economy to do for you.

Your cleverness is in vain, *Messieurs Protectionists,* it is useless to lower your tone, to boast of your latent generosity, or to deceive your opponents by sentiment. You cannot prevent logic from being logic.

You cannot prevent Mr. Billault from telling the legislators, "You have granted favors to one, you must grant them to all."

You cannot prevent Mr. Cremieux from telling

the legislators: "You have enriched the manufacturers, you must enrich the common people."

You cannot prevent Mr. Nadeau from saying to the legislators: "You cannot refuse to do for the suffering classes that which you have done for the privileged classes."

You cannot even prevent the leader of your orchestra, Mr. Mimerel, from saying to the legislators: "I demand twenty-five thousand subsidies for the workingmen's savings banks;" and supporting his motion in this manner:

"Is this the first example of the kind that our legislation offers? Would you establish the system that the State should encourage everything, open at its expense courses of scientific lectures, subsidize the fine arts, pension the theatre, give to the classes already favored by fortune the benefits of superior education, the most varied amusements, the enjoyment of the arts, and repose for old age; give all this to those who know nothing of privations, and compel those who have no share in these benefits to bear their part of the burden, while refusing them everything, even the necessaries of life?

"Gentlemen, our French society, our customs, our laws, are so made that the intervention of the State, however much it may be regretted, is seen everywhere, and nothing seems to be stable or durable if the hand of the State is not manifest in it. It is the State that makes the Sevres porcelain, and the Gobelin tapestry. It is the State that periodically gives expositions of the works of our artists, and of the products of our manufacturers; it is the State which recompenses those who raise its cattle and breed its fish. All this costs a great deal. It is a tax to which every one is obliged to contribute. Everybody, do you understand? And what direct benefit do the people derive from it? Of what direct benefit to the people are your porcelains and tapestries, and your expositions? This general principle of resisting what you call a state of enthusiasm we can understand, although you yesterday voted a bounty for linens; we can understand it on the condition of consulting the present crisis, and especially on the condition of your proving your impartiality. If it is true that, by the means I have indicated, the State thus far seems to have more directly benefited the well-to-do classes than those who are poorer, it is necessary that this appearance should be removed. Shall it be done by closing the manufactories of tapestry and stopping the exhibitions? Assuredly not; *but by giving the poor a direct share in this distribution of benefits.*"

In this long catalogue of favors granted to some at the expense of all, one will remark the extreme prudence with which Mr. Mimerel has left the tariff favors out of sight, although they are the most explicit manifestations of legal spoliation. All the orators who supported or opposed him have taken upon themselves the same reserve. It is very shrewd! Possibly they hope, *by giving the poor a direct participation in this distribution of benefits*, to save this great iniquity by which they profit, but of which they do not whisper.

They deceive themselves. Do they suppose that after having realized a partial spoliation by the establishment of customs duties, other classes, by the establishment of other institutions, will not attempt to realize universal spoliation?

I know very well you always have a sophism ready. You say: "The favors which the law grants us are not given to the *manufacturer*, but to *manufactures.* The profits which it enables us to receive at the expense of the consumers are merely a trust placed in our hands. They enrich us, it is true, but our wealth places us in a position to expend more, to extend our establishments, and falls like refreshing dew upon the laboring classes."

Such is your language, and what I most lament is the circumstance that your miserable sophisms have so perverted public opinion that they are appealed to in support of all forms of legalized spoliation. The suffering classes also say . "Let us by act of the Legislature help ourselves to the goods of others. We shall be in easier circumstances as the result of it; we shall buy more wheat, more meat, more cloth, and more iron; and that which we receive from the public taxes will return in a beneficent shower to the capitalists and landed proprietors."

But, as I have already said, I will not to-day discuss the economical effects of legal spoliation. Whenever the protectionists desire, they will find me ready to examine the *sophisms of the ricochets,* which, indeed, may be invoked in support of all species of robbery and fraud.

We will confine ourselves to the political and moral effects of exchange legally deprived of liberty.

I have said: The time has come to know what the law is, and what it ought to be.

If you make the law for all citizens a palladium of liberty and of property; if it is only the organization of the individual law of self-defense, you will establish, upon the foundation of justice, a government rational, simple, economical, comprehended by all, loved by all, useful to all, supported by all, entrusted with a responsibility perfectly defined and carefully restricted, and endowed with imperishable strength. If, on the other hand, in the interests of individuals or of classes, you make the law an instrument of robbery, every one will wish to make laws, and to make them to his own advantage. There will be a riotous crowd at the doors of the legislative halls, there will be a bitter conflict within; minds will be in anarchy, morals will be shipwrecked; there will be violence in party organs, heated elections, accusations, recriminations, jealousies, inextinguishable hates, the public forces placed at the service of rapacity instead of repressing it, the ability to distinguish the true from the false effaced from all minds, as the notion of justice and injustice will be obliterated from all consciences, the government responsible for everything and bending under the burden of its responsibilities, political convulsions, revolutions without end, ruins over which all forms of socialism and communism attempt to establish themselves; these are the evils which must necessarily flow from the perversion of law.

Such, consequently, gentlemen, are the evils for which you have prepared the way by making use of the law to destroy freedom of exchange; that is to say, to abolish the right of property. Do not declaim against socialism; you establish it.. Do not cry out against communism; you create it. And now you ask us Economists to make you a theory which will justify you! *Morbleu!* make it yourselves.

PART IV.

CAPITAL AND INTEREST.

My object in this treatise is to examine into the real nature of the Interest of Capital, for the purpose of proving that it is lawful, and explaining why it should be perpetual. This may appear singular, and yet, I confess, I am more afraid of being too plain than too obscure. I am afraid I may weary the reader by a series of mere truisms. But it is no easy matter to avoid this danger, when the facts, with which we have to deal, are known to every one by personal, familiar, and daily experience.

But, then, you will say, "What is the use of this treatise? Why explain what everybody knows?"

But, although this problem appears at first sight so very simple, there is more in it than you might suppose. I shall endeavor to prove this by an example. Mondor lends an instrument of labor to-day, which will be entirely destroyed in a week, yet the capital will not produce the less interest to Mondor or his heirs, through all eternity. Reader, can you honestly say that you understand the reason of this?

It would be a waste of time to seek any satisfactory explanation from the writings of economists. They have not thrown much light upon the reasons of the existence of interest. For this they are not to be blamed; for at the time they wrote, its lawfulness was not called in question. Now, however, times are altered; the case is different. Men, who consider themselves to be in advance of their age, have organized an active crusade against capital and interest; it is the productiveness of capital which they are attacking; not certain abuses in the administration of it, but the principle itself.

A journal has been established to serve as a vehicle for this crusade. It is conducted by M. Proudhon, and has, it is said, an immense circulation. The first number of this periodical contains the electoral manifesto of the *people.* Here we read, "The productiveness of capital, which is condemned by Christianity under the name of usury, is the true cause of misery, the true principle of destitution, the eternal obstacle to the establishment of the Republic."

Another journal, *La Ruche Populaire*, after having said some excellent things on labor, adds, "But, above all, labor ought to be free; that is, it ought to be organized in such a manner, *that money lenders and patrons, or masters, should not be paid* for this liberty of labor, this right of labor, which is raised to so high a price by the trafficers of men." The only thought that I notice here, is that expressed by the words in italics, which imply a denial of the right to interest. The remainder of the article explains it.

It is thus that the democratic Socialist, Thore, expresses himself:

"The revolution will always have to be recommenced, so long as we occupy ourselves with consequences only, without having the logic or the courage to attack the principle itself. This priciple is capital, false property, interest, and usury, which by the old *régime*, is made to weigh upon labor.

"Ever since the aristocrats invented the incredible fiction, *that capital possesses the power of reproducing itself*, the workers have been at the mercy of the idle.

"At the end of a year, will you find an additional crown in a bag of one hundred shillings? At the end of fourteen years, will your shillings have doubled in your bag?

"Will a work of industry or of skill produce another, at the end of fourteen years?

"Let us begin, then, by demolishing this fatal fiction."

I have quoted the above, merely for the sake of establishing the fact, that many persons consider the productiveness of capital a false, a fatal, and an iniquitous principle. But quotations are superfluous; it is well known that the people attribute their sufferings to what they call *the trafficing in man by man.* In fact, the phrase *tyranny of capital* has become proverbial.

I believe there is not a man in the world, who is aware of the whole importance of this question:

"Is the interest of capital natural, just, and lawful, and as useful to the payer as to the receiver?"

You answer, no; I answer, yes. Then we differ entirely; but it is of the utmost importance to discover which of us is in the right; otherwise we shall incur the danger of making a false solution of the question, a matter of opinion. If the error is on my side, however, the evil would not be so great. It must be inferred that I know nothing about the true interests of the masses, or the march of human progress; and that all my arguments are but as so many grains of sand, by which the car of the revolution will certainly not be arrested.

But if, on the contrary, MM. Proudhon and Thoré are deceiving themselves, it follows, that they are leading the people astray—that they are showing them the evil where it does not exist; and thus giving a false direction to their ideas, to their antipathies, to their dislikes, and to their attacks. It follows, that the misguided people are rushing into a horrible and absurd struggle, in which victory would be more fatal than defeat, since, according to this supposition, the result would be the realization of universal evils, the destruction of every means of emancipation, the consummation of its own misery.

This is just what M. Proudhon has acknowledged, with perfect good faith. "The foundation stone," he told me, "of my system is the *gratuitousness of credit.* If I am mistaken in this, Socialism is a vain dream." I add, it is a dream, in which the people are tearing themselves to pieces. Will it, therefore, be a cause for surprise, if, when they awake, they find themselves mangled and bleeding? Such a danger as this is enough to justify me fully, if, in the course of the discussion, I allow myself to be led into some trivialities and some prolixity.

CAPITAL AND INTEREST.

I address this treatise to the workmen of Paris, more especially to those who have enrolled themselves under the banner of Socialist democracy. I proceed to consider these two questions:

1st. Is it consistent with the nature of things, and with justice, that capital should produce interest?

2nd. Is it consistent with the nature of things, and with justice, that the interest of capital should be perpetual?

The working men of Paris will certainly acknowledge that a more important subject could not be discussed.

Since the world began, it has been allowed, at least in part, that capital ought to produce interest. But latterly it has been affirmed, that herein lies the very social error which is the cause of pauperism and inequality. It is, therefore, very essential to know now on what ground we stand.

For if levying interest from capital is a sin, the workers have a right to revolt against social order, as it exists; it is in vain to tell them that they ought to have recourse to legal and pacific means, it would be a hypocritical recommendation. When on the one side there is a strong man, poor, and a victim of robbery—on the other, a weak man, but rich, and a robber—it is singular enough, that we should say to the former, with a hope of persuading him, "Wait till your oppressor voluntarily renounces oppression, or till it shall cease of itself." This cannot be; and those who tell us that capital is, by nature, unproductive, ought to know that they are provoking a terrible and immediate struggle.

If, on the contrary, the interest of capital is natural, lawful, consistent with the general good, as favorable to the borrower as to the lender, the economists who deny it, the tribunes who traffic in this pretended social wound, are leading the workmen into a senseless and unjust struggle, which can have no other issue than the misfortune of all. In fact, they are arming labor against capital. So much the better, if these two powers are really antagonistic; and may the struggle soon be ended! But if they are in harmony, the struggle is the greatest evil which can be inflicted on society. You see, then, workmen, that there is not a more important question than this: "Is the interest of capital lawful or not?" In the former case, you must immediately renounce the struggle to which you are being urged; in the second, you must carry it on bravely, and to the end.

Productiveness of capital—perpetuity of interest. These are difficult questions. I must endeavor to make myself clear. And for that purpose I shall have recourse to example rather than to demonstration; or rather, I shall place the demonstration in the example. I begin by acknowledging, that, at first sight, it may appear strange that capital should pretend to a remuneration; and, above all, to a perpetual remuneration. You will say, "Here are two men. One of them works from morning till night, from one year's end to another; and if he consumes all which he has gained, even by superior energy, he remains poor. When Christmas comes, he is no forwarder than he was at the beginning of the year, and has no other prospect but to begin again. The other man does nothing, either with his hands or his head; or, at least, if he makes use of them at all, it is only for his own pleasure; it is allowable for him to do nothing, for he has an income. He does not work, yet he lives well; he has everything in abundance, delicate dishes, sumptuous furniture, elegant equipages; nay, he even consumes, daily, things which the workers have been obliged to produce by the sweat of their brow; for these things do not make themselves; and, as far as he is concerned, he has had no hand in their production. It is the workmen who have caused this corn to grow, polished this furniture, woven these carpets; it is our wives and daughters who have spun, cut out, sewed, and embroidered these stuffs. We work, then, for him and ourselves; for him first, and then for ourselves, if there is anything left. But here is something more striking still. If the former of these two men, the worker, consumes within the year any profit which may have been left him in that year, he is always at the point from which he started, and his destiny condemns him to move incessantly in a perpetual circle, and a monotony of exertion. Labor, then, is rewarded only once. But if the other, the 'gentleman,' consumes his yearly income in the year, he has, the year after, in those which follow, and through all eternity, an income always equal, inexhaustible, *perpetual.* Capital, then, is remunerated, not only once or twice, but an indefinite number of times! So that, at the end of a hundred years, a family, which has placed 20,000 francs, at five per cent., will have had 100,000 francs; and this will not prevent it from having 100,000 more, in the following century. In other words, for 20,000 francs, which represent its labor, it will have levied, in two centuries, a tenfold value on the labor of others. In this social arrangement, is there not a monstrous evil to be reformed? And this is not all. If it should please this family to curtail its enjoyments a little—to spend, for example, only 900 francs, instead of 1,000—it may, without any labor, without any other trouble beyond that of investing 100 francs a year, increase its capital and its income in such rapid progression, that it will soon be in a position to consume as much as a hundred families of industrious workmen. Does not all this go to prove, that society itself has in its bosom a hideous cancer, which ought to be eradicated at the risk of some temporary suffering?"

These are, it appears to me, the sad and irritating reflections which must be excited in your minds by the active and superficial crusade which is being carried on against capital and interest. On the other hand, there are moments in which, I am convinced, doubts are awakened in your minds, and scruples in your conscience. You say to yourselves sometimes, "But to assert that capital ought not to produce interest, is to say that he who has created instruments of labor, or materials, or provisions of any kind, ought to yield them up without compensation. Is that just? And then, if it is so, who would lend these instruments, these materials, these provisions? who would take care of them? who even would create them? Every one would consume his proportion, and the human race would never advance a step. Capital would be no longer formed, since there would be no interest in forming it. It will become exceedingly scarce. A singular step toward gratuitous loans! A singular means of improving the condition of borrowers, to make it impossible for them to borrow at any price! What would become of labor itself? for there will be no money advanced, and not one single kind of labor can be mentioned, not even the chase, which can be pursued without money in hand. And, as for ourselves, what would become of us? What! we are not to be allowed to borrow, in order to work in the prime of life, nor to lend, that we may enjoy repose in its decline? The law will rob us of the prospect of laying by a little property, because it will prevent us from gaining any advantage from it. It will deprive us of all stimulus to save at the present time, and of all hope of repose for the future. It is useless to exhaust ourselves with fatigue; we must abandon the idea of leaving our sons and daughters a little property, since modern science renders it useless, for we should become trafficers in men if we were to lend it on interest. Alas! the world which these persons would open before us as an imaginary good, is still more dreary and desolate than that which they condemn, for hope, at any rate, is not banished from the latter." Thus in all respects, and in every point of view, the question is a serious one. Let us hasten to arrive at a solution.

Our civil code has a chapter entitled, "On the manner of transmitting property." I do not think it gives a very complete nomenclature on this point. When a man by his labor has made some useful thing—in other words, when he has created a *value*—it can only pass into the hands of another by one of the following modes: as a gift, by the right of inheritance, by exchange, loan, or theft. One word upon each of these, except the last, although it plays a greater part in the world than we may think.

A gift, needs no definition. It is essentially voluntary and spontaneous. It depends exclusively upon the giver, and the receiver cannot be said to have any right to it. Without a doubt, morality and religion make it a duty for men, especially the rich, to deprive themselves voluntarily of that which they possess, in favor of their less fortunate brethren. But this is an entirely moral obligation. If it were to be asserted on principle, admitted in practice, or sanctioned by law, that every man has a right to the property of another, the gift would have no merit, charity and gratitude would be no longer virtues. Besides, such a doctrine would suddenly and universally arrest labor and production, as severe cold congeals water and suspends animation, for who would work if there was no longer to be any connection between labor and the satisfying of our wants? Political economy has not treated of gifts. It has hence been concluded that it disowns them, and that it is therefore a science devoid of heart. This is a ridiculous accusation. That science which treats of the laws resulting from the *reciprocity of services*, had no business to inquire into the consequences of generosity with respect to him who receives, nor into its effects, perhaps still more precious, on him who gives; such considerations belong evidently to the science of morals. We must allow the sciences to have limits; above all, we must not accuse them of denying or undervaluing what they look upon as foreign to their department.

The right of inheritance, against which so much has been objected of late, is one of the forms of gift, and assuredly the most natural of all. That which a man has produced, he may consume, ex change, or give; what can be more natural than that he should give it to his children? It is this power, more than any other, which inspires him with courage to labor and to save. Do you know why the principle of right of inheritance is thus called in question? Because it is imagined that the property thus transmitted is plundered from the masses. This is a fatal error; political economy demonstrates, in the most peremptory manner, that all value produced is a creation which does no harm to any person whatever. For that reason, it may be consumed, and, still more, transmitted, without hurting any one; but I shall not pursue these reflections, which do not belong to the subject.

Exchange is the principal department of political economy, because it is by far the most frequent method of transmitting property, according to the free and voluntary agreements of the laws and effects of which this science treats.

Properly speaking, exchange is the reciprocity of services. The parties say between themselves, "Give me this, and I will give you that;" or, "Do this for me, and I will do that for you." It is well to remark (for this will throw a new light on the notion of value), that the second form is always implied in the first. When it is said, "Do this for me, and I will do that for you," an exchange of service for service is proposed. Again, when it is said, "Give me this, and I will give you that," it is the same as saying, "I yield to you what I have done, yield to me what you have done." The labor is past, instead of present; but the exchange is not the less governed by the comparative valuation of the two services; so that it is quite correct to say, that the principle of *value* is in the services rendered and received on account of the productions exchanged, rather than in productions themselves.

In reality, services are scarcely ever exchanged directly. There is a medium, which is termed *money*. Paul has completed a coat, for which he wishes to receive a little bread, a little wine, a little oil, a visit from a doctor, a ticket for the play, etc. The exchange cannot be effected in kind; so what does Paul do? He first exchanges his coat for some money, which is called *sale*; then he exchanges this money again for the things which he wants, which is called *purchase*; and now, only, has the reciprocity of services completed its circuit; now, only, the labor and the compensation are balanced in the same individual,—"I have done this for society, it has done that for me." In a word, it is only now that the exchange is actually accomplished. Thus, nothing can be more correct than this observation of J. B. Say: "Since the introduction of money, every exchange is resolved into two elements, *sale* and *purchase*. It is the reunion of these two elements which renders the exchange complete."

We must remark, also, that the constant appearance of money in every exchange has overturned and misled all our ideas; men have ended in thinking that money was true riches, and that to multiply it was to multiply services and products. Hence the prohibitory system; hence paper money; hence the celebrated aphorism, "What one gains the other loses;" and all the errors which have ruined the earth, and imbrued it with blood.* After much research it has been found, that in order to make the two services exchanged of equivalent value, and in order to render the exchange *equitable*, the best means was to allow it to be free. However plausible, at first sight, the intervention of the State might be, it was soon perceived that it is always oppressive to one or other of the contracting parties. When we look into these subjects, we are always compelled to reason upon this maxim, that *equal value* results from liberty. We have, in fact, no other means of knowing whether, at a given moment, two services are of the same value, but that of examining whether they can be readily and freely exchanged. Allow the State, which is the same thing as force, to interfere on one side or the other, and from that moment all the means of appreciation will be complicated and entangled, instead of becoming clear. It ought to be the part

* This error will be combated in a pamphlet, entitled "*Cursed Money*."

of the State to prevent, and, above all, to repress artifice and fraud; that is, to secure liberty, and not to violate it. I have enlarged a little upon exchange, although loan is my principal object: my excuse is, that I conceive that there is in a loan an actual exchange, an actual service rendered by the lender, and which makes the borrower liable to an equivalent service,—two services, whose comparative value can only be appreciated, like that of all possible services, by freedom. Now, if it is so, the perfect lawfulness of what is called house-rent, farm-rent, interest, will be explained and justified. Let us consider the case of *loan*.

Suppose two men exchange two services or two objects, whose equal value is beyond all dispute. Suppose, for example, Peter says to Paul, "Give me ten sixpences, I will give you a five-shilling piece." We cannot imagine an equal value more unquestionable. When the bargain is made, neither party has any claim upon the other. The exchanged services are equal. Thus it follows, that if one of the parties wishes to introduce into the bargain an additional clause, advantageous to himself, but unfavorable to the other party, he must agree to a second clause, which shall re-establish the equilibrium, and the law of justice. It would be absurd to deny the justice of a second clause of compensation. This granted, we will suppose that Peter, after having said to Paul, "Give me ten sixpences, I will give you a crown," adds, "you shall give me the ten sixpences *now*, and I will give you the crown-piece *in a year;*" it is very evident that this new proposition alters the claims and advantages of the bargain; that it alters the proportion of the two services. Does it not appear plainly enough, in fact, that Peter asks of Paul a new and an additional service; one of a different kind? Is it not as if he had said, "Render me the service of allowing me to use for my profit, for a year, five shillings which belong to you, and which you might have used for yourself"? And what good reason have you to maintain that Paul is bound to render this especial service gratuitously· that he has no right to demand anything more in consequence of this requisition; that the State ought to interfere to force him to submit? Is it not incomprehensible that the economist, who preaches such a doctrine to the people, can reconcile it with his principle of *the reciprocity of services?* Here I have introduced cash; I have been led to do so by a desire to place, side by side, two objects of exchange, of a perfect and indisputable equality of value. I was anxious to be prepared for objections; but, on the other hand, my demonstration would have been more striking still, if I had illustrated my principle by an agreement for exchanging the services or the productions themselves.

Suppose, for example, a house and a vessel of a

value so perfectly equal that their proprietors are disposed to exchange them even-handed, without excess or abatement. In fact, let the bargain be settled by a lawyer. At the moment of each taking possession, the ship-owner says to the citizen, "Very well; the transaction is completed, and nothing can prove its perfect equity better than our free and voluntary consent. Our conditions thus fixed, I shall propose to you a little practical modification. You shall let me have your house to-day, but I shall not put you in possession of my ship for a year; and the reason I make this demand of you is, that, during this year of *delay*, I wish to use the vessel." That we may not be embarrassed by considerations relative to the detorioration of the thing lent, I will suppose the ship-owner to add, "I will engage, at the end of the year, to hand over to you the vessel in the state in which it is today." I ask of every candid man, I ask of M. Proudhon himself, if the citizen has not a right to answer, "The new clause which you propose entirely alters the proportion or the equal value of the exchanged services. By it, I shall be deprived, for the space of a year, both at once of my house and of your vessel. By it, you will make use of both. If, in the absence of this clause, the bargain was just, for the same reason the clause is injurious to me. It stipulates for a loss to me, and a gain to you. You are requiring of me a new service; I have a right to refuse, or to require of you, as a compensation, an equivalent service." If the parties are agreed upon this compensation, the principle of which is incontestable, we can easily distinguish two transactions in one, two exchanges of service in one. First, there is the exchange of the house for the vessel; after this, there is the delay granted by one of the parties, and the compensation correspondent to this delay yielded by the other. These two new services take the generic and abstract names of *credit* and *interest*. But names do not change the nature of things; and I defy any one to dare to maintain that there exists here, when all is done, a service for a service, or a reciprocity of services. To say that one of these services does not challenge the other, to say that the first ought to be rendered gratuitously, without injustice, is to say that injustice consists in the reciprocity of services—that justice consists in one of the parties giving and not receiving, which is a contradiction in terms.

To give an idea of interest and its mechanism, allow me to make use of two or three anecdotes. But, first, I must say a few words upon capital.

There are some persons who imagine that capital is money, and this is precisely the reason why they deny its productiveness; for, as M. Thoré says, crowns are not endowed with the power of reproducing themselves. But it is not true that capital and money are the same thing. Before the discovery of the precious metals, there were capitalists in the world; and I venture to say that at that time, as now, everybody was a capitalist, to a certain extent.

What is capital, then? It is composed of three things:

1st. Of the materials upon which men operate, when these materials have already a value communicated by some human effort, which has bestowed upon them the principle of remuneration—wool, flax, leather, silk, wood, etc.

2nd. Instruments which are used for working—tools, machines, ships, carriages, etc.

3rd. Provisions which are consumed during labor—victuals, stuffs, houses, etc.

Without these things, the labor of man would be unproductive, and almost void; yet these very things have required much work, especially at first. This is the reason that so much value has been attached to the possession of them, and also that it is perfectly lawful to exchange and to sell them, to make a profit of them if used, to gain remuneration from them if lent.

Now for my anecdotes.

THE SACK OF CORN.

Mathurin, in other respects as poor as Job, and obliged to earn his bread by day-labor, became, nevertheless, by some inheritance, the owner of a fine piece of uncultivated land. He was exceedingly anxious to cultivate it. "Alas!" said he, "to make ditches, to raise fences, to break the soil, to clear away the brambles and stones, to plough it, to sow it, might bring me a living in a year or two; but certainly not to-day, or to-morrow. It is impossible to set about farming it, without previously saving some provisions for my subsistence until the harvest; and I know, by experience, that preparatory labor is indispensable, in order to render present labor productive." The good Mathurin was not content with making these reflections. He resolved to work by the day, and to save something from his wages to buy a spade and a sack of corn; without which things, he must give up his fine agricultural projects. He acted so well, was so active and steady, that he soon saw himself in possession of the wished-for sack of corn. "I shall take it to the mill," said he, "and then I shall have enough to live upon till my field is covered with a rich harvest." Just as he was starting, Jerome came to borrow his treasure of him. "If you will lend me this sack of corn," said Jerome, "you will do me a great service; for I have some very lucrative work in view, which I cannot possibly undertake, for want of provisions to live upon until it is finished." "I was in the same case," answered Mathurin, "and if I have now secured bread for several months, it is at the expense of my arms and my stomach. Upon what principle of justice can it be devoted to the realization of *your* enterprise instead of *mine?*"

You may well believe that the bargain was a long one. However, it was finished at length, and on these conditions:

First. Jerome promised to give back, at the end of the year, a sack of corn of the same quality, and of the same weight, without missing a single grain. "This first clause is perfectly just," said he, "for without it Mathurin would *give*, and not *lend.*"

Secondly. He engaged to deliver *five litres* on *every hectolitre.* "This clause is no less just than the other," thought he; "for without it Mathurin would do me a service without compensation; he would inflict upon himself a privation—he would renounce his cherished enterprise—he would enable me to accomplish mine—he would cause me to enjoy for a year the fruits of his savings, and all this gratuitously. Since he delays the cultivation of his land, since he enables me to realize a lucrative labor, it is quite natural that I should let him partake, in a certain proportion, of the profits which I shall gain by the sacrifice he makes of his own."

On his side, Mathurin, who was something of a scholar, made this calculation: "Since, by virtue of the first clause, the sack of corn will return to me at the end of a year," he said to himself, "I shall be able to lend it again; it will return to me at the end of the second year; I may lend it again, and so on, to all eternity. However, I cannot deny that it will have been eaten long ago. It is singular that I should be perpetually the owner of a sack of corn, although the one I have lent has been consumed for ever. But this is explained thus: It will be consumed in the service of Jerome. It will put it into the power of Jerome to produce a superior value; and, consequently, Jerome will be able to restore me a sack of corn, or the value of it, without having suffered the slightest injury; but quite the contrary. And as regards myself, this value ought to be my property, as long as I do not consume it myself; if I had used it to clear my land, I should have received it again in the form of a fine harvest. Instead of that, I lend it, and shall recover it in the form of repayment.

"From the second clause, I gain another piece of information. At the end of the year, I shall be in possession of five litres of corn, over the 100 that I have just lent. If, then, I were to continue to work by the day, and to save a part of my wages, as I have been doing, in the course of time I should be able to lend two sacks of corn; then three; then four; and when I should have gained a sufficient number to enable me to live on these additions of five litres over and above each, I shall be at liberty to take a little repose in my old age. But how is this? In this case, shall I not be living at the expense of others? No, certainly, for it has been proved that in lending I perform a service; I complete the labor of my borrowers; and only deduct a trifling part of the excess of production, due to my lendings and savings. It is a marvellous thing, that a man may thus realize a leisure which injures no one, and for which he cannot be envied without injustice."

THE HOUSE.

Mondor had a house. In building it, he had extorted nothing from any one whatever. He owed it to his own personal labor, or, which is the same thing, to labor justly rewarded. His first care was to make a bargain with an architect, in virtue of which, by means of a hundred crowns a year, the latter engaged to keep the house in constant good repair. Mondor was already congratulating himself on the happy days which he hoped to spend in this retreat, declared sacred by our Constitution. But Valerius wished to make it his residence. "How can you think of such a thing?" said Mondor; "it is I who have built it; it has cost me ten years of painful labor, and now you would enjoy it!" They agreed to refer the matter to judges. They chose no profound economists—there were none such in the country. But they found some just and sensible men; it all comes to the same thing: political economy, justice, good sense, are all the same thing. Now here is the decision made by the judges: If Valerius wishes to occupy Mondor's house for a year, he is bound to submit to three conditions. The first is, to quit at the end of the year, and to restore the house in good repair, saving the inevitable decay resulting from mere duration. The second, to refund to Mondor the 300 francs, which the latter pays annually to the architect to repair the injuries of time; for these injuries taking place whilst the house is in the service of Valerius, it is perfectly just that he should bear the consequences. The third, that he should render to Mondor a service equivalent to that which he receives. As to this equivalence of services, it must be freely discussed between Mondor and Valerius.

THE PLANE.

A very long time ago there lived, in a poor village, a joiner, who was a philosopher, as all my heroes are, in their way. James worked from morning till night with his two strong arms, but his brain was not idle, for all that. He was fond of reviewing his actions, their causes, and their effects. He sometimes said to himself, "With my hatchet, my saw, and my hammer, I can make only coarse furniture, and can only get the pay for such.

If I only had a *plane*, I should please my customers more, and they would pay me more. It is quite just; I can only expect services proportioned to those which I render myself. Yes! I am resolved, I will make myself a *plane*."

However, just as he was setting to work, James reflected further: "I work for my customers 300 days in the year. If I give ten to making my plane, supposing it lasts me a year, only 290 days will remain for me to make my furniture. Now, in order that I be not the loser in this matter, I must gain henceforth, with the help of the plane, as much in 290 days, as I now do in 300. I must even gain more; for unless I do so, it would not be worth my while to venture upon any innovations." James began to calculate. He satisfied himself that he should sell his finished furniture at a price which would amply compensate for the ten days devoted to the plane; and when no doubt remained on this point, he set to work. I beg the reader to remark, that the power which exists in the tool to increase the productiveness of labor, is the basis of the solution which follows.

At the end of ten days, James had in his possession an admirable plane, which he valued all the more for having made it himself. He danced for joy—for, like the girl with her basket of eggs, he reckoned all the profits which he expected to derive from the ingenious instrument; but more fortunate than she, he was not reduced to the necessity of saying good-bye to calf, cow, pig, and eggs, together. He was building his fine castles in the air, when he was interrupted by his acquaintance William, a joiner in the neighboring village. William having admired the plane, was struck with the advantages which might be gained from it. He said to James:

W. You must do me a service.

J. What service?

W. Lend me the plane for a year.

As might be expected, James at this proposal did not fail to cry out, "How can you think of such a thing, William? Well, if I do you this service, what will you do for me in return?"

W. Nothing. Don't you know that a loan ought to be gratuitous? Don't you know that capital is naturally unproductive? Don't you know fraternity has been proclaimed? If you only do me a service for the sake of receiving one from me in return, what merit would you have?

J. William, my friend, fraternity does not mean that all the sacrifices are to be on one side; if so, I do not see why they should not be on yours. Whether a loan should be gratuitous I don't know; but I do know that if I were to lend you my plane for a year, it would be giving it to you. To tell you the truth, that is not what I made it for.

W. Well, we will say nothing about the modern

maxims discovered by the Socialist gentlemen. I ask you to do me a service; what service do you ask of me in return?

J. First, then, in a year, the plane will be done for, it will be good for nothing. It is only just, that you should let me have another exactly like it; or that you should give me money enough to get it repaired; or that you should supply me the ten days which I must devote to replacing it.

W. This is perfectly just. I submit to these conditions. I engage to return it, or to let you have one like it, or the value of the same. I think you must be satisfied with this, and can require nothing further.

J. I think otherwise. I made the plane for myself, and not for you. I expected to gain some advantage from it, by my work being better finished and better paid, by an improvement in my condition. What reason is there that I should make the plane, and you should gain the profit? I might as well ask you to give me your saw and hatchet! What a confusion! Is it not natural that each should keep what he has made with his own hands, as well as his hands themselves? To use without recompense the hands of another, I call slavery; to use without recompense the plane of another, can this be called fraternity?

W. But, then, I have agreed to return it to you at the end of a year, as well polished and as sharp as it is now.

J. We have nothing to do with next year; we are speaking of this year. I have made the plane for the sake of improving my work and my condition; if you merely return it to me in a year, it is you who will gain the profit of it during the whole of that time. I am not bound to do you such a service without receiving anything from you in return; therefore, if you wish for my plane, independently of the entire restoration already bargained for, you must do me a service which we will now discuss; you must grant me remuneration.

And this was done thus: William granted a remuneration calculated in such a way that, at the end of the year, James received his plane quite new, and in addition, a compensation, consisting of a new plank, for the advantages of which he had deprived himself, and which he had yielded to his friend.

It was impossible for any one acquainted with the transaction to discover the slightest trace in it of oppression or injustice.

The singular part of it is, that, at the end of the year, the plane came into James' possession, and he lent it again; recovered it, and lent it a third and fourth time. It has passed into the hands of his son, who still lends it. Poor plane! how many times has it changed, sometimes its blade, sometimes its handle. It is no longer the same plane, but it has always the same value, at least for James' posterity. Workmen! let us examine into these little stories.

I maintain, first of all, that the *sack of corn* and the *plane* are here the type, the model, a faithful representation, the symbol, of all capital; as the five litres of corn and the plank are the type, the model, the representation, the symbol, of all interest. This granted, the following are, it seems to me, a series of consequences, the justice of which it is impossible to dispute.

1st. If the yielding of a plank by the borrower to the lender is a natural, equitable, lawful remuneration, the just price of a real service, we may conclude that, as a general rule, it is in the nature of capital to produce interest. When this capital, as in the foregoing examples, takes the form of an *instrument of labor*, it is clear enough that it ought to bring an advantage to its possessor, to him who has devoted to it his time, his brains, and his strength. Otherwise, why should he have made it? No necessity of life can be immediately satisfied with instruments of labor; no one eats planes or drinks saws, except, indeed, he be a conjurer. If a man determines to spend his time in the production of such things, he must have been led to it by the consideration of the power which these instruments add to his power; of the time which they save him; of the perfection and rapidity which they give to his labor; in a word, of the advantages which they procure for him. Now, these advantages, which have been prepared by labor, by the sacrifice of time which might have been used in a more immediate manner, are we bound, as soon as they are ready to be enjoyed, to confer them gratuitously upon another? Would it be an advance in social order, if the law decided thus, and citizens should pay officials for causing such a law to be executed by force? I venture to say, that there is not one amongst you who would support it. It would be to legalize, to organize, to systematize injustice itself, for it would be proclaiming that there are men born to render, and others born to receive, gratuitous services. Granted, then, that interest is just, natural, and lawful.

2nd. A second consequence, not less remarkable than the former, and, if possible, still more conclusive, to which I call your attention, is this: *interest is not injurious to the borrower.* I mean to say, the obligation in which the borrower finds himself, to pay a remuneration for the use of capital, cannot do any harm to his condition. Observe, in fact, that James and William are perfectly free, as regards the transaction to which the plane gave occasion. The transaction cannot be accomplished without the consent of the one as well as of the other. The worst which can happen is, that James may be too exacting; and in this case, William, refusing the loan, remains as he was before. By the fact of his agreeing to borrow, he proves that he considers it an advantage to himself; he proves, that after every calculation, including the remuneration, whatever it may be, required of him, he still finds it more profitable to borrow than not to borrow. He only determines to do so because he has compared the inconveniences with the advantages. He has calculated that the day on which he returns the plane, accompanied by the remuneration agreed upon, he will have effected more work, with the same labor, thanks to this tool. A profit will remain to him, otherwise he would not have borrowed. The two services of which we are speaking are exchanged according to the law which governs all exchanges, the law of supply and demand. The claims of James have a natural and impassable limit. This is the point in which the remuneration demanded by him would absorb all the advantage which William might find in making use of a plane. In this case, the borrowing would not take place. William would be bound either to make a plane for himself, or to do without one, which would leave him in his original condition. He borrows, because he gains by borrowing. I know very well what will be told me. You will say, William may be deceived, or, perhaps, he may be governed by necessity, and be obliged to submit to a harsh law.

It may be so. As to errors in calculation, they

belong to the infirmity of our nature, and to argue from this against the transaction in question, is objecting the possibility of loss in all imaginable transactions, in every human act. Error is an accidental fact, which is incessantly remedied by experience. In short, everybody must guard against it. As far as those hard necessities are concerned, which force persons to burdensome borrowings, it is clear that these necessities exist previously to the borrowing. If William is in a situation in which he cannot possibly do without a plane, and must borrow one at any price, does this situation result from James having taken the trouble to make the tool? Does it not exist independently of this circumstance? However harsh, however severe James may be, he will never render the supposed condition of William worse than it is. Morally, it is true, the lender will be to blame; but, in an economical point of view, the loan itself can never be considered responsible for previous necessities, which it has not created, and which it relieves, to a certain extent.

But this proves something to which I shall return. The evident interests of William, representing here the borrowers, there are many Jameses and planes. In other words, lenders and capitals. It is very evident, that if William can say to James—"Your demands are exorbitant; there is no lack of planes in the world;" he will be in a better situation than if James' plane was the only one to be borrowed. Assuredly, there is no maxim more true than this—service for service. But let us not forget, that no service has a fixed and absolute value, compared with others. The contracting parties are free. Each carries his requisitions to the farthest possible point; and the most favorable circumstance for these requisitions is the absence of rivalship. Hence it follows, that if there is a class of men more interested than any other, in the formation, multiplication, and abundance of capitals, it is mainly that of the borrowers. Now, since capitals can only be formed and increased by the stimulus and the prospect of remuneration, let this class understand the injury they are inflicting on themselves, when they deny the lawfulness of interest, when they proclaim that credit should be gratuitous, when they declaim against the pretended tyranny of capital, when they discourage saving, thus forcing capitals to become scarce, and consequently interests to rise.

3rd. The anecdote I have just related enables you to explain this apparently singular phenomenon, which is termed the duration or perpetuity of interest. Since, in lending his plane, James has been able, very lawfully, to make it a condition that it should be returned to him, at the end of a year, in the same state in which it was when he lent it, is it not evident that he may, at the expiration of the term, lend it again on the same conditions. If he resolves upon the latter plan, the plane will return to him at the end of every year, and that without end. James will then be in a condition to lend it without end; that is, he may derive from it a perpetual interest. It will be said, that the plane will be worn out. That is true; but it will be worn out by the hand and for the profit of the borrower. The latter has taken into account this gradual wear, and taken upon himself, as he ought, the consequences. He has reckoned that he shall derive from this tool an advantage, which will allow him to restore it in its original condition, after having realized a profit from it. As long as James does not use this capital himself, or for his own advantage—as long as he renounces the advantages which allow it to be restored to its original condition—he will have an incontestable right to have it restored, and that independently of interest.

Observe, besides, that if, as I believe I have shown, James, far from doing any harm to William, has done him a *service* in lending him his plane for a year; for the same reason, he will do no harm to a second, a third, a fourth borrower, in the subsequent periods. Hence you may understand, that the interest of a capital is as natural, as lawful, as useful, in the thousandth year, as in the first. We may go still further. It may happen, that James lends more than a single plane. It is possible, that by means of working, of saving, of privations, of order, of activity, he may come to lend a multitude of planes and saws; that is to say, to do a multitude of services. I insist upon this point—that if the first loan has been a social good, it will be the same with all the others; for they are all similar, and based upon the same principle. It may happen, then, that the amount of all the remunerations received by our honest operative, in exchange for services rendered by him, may suffice to maintain him. In this case, there will be a man in the world who has a right to live without working. I do not say that he would be doing right to give himself up to idleness—but I say, that he has a right to do so; and if he does so, it will be at nobody's expense, but quite the contrary. If society at all understands the nature of things, it will acknowledge that this man subsists on services which he receives certainly (as we all do), but which he lawfully receives in exchange for other services, which he himself has rendered, that he continues to render, and which are quite real, inasmuch as they are freely and voluntarily accepted.

And here we have a glimpse of one of the finest harmonies in the social world. I allude to *leisure:* not that leisure that the warlike and tyrannical classes arrange for themselves by the plunder of the workers, but that leisure which is the lawful and innocent fruit of past activity and economy.

In expressing myself thus, I know that I shall shock many received ideas. But see! Is not leisure an essential spring in the social machine? Without it, the world would never have had a Newton, a Pascal, a Fenelon; mankind would have been ignorant of all arts, sciences, and of those wonderful inventions, prepared originally by investigations of mere curiosity; thought would have been inert—man would have made no progress. On the other hand, if leisure could only be explained by plunder and oppression—if it were a benefit which could only be enjoyed unjustly, and at the expense of others, there would be no middle path between these two evils; either mankind would be reduced to the necessity of stagnating in a vegetable and stationary life, in eternal ignorance, from the absence of wheels to its machine—or else it would have to acquire these wheels at the price of inevitable injustice, and would necessarily present the sad spectacle, in one form or other, of the antique classification of human beings into Masters and Slaves. I defy any one to show me, in this case, any other alternative. We should be compelled to contemplate the Divine plan which governs society, with the regret of thinking that it presents a deplorable chasm. The stimulus of progress would be forgotten, or, which is worse, this stimulus would be no other than injustice itself. But, no! God has not left such a chasm in his work of love. We must take care not to disregard his wisdom and power; for those whose imperfect meditations cannot explain the lawfulness of leisure, are very much like the astronomer who said, at a certain point in the heavens there ought to exist a planet which will be at last discovered, for without it the celestial world is not harmony, but discord.

Well, I say that, if well understood, the history of my humble plane, although very modest, is sufficient to raise us to the contemplation of one of the most consoling, but least understood, of the social harmonies.

It is not true that we must choose between the denial or the unlawfulness of leisure; thanks to rent and its natural duration, leisure may arise from labor and saving. It is a pleasing prospect, which every one may have in view; a noble recompense, to which each may aspire. It makes its appearance in the world; it distributes itself proportionably to the exercise of certain virtues; it opens all the avenues to intelligence; it ennobles, it raises the morals; it spiritualizes the soul of humanity, not only without laying any weight on those of our brethren whose lot in life devotes them to severe labor, but relieving them gradually from the heaviest and most repugnant part of this labor. It is enough that capitals should be formed, accumulated, multiplied; should be lent on conditions less and less burdensome ; that they should descend, penetrate into every social circle, and that, by an admirable progression, after having liberated the lenders, they should hasten the liberation of the borrowers themselves. For that end, the laws and customs ought to be favorable to economy, the source of capital. It is enough to say, that the first of all these conditions is, not to alarm, to attack, to deny that which is the stimulus of saving and the reason of its existence—interest.

As long as we see nothing passing from hand to hand, in the character of loan, but *provisions, materials, instruments*, things indispensable to the productiveness of labor itself, the ideas thus far exhibited will not find many opponents. Who knows, even, that I may not be reproached for having made great effort to burst what may be said to be an open door. But as soon as *cash* makes its appearance as the subject of the transaction (and it is this which appears almost always), immediately a crowd of objections are raised. Money, it will be said, will not reproduce itself, like your *sack of corn ;* it does not assist labor, like your *plane ;* it does not afford an immediate satisfaction, like your *house.* It is incapable, by its nature, of producing interest, of multiplying itself, and the remuneration it demands is a positive extortion.

Who cannot see the sophistry of this? Who

does not see that cash is only a transient form, which men give at the time to other *values*, to real objects of usefulness, for the sole object of facilitating their arrangements? In the midst of social complications, the man who is in a condition to lend, scarcely ever has the exact thing which the borrower wants. James, it is true, has a plane; but, perhaps, William wants a saw. They cannot negotiate; the transaction favorable to both cannot take place, and then what happens? It happens that James first exchanges his plane for money; he lends the money to William, and William exchanges the money for a saw. The transaction is no longer a simple one; it is decomposed into two parts, as I explained above in speaking of exchange. But, for all that, it has not changed its nature; it still contains all the elements of a direct loan. James has still got rid of a tool which was useful to him; William has still received an instrument which perfects his work and increases his profits; there is still a service rendered by the lender, which entitles him to receive an equivalent service from the borrower; this just balance is not the less established by free mutual bargaining. The very natural obligation to restore at the end of the term the entire *value*, still constitutes the principle of the duration of interest.

At the end of a year, says M. Thoré, will you find an additional crown in a bag of a hundred pounds?

No, certainly, if the borrower puts the bag of one hundred pounds on the shelf. In such a case, neither the plane, nor the sack of corn, would reproduce themselves. But it is not for the sake of leaving the money in the bag, nor the plane on the hook, that they are borrowed. The plane is borrowed to be used, or the money to procure a plane. And if it is clearly proved that this tool enables the borrower to obtain profits which he would not have made without it, if it is proved that the lender has renounced creating for himself this excess of profits, we may understand how the stipulation of a part of this excess of profits in favor of the lender, is equitable and lawful.

Ignorance of the true part which cash plays in human transactions, is the source of the most fatal errors. I intend devoting an entire pamphlet to this subject. From what we may infer from the writings of M. Proudhon, that which has led him to think that gratuitous credit was a logical and definite consequence of social progress, is the observation of the phenomenon which shows a decreasing interest, almost in direct proportion to the rate of civilization. In barbarous times it is, in fact, cent. per cent., and more. Then it descends to eighty, sixty, fifty, forty, twenty, ten, eight, five, four, and three per cent. In Holland, it has even been as low as two per cent. Hence it is concluded, that "in proportion as society comes to perfection, it will descend to zero by the time civilization is complete. In other words, that which characterizes social perfection is the gratuitousness of credit. When, therefore, we shall have abolished interest, we shall have reached the last step of progress." This is mere sophistry, and as such false arguing may contribute to render popular the unjust, dangerous, and destructive dogma, that credit should be gratuitous, by representing it as coincident with social perfection, with the reader's permission I will examine in a few words this new view of the question.

What is *interest?* It is the service rendered, after a free bargain, by the borrower to the lender, in remuneration for the service he has received by the loan. By what law is the rate of these remunerative services established? By the general law which regulates the equivalent of all services; that is, by the law of supply and demand.

The more easily a thing is procured, the smaller is the service rendered by yielding it or lending it. The man who gives me a glass of water in the Pyrenees, does not render me so great a service as he who allows me one in the desert of Sahara. If there are many planes, sacks of corn, or houses, in a country, the use of them is obtained, other things being equal, on more favorable conditions than if they were few; for the simple reason, that the lender renders in this case a smaller *relative service.*

It is not surprising, therefore, that the more abundant capitals are, the lower is the interest.

Is this saying that it will ever reach zero? No; because, I repeat it, the principle of a remuneration is in the loan. To say that interest will be annihilated, is to say that there will never be any motive for saving, for denying ourselves, in order to form new capitals, nor even to preserve the old ones. In this case, the waste would immediately bring a void, and interest would directly reappear.

In that, the nature of the services of which we are speaking does not differ from any other. Thanks to industrial progress, a pair of stockings, which used to be worth six francs, has successively been worth only four, three, and two. No one can say to what point this value will descend; but we can affirm, that it will never reach zero, unless the stockings finish by producing themselves spontaneously. Why? Because the principle of remuneration is in labor; because he who works for another renders a service, and ought to receive a service. If no one paid for stockings, they would cease to be made; and, with the scarcity, the price would not fail to reappear.

The sophism which I am now combating has its root in the infinite divisibility which belongs to *value*, as it does to matter.

It appears, at first, paradoxical, but it is well known to all mathematicians, that, through all eternity, fractions may be taken from a weight without the weight ever being annihilated. It is sufficient that each successive fraction be less than the preceding one, in a determined and regular proportion.

There are countries where people apply themselves to increasing the size of horses, or diminishing in sheep the size of the head. It is impossible to say precisely to what point they will arrive in this. No one can say that he has seen the largest horse or the smallest sheep's head that will ever appear in the world. But he may safely say that the size of horses will never attain to infinity, nor the heads of sheep to nothing.

In the same way, no one can say to what point the price of stockings nor the interest of capitals will come down; but we may safely affirm, when we know the nature of things, that neither the one nor the other will ever arrive at zero, for labor and capital can no more live without recompense than a sheep without a head.

The arguments of M. Proudhon reduce themselves, then, to this: since the most skillful agriculturists are those who have reduced the heads of sheep to the smallest size, we shall have arrived at the highest agricultural perfection when sheep have no longer any heads. Therefore, in order to realize the perfection, let us behead them.

I have now done with this wearisome discussion. Why is it that the breath of false doctrine has made it needful to examine into the intimate nature of interest? I must not leave off without remarking upon a beautiful moral which may be drawn from this law: "The depression of interest is proportioned to the abundance of capitals." This law being granted, if there is a class of men to whom it is more important than to any other that capitals be formed, accumulate, multiply, abound, and superabound, it is certainly the class which borrows them directly or indirectly; it is those men who operate upon *materials*, who gain assistance by *instruments*, who live upon *provisions*, produced and economized by other men.

Imagine, in a vast and fertile country, a population of a thousand inhabitants, destitute of all capital thus defined. It will assuredly perish by the pangs of hunger. Let us suppose a case hardly less cruel. Let us suppose that ten of these savages are provided with instruments and provisions sufficient to work and to live themselves until harvest time, as well as to remunerate the services of eighty laborers. The inevitable result will be the death of nine hundred human beings. It is clear, then, that since nine hundred and ninety men, urged by want, will crowd upon the supports which would only maintain a hundred, the ten capitalists will be masters of the market. They will obtain labor on the hardest conditions, for they will put it up to auction, or the highest bidder. And observe this—if these capitalists entertain such pious sentiments as would induce them to impose personal privations on themselves, in order to diminish the sufferings of some of their brethren, this generosity, which attaches to morality, will be as noble in its principle as useful in its effects. But if, duped by that false philosophy which persons wish so inconsiderately to mingle with economic laws, they take to remunerating labor largely, far from doing good, they will do harm. They will give double wages, it may be. But then, forty-five men will be better provided for, whilst forty-five others will come to augment the number of those who are sinking into the grave. Upon this supposition, it is not the lowering of wages which is the mischief, it is the scarcity of capital. Low wages are not the cause, but the effect of the evil. I may add, that they are to a certain extent the remedy. It acts in this way; it distributes the burden of suffering as much as it can, and saves as many lives as a limited quantity of sustenance permits.

Suppose now, that instead of ten capitalists, there should be a hundred, two hundred, five hundred—is it not evident that the condition of the whole population, and, above all, that of the "prolétaires,"* will be more and more improved? Is

* Common people.

it not evident that, apart from every consideration of generosity, they would obtain more work and better pay for it?—that they themselves will be in a better condition to form capitals, without being able to fix the limits to this ever-increasing facility of realizing equality and well-being? Would it not be madness in them to admit such doctrines, and to act in a way which would drain the source of wages, and paralyze the activity and stimulus of saving? Let them learn this lesson, then; doubtless, capitals are good for those who possess them: who denies it? But they are also useful to those who have not yet been able to form them; and it is important to those who have them not, that others should have them.

Yes, if the "prolétaires" knew their true interests, they would seek, with the greatest care, what circumstances are, and what are not favorable to saving, in order to favor the former and to discourage the latter. They would sympathize with every measure which tends to the rapid formation of capitals. They would be enthusiastic promoters of peace, liberty, order, security, the union of classes and peoples, economy, moderation in public expenses, simplicity in the machinery of Government; for it is under the sway of all these circumstances that saving does its work, brings plenty within the reach of the masses, invites those persons to become the formers of capital who were formerly under the necessity of borrowing upon hard conditions. They would repel with energy the warlike spirit, which diverts from its true course so large a part of human labor; the monopolizing spirit, which deranges the equitable distribution of riches, in the way by which liberty alone can realize it; the multitude of public services, which attack our purses only to check our liberty; and, in short, those subversive, hateful, thoughtless doctrines, which alarm capital, prevent its formation, oblige it to flee, and finally to raise its price, to the special disadvantage of the workers, who bring it into operation. Well, and in this respect is not the revolution of February a hard lesson? Is it not evident, that the insecurity it has thrown into the world of business, on the one hand; and, on the other, the advancement of the fatal theories to which I have alluded, and which, from the clubs, have almost penetrated into the regions of the Legislature, have everywhere raised the rate of interest? Is it not evident, that from that time the "prolétaires" have found greater difficulty in procuring those materials, instruments, and provisions, without which labor is impossible? Is it not that which has caused stoppages; and do not stoppages, in their turn, lower wages? Thus there is a deficiency of labor to the "prolétaires," from the same cause which loads the objects they consume with an increase of price, in consequence of the rise of interest. High interest, low wages, means in other words that the same article preserves its price, but that the part of the capitalist has invaded, without profiting himself, that of the workman.

A friend of mine, commissioned to make inquiry into Parisian industry, has assured me that the manufacturers have revealed to him a very striking fact, which proves, better than any reasoning can, how much insecurity and uncertainty injure the formation of capital. It was remarked, that during the most distressing period, the popular expenses of mere fancy had not diminished. The small theaters, the fighting lists, the public houses, and tobacco depôts, were as much frequented as in prosperous times. In the inquiry, the operatives themselves explained this phenomenon thus: "What is the use of pinching? Who knows what will happen to us? Who knows that interest will not be abolished? Who knows but that the State will become a universal and gratuitous lender, and that it will wish to annihilate all the fruits which we might expect from our savings?" Well! I say, that if such ideas could prevail during two single years, it would be enough to turn our beautiful France into a Turkey—misery would become general and endemic, and, most assuredly, the poor would be the first upon whom it would fall.

Workmen! They talk to you a great deal upon

the *artificial* organization of labor;—do you know why they do so? Because they are ignorant of the laws of its *natural* organization; that is, of the wonderful organization which results from liberty. You are told, that liberty gives rise to what is called the radical antagonism of classes; that it creates, and makes to clash, two opposite interests —that of the capitalists and that of the "prolétaires." But we ought to begin by proving that this antagonism exists by a law of nature; and afterwards it would remain to be shown how far the arrangements of restraint are superior to those of liberty, for between liberty and restraint I see no middle path. Again, it would remain to be proved, that restraint would always operate to your advantage, and to the prejudice of the rich. But, no; this radical antagonism, this natural opposition of interests, does not exist. It is only an evil dream of perverted and intoxicated imaginations. No; a plan so defective has not proceeded from the Divine Mind. To affirm it, we must begin by denying the existence of God. And see how, by means of social laws, and because men exchange amongst themselves their labors and their productions, see what a harmonious tie attaches the classes, one to the other! There are the landowners; what is their interest? That the soil be fertile, and the sun beneficent: and what is the result? That corn abounds, that it falls in price, and the advantage turns to the profit of those who have had no patrimony. There are the manufacturers; what is their constant thought? To perfect their labor, to increase the power of their machines, to procure for themselves, upon the best terms, the raw material. And to what does all this tend? To the abundance and low price of produce; that is, that all the efforts of the manufacturers, and without their suspecting it, result in a profit to the public consumer, of which each of you is one. It is the same with every profession. Well, the capitalists are not exempt from this law. They are very busy making schemes, economizing, and turning them to their advantage. This is all very well; but the more they succeed, the more do they promote the abundance of capital, and, as a necessary consequence, the reduction of interest? Now, who is it that profits by the reduction of interest? Is it not the borrower first, and finally, the consumers of the things which the capitals contribute to produce?

It is, therefore, certain that the final result of the efforts of each class, is the common good of all.

You are told that capital tyrannizes over labor. I do not deny that each one endeavors to draw the greatest possible advantage from his situation; but, in this sense, he realizes only that which is possible. Now, it is never more possible for capitals to tyrannize over labor, than when they are scarce; for then it is they who make the law—it is they who regulate the rate of sale. Never is this tyranny more impossible to them, than when they are abundant; for, in that case, it is labor which has the command.

Away, then, with the jealousies of classes, ill-will, unfounded hatreds, unjust suspicions. These depraved passions injure those who nourish them in their hearts. This is no declamatory morality; it is a chain of causes and effects, which is capable of being rigorously, mathematically demonstrated. It is not the less sublime, in that it satisfies the intellect as well as the feelings.

I shall sum up this whole dissertation with these words: Workmen, laborers, "prolétaires," destitute and suffering classes, will you improve your condition? You will not succeed by strife, insurrection, hatred, and error. But there are three things which cannot perfect the entire community without extending these benefits to yourselves; these things are—peace, liberty, and security.

www.ingramcontent.com/pod-product-compliance
Lightning Source LLC
LaVergne TN
LVHW020058110826
845151LV00001B/11

* 9 7 8 1 4 2 5 5 4 5 4 0 6 *